REGIONAL DEVELOPMENT AT THE NATIONAL LEVEL

JL
27
·R44
1985

Volume I

Canadian and African Perspectives

Edited by

Timothy M. Shaw
Yash Tandon

Published for the
African Association of Political Science and the
Canadian Political Science Association
with funds provided by CIDA and IDRC.

UNIVERSITY
PRESS OF
AMERICA

LANHAM • NEW YORK • LONDON

Copyright © 1985 by

University Press of America,® Inc.

4720 Boston Way
Lanham. MD 20706

3 Henrietta Street
London WC2E 8LU England

Library of Congress Cataloging in Publication Data
Main entry under title:

Regional development at the national level.

  Papers from a conference held at the University of
Zimbabwe, Feb. 1984, which was sponsored by the
African Association of Political Science and the
Canadian Political Science Association.
  "Published for the African Association of Political
Science and the Canadian Political Science
Association."
  Includes index.
  1. Regionalism—Canada—Congresses. 2. Regionalism
—Africa—Congresses. 3. Regional economics—
Congresses. I. Shaw, Timothy M. II. Tandon,
Yashpal, 1939-   . III. African Association of
Political Science. IV. Canadian Political Science
Association.
JL27.R44   1985   320.1'2   85-15034
ISBN 0-8191-4850-4 (alk. paper)
ISBN 0-8191-4851-2 (pbk. : alk. paper)

Table of Contents

iii

Table of Contents (continued)

Part Two: Regional Policies (continued)

iv

List of Tables, Figures and Maps

T A B L E S

List of Tables, Figures and Maps (continued)

FIGURES

MAPS

List of Abbreviations

AAPS	-	African Association of Political Science
ACP	-	African, Caribbean and Pacific Countries (associated with EEC)
BLS	-	Botswana, Lesotho and Swaziland
CIDA	-	Canadian International Development Agency
CPSA	-	Canadian Political Science Association
DREE	-	Department of Regional Economic Expansion (Canada)
EAC	-	East African Community
EACM	-	East African Common Market
ECA	-	(UN) Economic Commission for Africa
ECOWAS	-	Economic Community of West African States
EDC	-	Export Development Corporation (Canada)
EEC	-	European Economic Community
ERDF	-	European Regional Development Fund
GATT	-	General Agreement on Tariffs and Trade
IBRD	-	International Bank for Reconstruction and Development (World Bank)
IMF	-	International Monetary Fund
KBO	-	Kagera Basin Organization
MNCs	-	Multinational Corporations
NIC	-	Newly Industrializing Country
OAU	-	Organization of African Unity
OECD	-	Organization for Economic Cooperation and Development
PAFMECSA	-	PanAfrican Freedom Movement for Eastern, Central and Southern Africa
PTA	-	Preferential Trade Area (for Eastern, Central and Southern Africa)
RSA	-	Republic of South Africa
SACU	-	Southern African Customs Union
SADCC	-	Southern African Development Coordination Conference
SDRW	-	Societé de Développement Régional Wallon
TNCs	-	Transnational Corporations
ZANU	-	Zimbabwe African National Union
ZAPU	-	Zimbabwe African People's Union

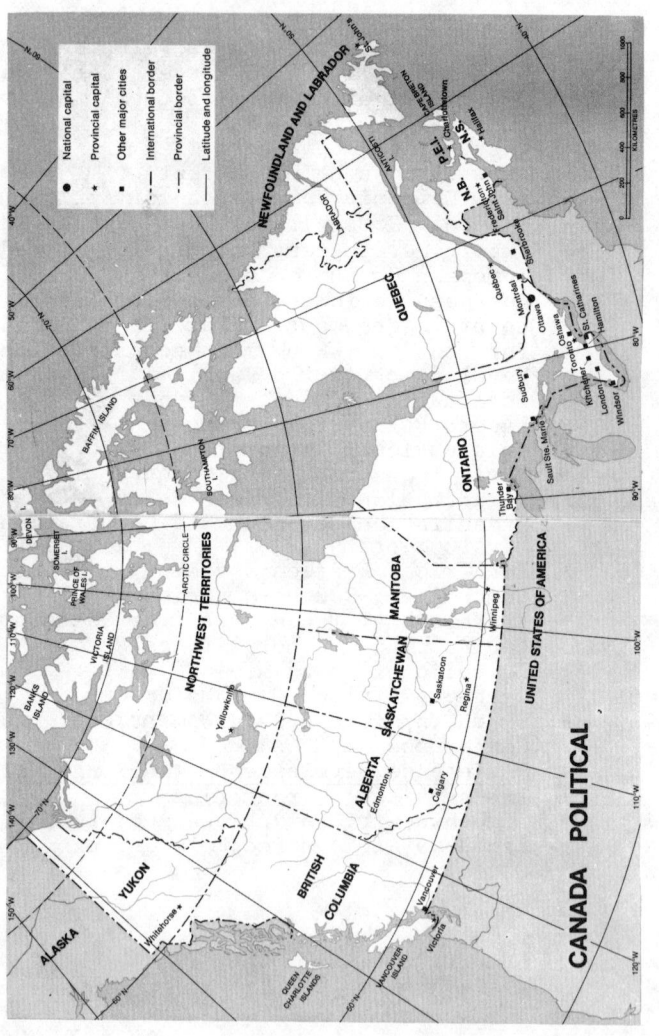

CANADA POLITICAL

Legend:
● National capital
★ Provincial capital
■ Other major cities
–··– International border
–·– Provincial border
— Latitude and longitude

viii

Map 2

Africa Political

PREFACE

Regional Development in Africa and Canada:

public policy and political economy

Timothy M. Shaw

1984-85 was full of symbols and surprises for students
of Africa, Canada and other parts of the world system.
The year of George Orwell's cautionary novel was also
the centenary of the notorious Treaty of Berlin which
first divided Africa. This "balkanization" has yet to
be transcended: one element in Africa's dream of
development and dignity. The year also saw the return
to power in federal Canada of the Tory party and the
demise of seperatiste nationalism in the province of
Quebec. If such topical concerns overlaid efforts by
political scientists in Canada and Africa to meet to
identify, discuss and compare seemingly mutual interests,
then the anticipated yet unacceptable drought and famine
in Ethiopia and its neighbors reinforced the sense of
timeliness, urgency and commonality. 1984 saw bad rainy
seasons and grain harvests in the Canadian prairies,
Southern African plateau and Ethiopian highlands. If
the first was mitigated by irrigation and stocks, and
the second moderated by some previous good years and
alternative resources, then the last was but a further
disaster: Ethiopia is well into an apparently relent-
less cycle of seven lean years. The regional as well
as global incidences and impacts of drought are well-
known: mass migrations, border tensions, refugee
camps, exponential desertification, and dissident movements. The continuing African crisis of the mid-1980s
provided a compelling backdrop to our more modest yet
not unrelated purpose: to exchange ideas, analyses and
proposals of relevance to regional problems and
potentials in Africa and Canada.

i) Regionalisms Compared

The first joint international activity of the
African Association of Political Science (AAPS) was,
then, with its fellow Canadian organization: CPSA.
Based on general historical awareness and particular
personal linkges--doctorates, lectureships, research
projects, publications etc.--some dozen Canadian and
two dozen African political scientists gathered on the

1

campus of the University of Zimbabwe for three days in mid-February 1984. The intricate plans and high hopes were not disappointed by the seven sessions and twenty-two papers (11 each from AAPS and CPSA). For the compatible perceptions and orientations which brought us together permeated and reinforced the presentations and discussions; despite different histories and milieus there were indeed shared problems and perspectives. These were identified in the opening remarks of Dr. Nathan Shamuyarira, Honorary President and a founding father of AAPS, now minister in the government of Zimbabwe. He concentrated on the constraints to regional integration and development in Africa and elsewhere and suggested ways to break the barriers to regional exchange, focusing in particular on a quintessentially Canadian response: industrial strategy.2

In both preparing for and participating in this joint AAPS/CPSA conference there was an unmistakeable tension between inter- and intra-state regionalisms. The former tended to be the concern of more radical and African scholars, the latter the preference of more orthodox and Canadian students. Yet in debate, if not in this pair of volumes, the two were joined: the pre-occupation throughout was on regionalism(s) and (under) development in the 1980s. Regional inequalities both inside and outside states have increased with the demise of the post-war Bretton Woods political economy: the post-industrial global division of labor poses major challenges to political policies, processes, and practices likely to last well into the twenty-first century. So the countinuing demands from the Canadian North are not so dissimilar from those emanating from disadvantaged peripheries in Africa. Likewise, the difficulties of coordination among Canadian provinces are not so different from those in African regional organizations such as ECOWAS and SADCC. And the continuing Canadian debates over free trade with the United States are not unlike those in Africa over inter-African or EurAfrican exchange; ie. PTA or ACP-EEC. Moreover, inter- and intra-regional issues spill-over supposed political and territorial boundaries: offshore resources in both Africa and Canada have myriad international connections. Similarly, external relations impact upon internal differences in both continents.

The overarching element which permitted fruitful comparisons among a diverse group of participants-- neither African nor Canadian "delegates" meet very often in their own organizations let alone between such continental groupings--was a shared acceptance of the salience of both political economy and political culture in the world of the 1980s. Regionalism is a response to both economic and social fragmentation, articulation and externalization. Whilst the emphasis between economy and society may vary and be reflective of underlying conceptual and theoretical divergencies, at the level of policy they may be rendered compatible. Certainly in the Harare workshop, questions of language and culture in Canadian regions were readily appreciated by African scholars. Likewise, issues of production and exchange in Africa were quite understandable by Canadian participants.

One of the distinctive intellectual traditions in Canada rather than in some other OECD states is that of political economy. To be sure this may be less rather than more materialist: the interaction of economics and politics rather than the more Marxist notion of dialectic between sub- and super-structure. Regionalism is, in part, at the level of both analysis and praxis, a response to economic and social inequalities. So the familiarity of Canadian colleagues with concepts and situations of primary interest to African political scientists made for an empathetic and candid discussion. Indeed, one of the major points of mutual experience and education was political economy: from staples to colonial economies and from Canadian culture to African authenticity. The familiarity of Canadian social scientists with the everyday issues of Canadian nationalism--academic, social, political and economic-- provided an invaluable preparation for treating African frustrations, aspirations and experiments in a post-independence yet still very dependent continent.3

Regionalism as both ideology and policy as well as level and mode of analysis is in part, of course, a response not only to uneven development but also to dependence. Canadian as well as African scholars are very conscious of such an inheritance or context and have devoted considerable attention to both analyzing and transcending it. For example, the National Energy Program and Foreign Investment Review Agency initiatives in the mid-1970s were early attempts to respond to nationalist pressures in a world of energy shocks and inter-imperial rivalries. Likewise, the OAU's Lagos Plan of Action as well as ECOWAS, PTA and SADCC constitute African responses to inappropriate development strategies, disappointing economic performances and unpromising social projections.4

Underlying many of these concerns for regionalist responses within a political culture/economy mold are different notions of the state which transcend any existential or historical differences between Canada and Africa. Rather, they are correlates of distinctive modes of analysis which bridge the North-South divide, in Canada and Africa as well as between them. Whilst we might expect African scholars to be more amenable to dependency and radical analysis there are many orthodox social scientists on the continent. Conversely, whilst Canadian like other North American "behavioralists" may as a group be inclined towards established paradigms, there is a significant and respected materialist tradition in the country. Such profound questions were not about to be resolved in one conference in either their abstract and/or relevant forms as related to regionalism, dependence and development. But at least they were on the agenda, as reflected in this set of papers.

Finally, aside from intellectual and institutional, pedagogical and informational purposes, the joint conference did treat issues of public policy. These served to bring together not only diverse perspectives-- political culture and political economy--and not only diverse sub-fields--public administration and international relations, comparative political and policy analysis--but also to inject a note of relevancy and urgency: the drought in southern, eastern and western Africa and the continuing imperative of global economic reform and ecological renewal. The history of regional policy in Africa, Canada and Europe is not inspiring. Moreover, the challenges of new technologies in both African and Canadian regions are undermining old assumptions and prescriptions. There was a sense, then, that bioengineering, microchips, laser and other post- industrial technologies together constitute a new context to which all states, including Canada and Africa, have to respond. These innovations may, through satellite communications, reduce the need for spatial and capital concentration or, alternatively, they may further concentrate R&D, power and growth, as in the world's 'silicon vallies' and NICs. The place of both Africa and Canada in such new divisions of labor is quite problematic given our respective commodity-based economies.

In short, despite apparently diverse positions and assumptions, Canadian and African political scientists

have a range of mutual interests and problems clustered
around the notion "regional development": uneven growth
and regional inequalities, political economy and political culture, dependence and nationalism, public policy
and development strategy. And these in turn are aspects
of broader questions of industrialization, technology,
communications and resources: unequal patterns of
capital, production, distribution and consumption in
the new international division of labor. Thus the scope
of the presentatons and discussions went somewhat
beyond the relatively modest objectives which we set
for ourselves when applying for funding in Ottawa:

> To promote increased knowledge of
> regional development issues in
> Africa and Canada on the part of
> Canadian and African political
> scientists respectively; to promote
> the development of research between
> African and Canadian political
> scientists on regional development
> issues; to promote the teaching of
> regional development policy,
> particularly in African and compara-
> tive perspective; (and)...to foster
> comparative research within Africa
> and between Africa and Canada.5

ii) Regionalisms Projected

An enhanced awareness of mutual problems and
perspectives arose out of the conference itself. The
promotion of research and teaching in both Africa and
Canada on regional issues is being advanced through
this and related pubications. Moreover, arising out of
several central conference themes--comparative federalism; regional development structures and processes;
SADCC in comparative perspective; communications and
regionalism; ethnicity and national development; and
external capital: private and state--a set of joint
AAPS/CPSA research groups were identified for ongoing
contact and comment.6 Details of these and their joint
coordinators can be obtained from either AAPS in Harare
or CPSA in Ottawa.7 It is hoped that both organizational and intellectual arrangements between CPSA and
AAPS will be discussed and advanced at the International
Political Science Conference in Paris in mid-July 1985.

Both Africa and Canada have a history of regional
problems, policies and politics. These papers are
intended to further the analysis of these and thereby
advance appropriate strategies for regional development
within and between countries. The volumes are somewhat
abitrarily divided into two emphases: national and
international, respectively. But they both contain
African and Canadian contributions, cases and content
and are designed to be read in tandem. The very production of a two-volume, twenty-three chapter set of
joint papers is illustrative of the potential for
mutual enlightenment, encouragement and advancement.
As a recent survey collection on African Regional
Organizations indicates, regionalism in Africa is in
the process of being redefined as problems and
potentials are juxtaposed with the emerging international
division of labor.8 We are excited as well as apprehen-
sive about this process--will redefinition lead to
renewed development?--but at least inherited structures
and assumptions are being questioned. And Canadian
experience may both advance Africa's reevaluation as
well as be challenged by it. 9

For such a stimulating and suggestive outcome we
are indebted to several Canadian agencies for timely
assistance: Canadian International Development Agency
(CIDA), International Development Research Centre
(IDRC), Social Sciences and Humanities Research Council
of Canada (SSHRCC), and Department of External Affairs.
In addition, AAPS invested its own scarce resource as
did the University of Zimbabwe. This exercise in comparative regionalism was auspicious. Hopefully, it
will help to generate continuing exchanges and
challenges in both public policy and political economy
in Africa and Canada.

Notes

1. See "Programme for Joint Workshop of AAPS and CPSA in association with the Department of Political and Administrative Studies, University of Zimbabwe, Harare, 13 to 17 February 1984 on Regional Development in Canada and Africa: issues in public policy".

2. See Dr. Nathan Shamuyarira "Opening Speech: regional development in Canada and Africa", University of Zimbabwe, 13 February 1984.

3. See "Welcome Remarks by Professor W. J. Kamba, Vice-Chancellor: Joint AAPS and CPSA Workshop," University of Zimbabwe, 13 February 1984.

4. See inter alia, David Fasholé Luke and Timothy M. Shaw (eds.) Continental Crisis: the Lagos Plan of Action and Africa's future, (Washington: University Press of America, 1984).

5. See CPSA/AAPS, "Project Submission Form" to NGO Division of CIDA for support in late-1982.

6. See AAPS/CPSA memo on "Follow-up to Joint Workshop in Regional Development", Harare, 17 February 1984.

7. For some details of the Harare discussions and subsequent CPSA delegates' visits to Kenya and Nigeria, see CPSA Bulletin, 14(1), June 1984, 7-9 and IPSA Participation 8(3), Winter 1984, 16. The addresses for CPSA and AAPS are c/o University of Ottawa, 12 Henderson Avenue, Ottawa, Ontario, Canada K1N 6N5, and c/o University of Zimbabwe, P O Box MP 167, Mount Pleasant, Harare, Zimbabwe, respectively.

8. See Domenico Mazzeo, "Introduction: the regional trend" and "Conclusion: problems and prospects of intra-African cooperation" in his collection on African Regional Organizations, (Cambridge: Cambridge University Press, 1984) 1-12 and 225-242.

9.   For one such byproduct see the "Discussion"
     prepared for a February 1984 Nigerian-Canadian
     "Dialogue" on ethnicity at Bayero University,
     Kano: Y. R. Barongo "Ethnic and Cultural Puralism
     in Nigeria and Canada: the problems of political
     conflict and national integration", Journal of
     General Studies 4(1), December 1983, 142-148.

Part One

REGIONAL POLITICS

Chapter One

Regionalism and National Unity in Canada:

the dialectics of political discontent

in a liberal state

H. M. Stevenson

i) Introduction

Most participants at this and other conferences on
regional development want to concentrate upon the hard
practicalities of how to stimulate economic development
in regions underdeveloped by the uneven history of
capitalist growth. I hope, however, that I can be
excused my ignorance of these matters and deal with the
rather more nebuluous, socio-psychological aspects of
regional development and underdevelopment--the general
problem of competing regional and national political
identities, and for forging national integration in
ethnically and regionally heterogeneous states.

That this problem has become an almost pathological
political concern in Canada has been widely remarked,
and for many African countries the same can probably be
said. A pathlogical concern, not because there are not
real problems, but because those problems are so
ideologically distorted in political practise and
analysis. I will not rehearse the errors in most treat-
ments of regionalism, ethnicity, and political

The research reported here is part of the Research
Programme on Social Change in Canada at the Institute
for Behavioural Research, York University, supported by
the Social Sciences and Humanities Research Council of
Canada (Grant #S75-0332) and by York University, and
directed by T. Atkinson, B. Blishen, M. Ornstein and the
author. Data processing for this chapter was carried
out by J. Tibert, Director of Programming at the
Institute for Behavioural Research. The author is
grateful for the assistance of all these individuals and
institutions.

integration, which are better known in Africa than in Canada.1 I am well aware of the problems in the American political science paradigm of national integration and political development and my sympathies lie with the rival Marxist paradigm. These sympathies do not, however, include the tendency among too many of its proponents to dismiss the problems of ethnic and regional politics as simply ideological mystification and manipulation, "based" upon the economic distortions of capitalist and imperialist expansion. The politics and ideology of ethnic or regional identity and discontent have, as much recent Marxist scholarship agrees, a relative autonomy from the economic forces and relations of production.2 The analytic and empirical problem for Marxists is how to understand that autonomy in the context of changing economic and class forces.

This chapter attempts such an understanding of recent Canadian politics. The general questions addressed are first, to what extent, and in what ways, do class relations rather than regional identities affect political attitudes and political action? Second, to what extent are class rather than regional cleavages in political life intensified by worsening economic conditions? And third, to what extent are the political problems of regionalism amenable to integrative solutions through political and ideological campaigns for national unity, when such campaigns do not involve a critique of the existing economic order nor an appeal to new coalitions of classes in order to realize an alternative political and economic order.

Canada is a particularly interesting case for the examination of these questions. It is a country with sharply defined regional cleavages, which are commonly thought to reduce the effects of class cleavages on national politics to insignificance.3 It is, therefore, a particularly challenging case for a Marxist understanding of regionalism in terms of class relations. Canada is also peculiarly suited to an examination of the prospects for liberal rather that socialist solutions to the problems of national unity in ethnically and regionally divided states. In the 20th century, Canada has had the only official "Liberal" national government in advanced capitalist states, and it has had such a government for more than three-quarters of the last eighty-four years; until late-1984. This experience provides an excellent basis for the examination of liberal as opposed to conservative or socialist responses to the problems of national unity--the latter

10

two alternatives being weakly, but distinctively present in Canadian politics as a foil for the articulation of liberal thought. In the last fifteen years, moreover, the politics of national unity have monopolized the Canadian political agenda, involving most recently a substantial change in the constitution of the country. The effects of this liberal campaign for national unity are much disputed, with politicians and academics arguing either that regional conflict is more intense than ever, or that national integration has been substantially advanced.

The difficulty involved in trying to take sides in this dispute lies in the dialectical character of regionalism and national integration as processes of change in liberal states. Just as class and region are not independent and mutually exclusive but interacting determinants of political activity, so regionalism and national unity are coexisting and dialectically related, rather than mutually exclusive tendencies in the life of liberal states. Regionalism is typically produced by the economic underdevelopment of different parts of country, but it is also reinforced by economic growth and development in those parts at later periods, as the cases of Quebec and Alberta illustrate. Regionalism muted class politics, but regional political movements also reflect definite class interests, as recent analysis of the key roles of the "arriviste" bourgeoisie in Alberta or the state middle class in Quebec suggests. Ideological appeals to nationalism and national unity may, as intended, mute regional conflicts, but are likely to be really successful in this regard only when they entail substantial promises of social, economic and political change. In the politics of national unity too little is always too late. Governments that wrap themselves in the mantle of national unity without substantial offers to regionally alienated constituencies or to new nation-wide coalitions of classes are likely simply to provoke more intense regional antagonism, as much of the recent record of the federal government of Canada suggests.

The failure of liberal governments to make sufficiently substantive appeals to national unity as against regional conflicts is explained by another paradoxical feature of the politics of regionalism and national unity: where genuine social transformation is offered to a national political coalition, national integration on this basis invariably provokes class conflict. The real dialectical irony, however, may be

11

that almost any but the most vacuous of campaigns for
national unity tends to stimulate class conflict--that
even liberal compromises in the politics of national
unity produce both increased regional conflict and
increased class conflict. In recent Canadian developments, there is little evidence of this tendency for
appeals to national unity to invigorate class conflict.
In part this is because active intervention by the left
in the constitutional debate was limited by the alliance
of labor in Quebec with the government hostile to federal
constitutional initiatives. In addition it was limited
by the general economism of the labor movement and the
New Democratic Party (NDP) for which the debate over
economic policy, and by the split between the federal
and provincial NDP over the implications of constitutional change for diminishing the powers of provincial
governments that the party in Western Canada controlled
or was in a position to control.7 There has, nevertheless, been some evidence that the recent politics of
national unity has stimulated class politics in Canada,
albeit in a predominantly regionalized form. On major
issues of national policy--particularly questions of
national energy policy, economic autonomy vis-a-vis
foreign investment, and the maintenance of the national
medicare system--there has been a tendency for federal-
provincial conflict to be expressed in terms of ideological arguments about the defense of a truly capitalist
society.8 The increasingly ideological tenor of this
argument between the Liberal federal government and
Conservative provincial governments has further been
reflected in efforts to reorient the federal Liberal
and Conservative parties, although current electoral
politics continues to avoid ideological confrontation
over issues.

    These introductory remarks outline a dialectical
concept of the interplay of class and region in political change, and of processes of regionalism and
national integration in liberal states like Canada.   In
the next section I give a brief account of Canadian
political history to provide some concrete feel for the
applicability of this concept. In the third section I
go on to a systematic examination of changes in Canadian
political culture in the period 1979 to 1981, again
attempting to expose the interrelationships of class
and region in political life, and the ambiguous dynamics
of national integration and regionalism as processes of
political change.

ii) National Unity and Regionalism in Canada:
    historical background

    In the Canadian case, contradictory tendencies
towards national integration and regional disintegration
are well identified historically. Canada, despite its
qualitatively more extensive economic development and
its quantitatively greater experience of economic growth,
shares with many African states a pattern of uncertain
success in achieving the ambitions of its founders for
political and economic autonomy from imperial power. As
in many African cases, this uncertainty derives in part
from the ambiguity of the founders' own project of
decolonization--loyalism being a key element of English
Canadian political culture. Primarily, however, the
uncertainty derives from the country's location in the
world economies organized by the successively hegemonic
powers of Britain and the United States.

    In these terms, Canadian development, like much of
subsequent African development, has been "stapled" to
the export of primary commodities. The leading primary
commodity staples have shifted historically and geographically from fur to timber to wheat, and in the
contemporary period to oil and gas, creating in the
process regionally uneven growth spurts and declines.
A national manufacturing and industrial sector, though
longer lived and more extensive than those of Third
World nations, has a similar lineage. Raised under
tariff protected import substitution industrialization,
dependent initially upon foreign technology and capital,
the Canadian economy was vulnerable to imperial demands
for free trade and soon succumbed to very heavy competition from foreign multinational enterprises that
controlled more than half of total manufacturing and
mining activity in Canada in the late 1970s. And as
the case of the regionally uneven growth of primary
commodity staples, the growth of manufacturing activity has been highly uneven, creating a clear structure
of center and periphery in the Canadian economy and
society.

    If the pattern of economic development in Canada,
as in much of Africa, has tended to contradict in
practice the original intentions of the founding
nationalists--producing relatively weak, structurally
distorted, dependent and fragmented, rather than
strong, diversified, autonomous and unified economies--
the pattern of political development has been likewise
contradictory. Instead of the more stable unity under

13

a more centralized state than in the neighboring United States, as intended in 1867, Canada has developed a relatively radical political decentralization, and a highly visible pattern of political conflict over regional interests. A federal system, conceived to impose unity on an ethnically divided society, became transformed under the pressures of uneven economic development and the unambiguous reality of the ethnic stratification of economic power, into an instrument that resonated not with the harmonies of the national interest but with the discordant strains of defensive and aggressive regional claims against the central power. This transformation from centralization to decentralization, from a weighting of institutional powers in favor of national interests to one in favor of regional interests, was the more easy because of the ironic and unforeseeable circumstance that the original constitutional grants of power over culture and natural resources to the provinces--inconsequential in the 19th century relative to the economic management powers of the federal government--turned out to be the principal sources of revenue and of growth in state activity in the 20th century.

Both of the preceeding paragraphs violate my introductory remarks by suggesting a linear, uncompli-cated tendency toward the negative inversion of the positive intentions of Canada's founders for a unified economy and society. The dialectical alternation of patterns of growth and stagnation, of centralization and decentralization, of nationalism and regionalism, is, however, more cyclical than linear in the long run, and more contradictory than unidirectional in the short run. Further, the abstract logics of capitalism, imperialism and geography do not, as suggested in the last paragraph, adequately explain the historical patterns. These are rather the products of concrete social forces--classes, parties, social movements--whose definition of the situation in political and ideological practice is as important to the analysis as the constraints imposed upon them by the "external world."

In these terms, the post-1867 National Policy--based upon tariff protection, the export of the wheat staple to generate the capital and income necessary for domestic manufacturing, and railway development to integrate the society from sea to shining sea by moving the staples to export and the manufactures of central Canada to the staple-producing-hinterlands--reached its

14

height under the impetus of economic and political
centralization during the First World War. However,
the result of the centralism under union government was
the breakdown of the two party system, and the emergence
of class and regional politics on an unprecedented
scale. In response to the meteoric rise in the west of
agrarian socialist movements, and the intensified class
struggles of the depression, the long era of Liberal
federal govenment was intitiated under a second
National Policy.

This policy, though less coherently defined than
the first, was based upon Keynesian principles of
entrenching federal power over management of the economy
and expanding these powers in areas of redistributive
social programming for economic and political stabilization; as well as upon a principle of functional integration into the international system. This last internationalist modification of the previously more protec-
tive and defensive nationalism gave rise to the rapid
Americanization of investment, production, and culture
in Canada, the negative effects of which were disguised
in the post-war boom, but which nevertheless laid the
ground for the left nationalism in English Canada that
bourgeoned in the 1960s, and which had an effect on the
discourse of cultural and economic nationalism in
Quebec. The effects of Keynesian economic and social
policy, though initially re-enforcing tendencies toward
federal centralization, stimulated provincial government
growth as a result of the constitutional requirement to
channel health, education, welfare and cultural expenditures through provincial governments. This cooperative,
but essentially centralized federalism, lasted less
than a quarter century, however, before provoking
provincial appetites for conserving and autonomizing
the powers associated with their expanding jurisdictions
and budgets.

The second National Policy withered, therefore,
under the sustained counter attack of Quebec nationalism
and the more recent enterprise of province building in
other areas, notably Alberta. In this new cycle of
decentralization, there was conceived a third National
Policy, even more contradictory and less coherently
stated than its predecessor, but visible nevertheless
in its general policy commitments, and personified in
that most enigmatic charismatic, Pierre Trudeau.
Trudeau's extraordinary career sums up the contradictions: anti-nationalist become Canadian super patriot;
internationalist transformed into economic nationalist;

Liberal champion of the autonomy of civil society and
the free market become the godfather of state regulation
and investment in culture, the state control of wages
and prices, and overtures to business and labour to
enter into "tripartite," corporatism; civil Libertarian
become warrior against internal insurrection and the
"bleeding hearts" who lack the will to confront it;
high theoretician of the virtues of a balanced federalism transformed into the chief prosecutor of provincialism and the most intense advocate of the national as
opposed to provincial interest; the literate and effete
exponent of classical political theory and epigramatic
philosophy become the churlish speaker of vulgarity and
platitude; architect of expanded participation and
rational decision making in government appearing as a
aloof, autocratic leader contemptuous of the public and
its representatives.

For all the contradiction, the dominating influences
of this leader and his party during progressively
troubled times are inconceivable without a sense of the
emerging national policy they have proclaimed. The key
elements of this policy include national independence
through patriation of the constitution, and the removal
thereby of constraints upon constitutional adjustment
in the internal balance of powers; the development of a
bilingual and multicultural society as an antidote to
ethnic nationalism; the constitutional entrenchment of
civil liberties, with the associated increase in the
powers of the federal supreme court, as a means to
building a national political culture; the development
of a national economy through foreign investment review
and a national energy policy; finally, and least pro-
minently because of the ravages of fiscal crisis and
the accommodation to provincial prerogatives in these
areas, the continuing identification of a national
interest and federal government responsibility in
social policy--health, education, income maintenance,
etc.

The third national policy has been both less
coherently formulated, and less able to succeed against
the tide of world-wide economic crisis, than its prede-
cessors which succeeded in buoyant periods of cyclical
recovery and war economy. Apart from its draining
legitimacy as a result of economic ineffectiveness, the
Trudeau government has seemed to fall two steps back
for every step forward in its national policy. Federal
victory in the 1980 referendum on the proposition for
Quebec's sovereignty with economic association in the

16

rest of Canada, was followed by the revitalization and stunning electoral return of the Parti Quebecois, and it can by no means be taken for granted--as it, nevertheless, mostly is--that the independence movement is dead for another generation at least. Accommodation by all provinces other than Quebec to the final patriation of the constitution, was purchased at the price of allowing unilateral provincial exclusion from the application of the national Charter of Rights to their legislation, for no subsequent return in reduced provincial antagonism to the federal government. National energy policy and foreign investment review have been progressively emasculated to allay the protests of foreign capital and provincial governments. Social policy and national standards in health, education and welfare have been seriously curtailed by budget constraints and provincial deviations from principles underlying federal social policy. Bilingual and multicultural policy have accelerated fractional ethnic competition for resources, and while more has been gained here than lost, "backlash" effects are nevertheless observable. Finally, the hold on federal power was maintained at the cost of the elimination of the Liberal party from government in all of the provinces, and the growing regional isolation of the federal Liberal party, especially in western Canada.

It is not surprising, in these circumstances that excellent scholars disagree about the extent to which the country is becoming more or less integrated. Federal-provincial conflict is as intense as ever before, and the regionalization of party competition is more evident than ever. There is at the same time, however, a sense that this conflict and competition has moved from the narrow discourse of regional <u>versus</u> national interests to a broader debate on question of economic and political philosophy. Rather than being antithetically related, as is commonly supposed in the literature, regionalism has become the medium of class politics, at least in the different ideological positions enunciated by provincial and federal governments. The traditional weaknesses of Canada's nationalism based upon economic form rather than cultural and ideological content have been exposed more than ever by the weaknesses of its economy, but at the same time there have developed strong national coalitions around ideological positions in the recent constitutional debate: support for the rights of women and native people; support for the entrenchment of civil liberties; and support for universal, national standards of social

17

welfare policy. Regional identities and separatist movements have increased in power but, at the same time, there has been evidence of a highly flexible, pragmatic accommodation to dual regional and national identities by most Canadians, even in Quebec and Alberta where the resilience of national loyalties would seem to be most suspect.

It is my aim in the rest of this chapter, there-fore, to examine more precisely this balance of opposing tendencies. For this purpose, I have access to sample surveys of the social and political attitudes of the Canadian population in 1977, 1979 and 1981, including a national panel of individuals surveyed in each of those three years. Using these data, I propose to investi-gate the increasing or decreasing relevance of regional divisions as opposed to national class based divisions in the Canadian political culture. In this connection I take up an argument, that my colleagues and I have initiated elsewhere, to the effect that the regional-ism of Canadian political culture has been exaggerated, and that its significance declines as one moves between "layers" of political culture: from attitudes towards political parties and government institutions, to attitudes favoring political participation and, finally, to attitudes which structure ideological arguments about the goals of political action and the appropriate distribution and uses of political power. For each of the three years in the five year span, I will examine the relative influence of class and region on these three areas of the political culture, looking in the last at issues directly related to elements of the national policy--i.e., economic nationalism, social welfare policy, civil liberties, and bilingualism. What is of particular interest to me is to establish whether the long-term influence of economic crisis has increased the salience of class rather than regional divisions across dimensions of political culture; whether the national policy of the federal government has had such an effect; and whether, if regional rather than class influences have increased, there are unique patterns of class mobilization in support of different regional interests.

iii) Survey Analysis: region, class, and political culture, 1979-81

The period with which we are concerned in this section begins in 1977 with the tenth year of Trudeau's tenure as Prime Minister, following three years of his

second majority government; it includes the defeat of
that Liberal government and the election in 1979, just
before our second survey, of the Progressive Conservative government under Clark; the defeat eleven months
later of that government, and the re-election of another
majority government under Trudeau; the defeat of the
Parti Quebecois' (PQ) referendum on sovereignty-
association, and the initiation of the Liberal government's proposals for renewed federalism through constitutional change to satisfy Quebec; the decisive
re-election of the PQ in Quebec after the referendum
defeat; the ambiguous fortunes of the NDP, elected to
govern in Manitoba but defeated as the government of
Saskatchewan, and the decisive re-elections of Progressive Conservative (PC) governments in Newfoundland, New
Brunswick, Ontario and Alberta.

These political changes took place in a period of
significant economic change. The overall picture in
this period was one of descent into "lean times," as
the Economic Council of Canada entitled its 1982 Annual
Review. After the recession of 1974-75, average annual
growth in real gross domestic product declined from the
5% registered in 1970-75 to 3% in 1975-80. 1980 was in
turn the first of three successive years of recession,
in which there was negative real growth for more than
six months in each year. Inflation which had risen
sharply after the 1973-74 oil shock to over 11 per
cent, declined to 7 per cent in 1976 following the
imposition of wage and price controls. Thereafter,
however, prices rose and real wages fell. The consumer
price index rose steadily from 1977 to 1981, and real
personal disposable income fell almost 4 per cent between the first quarter of 1978 and the first quarter of
1980. Unemployment after the recession of the mid-70s
rost to 8% in 1977; declined to 7.5% in 1979, but rose
steeply thereafter to 10% by the end of 1982.

Our survey data, therefore, cover a period of considerable political and economic change in Canada.
They should as a result be a useful guide to the understanding of how changing economic circumstances are
reflected in political action, and of the general
problems raised in this chapter. Perhaps the most
significant general statement to be made from our data
in application to these questions, however, is that
there is very little change in the aggregate distribution of public political preferences as compared to the
rapidity and apparent significance of the political and
economic changes just reviewed. This reflects a number

19

of conservative influences: the confusion among politicians, economists, business persons and other elites as
to the nature of the economic malaise; the contradictory
and incoherent nature of public policy in response to
that malaise; the shapeless musical chairs of electoral
politics in which most, though not all, incumbents were
thrown out, and in which new governments of every ideological hue and party label were elected in this period
in one place or another. All these factors leave a
justifiable confusion about public issues in the mind
of the average citizen. In response to such confusion,
the most likely response is a conservation of past
commitments or random change in public political pre-
ferences--the combination of the two producing little
if any change in the aggregate distributions of
attitudes across the whole population.

Despite this general stability of public political
attitudes, it is worth noting marginal changes that
have occurred. And since so much of the debate about
regionalism in Canada focuses on voting behavior and
party politics, it is useful to start with changes in
federal political party identification. As Table 1.1
shows, these data do not indicate the massive decline in
the popularity of the Liberal party observed in 1982-84
after our surveys were conducted, but the changes
registered in Table 1.1 were a definite indication of
what was to come.

The most significant changes for the Canadian
public as a whole during this period were (a) the
decline in the proportion of the population who
regularly think of themselves as independents, and of
those who have no concern for political parties at
all; (b) an equivalent growth in the proportion of
the population who regularly identify with the two
major federal parties; and (c) among those two
parties, a proportionately more marked and consistent
increase in the identification with the Progressive
Conservatives rather than the Liberals. This indication of increasing Tory identification is particularly
significant in as much as Liberal identification in 1981
was no doubt inflated by the halo effect of the recent
federal election victory, and PC identification
increased by almost as much from 1979 to 1981, after
its defeat in the '81 election, as it did between 1977
and 1979, when the level of PC identification was
similarly inflated by a recent election victory. These
data, that is, underestimate the extent of increasing
Tory identification, and decreasing Liberal identifica-

20

Table 1.1

Political Party Identification
1977 - 1981

	Atlantic 77 %	79 %	81 %	Quebec 77 %	79 %	81 %	Ontario 77 %	79 %	81 %	Prairies 77 %	79 %	81 %	B.C. 77 %	79 %	81 %	CANADA 77 %	79 %	81 %
Liberal	35	35	39	46	54	57	35	36	41	26	20	23	27	24	23	35	37	40
Progressive Conservative	28	29	29	5	8	7	22	26	27	32	38	46	16	26	25	19	23	25
New Democratic Party	6	10	9	3	5	5	13	13	13	9	12	11	21	28	25	10	12	11
Other	1	1	1	6	12	9	0	1	2	3	6	2	6	4	4	3	5	4
Independent	15	13	10	24	8	12	16	12	9	13	9	8	11	8	8	17	10	9
D. K./Missing	14	13	10	17	13	10	14	13	10	17	15	11	17	8	16	16	13	11
N 1977	315			879			1198			540			357			3290		
1979	285			811			1070			499			314			2979		
1981	283			782			1091			482			311			2948		

21

tion in this period. Overall, the data suggest that
federal party politics in this period was becoming more
competitive in two senses: the salience of federal
party politics was increasing, and the balance of
identification among the two major parties was becoming
more even.

If party political competition generally increased
in this period as just indicated, how much of this
increase can be accounted for by increasing regional
cleavages in partisanship? The long remarked bias in
electoral outcomes, indicated by regional disproportions
in seats won to votes cast for different parties,
worked to isolate the federal Liberals from representation in the West during this period, and our data are
consistent with this result. Although the growth in
PC identification was 6 per cent in the nation as a
whole from 1977 to 1979, the equivalent growth was 9
per cent in British Columbia and 14 per cent in the
Prairies. Since elsewhere there was almost no change,
it is clear that the increasing party competitiveness
we have observed in this period is almost entirely a
regional phenomenon--attributable to the proportionately increaed identification of Western Canadians with
the PC party.

This increasing regionalism of Canadian federal
party politics can be expected to influence the balance
of regional and class cleavages in other aspects of
public political attitudes--presuming that there is
some connection between partisan preferences and
attitudes towards public policy issues. Though such
connections are normally weak, they might be expected
to have increased during a period of increasing party
competitiveness, especially when the period involved
major political campaigns for national unity couched in
terms of social, cultural and economic policy as well
as constitutional change.   In order to see whether
regionalism increased in other areas of the political
culture, we have chosen a variety of indicators of
attitudes towards government, toward political participation, and towards the substantive policy and
constitutional issues involved in the recent politics
of national unity. The data on attitudes towards
government and political participation are summarized
in Table 1.2

As in the case of party identification, there is a
great deal of stability in public opinion on the issues
described here. The first five items deal with

22

Table 1.2
Attitudes Towards Government
1977 - 1981

	Atlantic 77 %	79 %	81 %	Quebec 77 %	79 %	81 %	Ontario 77 %	79 %	81 %	Prairies 77 %	79 %	81 %	B.C. 77 %	79 %	81 %	CANADA 77 %	79 %	81 %
1. Dissatisfaction with the Federal Government (a)	33	36	44	23	39	29	32	39	39	46	43	59	52	51	53	33	37	43
2. Unfair treatment of Province by Federal Government	59	63	67	57	54	58	31	33	36	60	56	71	63	59	67	52	48	54
3. Federal Government too much power	43	43	45	44	44	47	34	35	44	49	48	67	45	38	47	42	40	50
4. Provincial Government too much power		15	15		30	23		28	33		28	28		28	37	27	27	28
5. Future balance of power should favour Provinces	39	37	41	58	59	56	31	26	22	46	40	48	42	37	46	40	40	40
6. Parliament loses touch with the people	76	72	80	76	75	75	69	74	74	78	74	74	76	68	71	75	72	75
7. Government doesn't care what people like me think	61	65	66	65	68	64	56	60	62	62	59	69	64	61	63	60	63	64
8. Politics and government too complicated	73	71	69	63	68	59	68	74	71	73	71	65	65	69	62	67	70	66
9. Have no say about what government does	62	59	59	55	57	51	52	55	54	58	60	59	46	50	55	54	56	55

(a) % below neutral point on a 11 point scale. All other entries are the % who agree or agree strongly with the item as opposed to those neutral or disagreeing with the item. In this and the following tables, the % is calculated excluding missing data--excluding those who did not answer the question.

23

attitudes towards government and the governmental
system. On only two of them is there a definite
change--in both cases indicating increasing dissatisfaction with the federal government. The proportion of
the population who were dissatisfied with the federal
government increased by 10 per cent from 1977 to 1981.
In that year, 43 per cent of the population were
dissatisfied with the federal government--a far greater
proportion than were dissatisfied with any other aspect
of their community or private life. In similar fashion,
there was close to a 10 per cent increase in the
proportion of the population who felt that the federal
government had too much power--almost twice as many
Canadians complained of the excessive power of the
federal government as opposed to those complaining of
the excessive power of the provincial governments,
although still larger numbers complained of the
excessive powers of trade unions and large corporations.

The increasing dissatisfaction with the national
government was, however, distinguishable in this period
from dissatisfaction with the federal system, which,
though widespread, did not increase to the same extent.
The proportion of the population who felt that their
provinces were not fairly treated by the federal government dropped slightly after the election of the Clark
government in 1979, and then increased rapidly to 54
per cent in 1981: more than it was in 1977. On the
other hand, the smaller proportion of the population
who felt that the balance of powers between the federal
and the provincial governments should be changed in the
future to favor the provinces declined after the
election of Clark and did not rise again after the re-
election of Trudeau. The question of fair treatment is
more directly an evaluation of the federal government,
and change on this question is therefore more like the
increasing dissatisfaction with the federal government
than is change on the question of the balance of
powers. This latter question deals more with the issue
of the federal system. These data suggest, therefore,
that increasing political dissatisfaction in this
period reflected more an evaluation of the national
government's incompetence to handle problems of the
day, rather than a perception of constitutional defects
that limited governmental competence. At the same
time, it is clear that a very substantial proportion--
between 40 and 55 per cent--of all Canadians in 1981
favored some form of greater accommodation to their
provincial interests by the national government.

24

This "provincialism" was, in addition, much more
marked in some regions than in others, and regionalism
in these terms, as in the associated terms of party
identification, increased over this period. Dissatisfaction with the federal government remained constant
in British Columbia, but increased more markedly in the
other peripheral regions--the Atlantic and Prairie
provinces--as compared to central Canada. Regionalism
in this respect is further marked by the strong sensitivity of public dissatisfaction with the federal government to the character of the party in power. The
decline in dissatisfaction in the West after the
election of the Clark government and the subsequent
rise after the re-election of Trudeau is inversely
mirrored in Quebec, where dissatisfaction increased and
then decreased following the same changes in governing
party. The distinctive position of Quebec is shown
further by the evidence that although Quebeckers are
least dissatisfied with the federal government, they
are the most in favor of constitutional changes to give
increased powers to the provincial governments. In
Quebec, that is, unlike the rest of the country, there
is more public criticism of the governmental system
rather than of particular national governments.

If we move from these attitudes to government and
the system of government to questions of political
efficacy--perceptions of adequate representation and of
competence to effect government--we find interesting
sidelights on the nature of public dissatisfaction with
government in Canada. As indicated by items 6-9 in
Table 1.2, political alienation, in the sense of a low
sense of political efficacy, was remarkably widespread
and stable between 1977 and 1981. Comparable data from
other surveys show increasing political alienation on
these measures since 1965, and the relative absence of
change after 1977 probably reflects a "ceiling effect"
of high levels of political alienation rather than the
lack of response to changing economic and political
conditions, or a lack of association between political
alienation and the increasing dissatisfaction with
government noted above. The extent of alienation
measured in these terms is very striking: 55% of the
Canadian population feel they have no say about what
the government does; close to two-thirds feel that
politics and government is too complicated, or that
government does not respond to what people like them
think; and three-quarters feel that parliament is out
of touch with the people. Although one of the classic
accounts of regionalism in Canada describes the

phenomenon in terms of political efficacy--i.e., of lower levels of political efficacy in some regions rather than others--our data in Table 1.2 show no such regional pattern. In any event, however, the high overall levels of political alienation are a meaningful context in which to understand the escalating dissatisfaction with government in this period.

We move now from these attitudes towards government and political participation to more general questions of ideology, beginning with questions of civil liberties and tolerance.

The data in Table 1.3, show substantial popular support for key aspects of the Trudeau government's campaign for linguistic rights and bilingualism as an aid to national unity. A very solid national majority (77%) favored official bilingualism in 1977, some years after the introduction of legislation requiring French qualifications for promotion to senior positions in the federal civil service. Criticism of the implementation of these requirements had already been widely publicized, and it is unlikely that there was much more negative public reaction after 1977 for these reasons, although we do not have repeated measures of that item to establish this. Popular approval of Liberal policy on bilingualism also covered the extension of French schooling outside of Quebec (64% approval), and even more so, predictably, the provision of English school for non-English immigrants to Quebec (77% approval).

This and other questions of language policy in Quebec indicate, however, serious ambiguities in the justification of language policy in terms of civil liberties, and the distinctive position of Quebec in this regard. The provision of English schooling for non-English speaking immigrants to Quebec was opposed by the independentist government of the province, and Quebeckers throughout the period were substantially less likely than other Canadians to agree with this notion of bilingualism. In 1977, less than half of the Quebec population--and much less than half of the French-speaking Quebeckers--approved of this extension of bilingualism, although support for hard-edged PQ policy on this matter declined subsequently. The other major question of language rights in Quebec--the institution of French as the language of work--also affected Quebeckers and other Canadians very differently. Seventy to eighty per cent of the Quebec population--in effect, all French-speaking Quebeckers--approved of this

Table 1.3.1

Attitudes Towards Civil Liberties and Out-Groups

1977 - 1981

	Atlantic 77 %	79 %	81 %	Quebec 77 %	79 %	81 %	Ontario 77 %	79 %	81 %	Prairies 77 %	79 %	81 %	B.C. 77 %	79 %	81 %	CANADA 77 %	79 %	81 %
1. French schooling outside Quebec	66	64	80	91	90	89	56	58	58	54	50	49	40	45	44	64	64	64
2. English schooling for non-English immigrants to Quebec	84	83	88	45	64	61	79	84	82	89	89	85	79	80	78	71	77	77
3. French should be language of work in Quebec	24	28	31	71	85	80	24	23	24	19	18	17	22	28	24	36	38	39
4. French requirement for senior civil servants	75	–	–	90	–	–	75	–	–	65	–	–	69	–	–	77	–	–
5. Immigrants should try harder to be like other Canadians	59	59	61	83	83	82	64	66	63	63	63	62	64	63	62	68	69	68
6. Immigrants not prepared to work as hard as other Canadians	15	12	13	21	16	20	12	8	8	10	12	10	6	4	6	13	11	12

Table 1.3.2

Attitudes Towards Civil Liberties and Out-Groups
1977 - 1981

	Atlantic 77 %	79 %	81 %	Quebec 77 %	79 %	81 %	Ontario 77 %	79 %	81 %	Prairies 77 %	79 %	81 %	B.C. 77 %	79 %	81 %	CANADA 77 %	79 %	81 %
7. Immigrants bring discrimination upon themselves	64	56	56	67	65	63	73	68	67	67	64	64	75	75	74	69	67	66
8. More effort to protect rights of native people	51	49	40	53	54	49	58	52	50	41	42	42	55	52	52	53	51	47
9. More effort to eliminate discrimination against women	49	48	50	60	59	66	48	44	54	46	38	51	49	45	48	52	48	55
10. Constitutional right of women; equal pay for equal pay	-	-	92	-	-	91	-	-	90	-	-	86	-	-	87	-	-	90
11. Affirmative action programs for women and minorities	-	-	56	-	-	68	-	-	50	-	-	46	-	-	44	-	-	54
12. Native peoples right to limited self-government	-	-	47	-	-	52	-	-	43	-	-	42	-	-	47	-	-	46

extension of French rights, but less than one quarter of Canadians outside of Quebec agreed.

These items indicate the difficulties of a liberal conception of language rights, and the extent to which attitudes towards linguistic rights and bilingualism differ by region. Freedom of choice in matters of language is, in practice, a freedom not to be understood in different parts of a country in which majorities are unilingual in French or English. The logic of official bilingualism is easily approved, therefore, as ensuring the right of all citizens to have access to services of the national government in either official language. In effect, making French the official language of work in Quebec establishes a similar right for the vast majority of Quebec workers who are French speaking in their dealing with the majority of private sector employers who are English speaking. But it deprives the small proportion of English speaking workers of that right, and is correspondingly strongly opposed by them.

There is, of course, more involved for most French speaking Quebeckers than the individual right to participate fully in government and the economy. What is more at issue in questions of the language of work, and schooling for immigrants, is the collective right to preserve an essentially French society and culture in Quebec. For French Quebeckers, simply the achievement of that collective right is the precondition for a meaningful right to choose among Canada's official languages. This confusion of individual and collective rights, and the opposition of English Canadians to the claim of a collective right to the preservation of a French society in Quebec, seriously limits the ability to promote national unity through language policy.

Items 5-7 in Tables 1.3.1 and 1.3.2 deal with attitudes towards immigrants. The data reveal a very stable distribution of opinion over the five years, and there is no evidence here that worsening economic conditions have, for example, increased prejudice against immigrants. The proportion of the population who indicate a prejudiced attitude towards immigrants is, however, very high on two of these items. More than two thirds of the population indicate that they think "immigrants should try harder to be like other Canadians," and that "immigrants bring discrimination upon themselves." These data indicate serious limits to public acceptance of the liberal orientation towards

tolerance of ethnic and cultural differences, and of the
Liberal government's operational defence of that orientation in policy promoting multiculturalism. Such
policy has, however, been less forceably stated than
policy on bilingualism, and it should be noted that
Canadian prejudice against immigrants is not without
qualification. As indicated in Tables 1.3.1 and 1.3.2
not more than 13 per cent of Canadians agreed with the
assertion that "immigrants are not prepared to work as
hard as other Canadians."

As in attitudes towards bilingualism, the major
regional differences in attitudes towards immigrants
reflect the peculiar position of Quebec. Quebeckers
are substantially more likely than other Canadians to
agree that immigrants should try harder to be like
other Canadians and that they are not prepared to work
as hard as other Canadians. However, they are less
likely than Ontarians or British Columbians to agree
that immigrants bring prejudice upon themselves.
Furthermore, as in reference to bilingualism, there is
an obvious sense in which these questions about
immigrants involve significantly different issues in
Quebec as compared to the rest of the country. For
Quebeckers, clearly, an important issue in answering
these questions is the lack of willingness of many
immigrants to Quebec to become more like the majority
of French speaking rather than the minority of English
speaking citizens, and the concern that they are not as
prepared to work as hard as other Canadians at learning
French. This is less a matter of intolerance of ethnic
and cultural diversity, or simple prejudice against
immigrants, than it is a matter of defending the collective identity of Quebec. Although this concern may well
lead to greater prejudice against immigrants in Quebec,
the differences in prejudice between regions are not
likely to be as great as the numbers in Tables 1.3.1
and 1.3.2 suggest.

Items 8-12 refer to proposals to giver greater
recognition to the rights of women and native peoples.
These data indicate that prejudice against women and
native peoples is much less than appears to be the case
for immigrant groups, although public support for the
entrenchment of civil rights for the former out-groups
is not by any means overwhelming. In 1981, the principle of equal pay for equal work was all but universally
approved, but only a slim majority (55%) agreed with a
harder edged proposition to eliminate discrimination
against women. On the complex issue of affirmative

action programs for the hiring and promotion of women
and minorities, there was a similarly narrow majority
(54%) in support of such action.

There is a suggestion that support for the elimination of discrimination against women increased over the
five years, but the evidence is not strong. Approval
of the rights of native people seems in fact to have
declined, and in 1981 less than a majority advocated
greater government effort to protect the rights of
native people, or their constitutional right to limited
self-government. There are no pronounced or consistent
regional differences in attitudes towards the civil
rights of women and native people. Quebec appears to
be slightly more supportive of the extension of the
civil liberties of these out-groups, and the Prairies
less so, but the differences are minor.

I turn, finally, to a consideration of attitudes
towards social welfare, economic nationalism and labor
relations. The full range of debate over problems of
social welfare cannot be revealed by the first three
items in Table 1.4, but they are nevertheless illustrative. There is widespread (more than two-thirds)
agreement in Canada--and apparently increasing agreement
during this period of economic stagnation or
recession--that income inequalities are too pronounced.
There is also very widespread (more than 70 per cent)
but apparently declining support for the principle that
the government should provide employment for those who
cannot find jobs. Finally, there is majority (between
55 and 60 per cent) support, though not overwhelming and
again apparently declining support, for measures which
might alleviate income inequalities by more redistributive taxation. In sum, there is general agreement that
there are unacceptable levels of inequality in Canadian
society; general approval of social measures which
provide minimal income security or job opportunity to
the most deprived, but considerable disagreement over
the means of attaining the object of greater overall
justice in the distribution of income and wealth. The
effects of economic decline have been to accentuate the
perception of inequalities, but to reduce the level of
public support for measures to alleviate these
inequalities. There is, that is, some partial support
in these data for a shift to the right during this
period, although the majority of Canadians remain
generally supportive of the welfare state.

Table 1.4

Attitudes Towards Social Welfare
Economic Nationalism and Labor Relations
1977 - 1981

	Atlantic 77 %	79	81	Quebec 77 %	79	81	Ontario 77 %	79	81	Prairies 77 %	79	81	B.C. 77 %	79	81	CANADA 77 %	79	81
1. Too much difference between rich and poor	(25)a 72	75	80	(26)a 70	79	72	(16)a 62	64	65	(18)a 63	62	66	(17)a 57	63	63	(20)a 64	67	69
2. Government should provide jobs for those who can't find them	(31) 86	69	77	(42) 88	89	88	(19) 73	68	65	(17) 78	63	62	(22) 70	62	61	(27) 79	72	70
3. High income people should pay more taxes	(16) 55	61	60	(41) 69	69	67	(15) 57	50	55	(16) 54	48	53	(19) 58	53	50	(20) 60	57	58
4. Results of foreign investment mixed or bad	61	64	60	54	48	59	54	57	58	61	61	55	58	60	63	57	55	58
5. Teachers no right to strike (disagree/neutral)	52	57	58	(b) 78	44	40	42	44	43	55	54	54	51	54	57	(b) 52	47	47
6. Laws against hiring workers to replace those on strike	53	52	60	65	65	71	55	49	53	54	36	40	56	55	55	58	52	57
7. Workers on boards of governors of firms where they work	(10) 75	74	76	(17) 77	77	76	(8) 65	71	70	(11) 71	71	73	(13) 71	73	73	(12) 70	73	73

a - Figures in parentheses refer to the proportion who "strongly agree"; while all other figures include simple agreement.

b - The question on this issue was worded positively, in favor of the right of teachers to strike, in French but negatively in English. This inflates the figure in Quebec relative to other areas.

32

Although we expect, and will show later that class divisions are important to this debate over social welfare, there are regional differences on these matters shown in Table 1.4. Quebec as always is distinctive-- consistently more to the left. Comparison with the other central Canadian region makes this clearest: 10 per cent more Quebeckers than Ontarians strongly agreed that there is too much difference between rich and poor; 15 to 20 per cent more Quebeckers approved of government as employer of last resort; and 12 to 20 per cent more Quebeckers favored more redistributive taxation. The poorest, Atlantic region is, like Quebec, substantially more likely than other regions to see unacceptable differences in wealth, and to support government as an employer of last resort, but it is not as different as Quebec is from other regions in endorsing redistributive taxation.

We have regretably little time series information on public attitudes towards economic nationalism. Our data do suggest, however, that there was some increase in opposition to foreign investment in Canada over this period. The proportion of the population who said that there was "enough U.S. capital in Canada" increased by over ten per cent in this period, until more than 80% of the population expressed this partial indictment of foreign investment. Overall evaluations of foreign investment were, however, less critical. Only 55 per cent of the population felt that the result of foreign investment had been less than unambiguously beneficial to Canada, and there is no evidence of any consistent increase in this critical attitude towards the long term effect of foreign capital in Canada. There was also no pronounced regional differences in these attitudes towards foreign investment, although overall evaluations of foreign investment were somewhat more favorable in central Canada--Quebec and Ontario--than in the peripheral regions.

Finally, the first of the last three items in Table 1.4 indicates, as expected, major disagreements over questions of labor relations. A minority of Canadians--although just less than half--upheld the right of teachers to strike. Close to 60 per cent, however, were prepared to protect the strike power of unions by legislation against scab labor, and over 70 per cent favored the principle of representation of workers on the governing boards of firms in which they work. As in relation to foreign investment, there is no consistent pattern of change here, and again,

33

therefore, no evidence for the slight shift to the right observed in attitudes towards social welfare. Further, there is again no evidence of any pronounced regional differences, although there is consistently but marginally lower support for labor in Ontario as opposed to other regions, and marginally greater support for labor in Quebec.

On balance, the preceding review of regionalism in Canadian political culture can be summarized as follows:

(a)   There are very pronounced regional differences in political party loyalties and in public dissatisfaction with the national government and the federal system;

(b)   There are no regional differences in the rooting of a "participant political culture" which is everywhere very weak in Canada;

(c)   There are pronounced regional differences on questions of civil liberties--the rights of linguistic, sexual and racial or ethnic out-groups;

(d)   Regional differences on general ideological issues of social welfare, economic nationalism, and labor rights are not pronounced, except perhaps on social welfare; and

(e)   There is consistent evidence in all dimensions of political culture that Quebec is a distinctive political community as compared to other regions of the country, and the strongest component of the regionalism identified in (a), (c), and (d) is the distinctive position of Quebec.

These findings confirm our past assertions that regionalism in political culture is expressed less in matters most directly tied to the class logic of a capitalist society--such as questions of social welfare, economic policy and labor relations, or the general questions of participation, trust and efficacy in the political system--than it is in matters of identification with particular political institutions like political parties and governments. These findings reinforce also our past assertion that the "national question" of the relationship between Quebec and the rest of Canada should not be confused as a general problem of regional differences across the country as a

34

whole. If the extent of regionalism in Canadian
political life should be qualified in these ways, it
may still be argued, however, that regionalism is the
dominant influence in Canadian politics, and that it
has been becoming more so. I turn, therefore, to
examine these latter issues.

Tables 1.5.1 and 1.5.2 present the results of a
systematic comparison of the direct or unique effects
of region and class, as well as the effect of their
interaction on the different aspects of political
culture I have been examining. Region is characterized
as in Tables 1.1-4, while class is classified in eight
categories (a) professional and managerial; (b) small
business, technical/semi-professional, mid-managers and
farmers; (c) supervisors and foremen; (d) skilled
workers; (e) semi-skilled workers; (f) unskilled labor;
(g) house-workers; and (h) others, including students,
retired, etc.). Items 1 and 2 in Table 1.5 are the
single items reported earlier, but items 3-9 are the
summed scores on the mutually correlated multiple items
on each topic reported earlier. Differences in the distributions of each item make comparison of the relative
effects of class and region on one dependent variable
rather than another difficult. We cannot, for example,
say that region has a stronger effect on attitudes
towards the extension of French language rights than it
does on any other attitudes; although it is theoretically
plausible that this should be so, the data look that
way, and it may be the case. The data nevertheless
shed very useful light on the questions raised in this
chapter and they can be summarized as follows:

(a)   There are statistically significant effects of
      region in every dimension of political culture,
      even in those dimensions where our previous analysis
      has shown that the regional differences are not so
      pronounced.

(b)   By comparison, the effects of class are somewhat
      less often and less strongly statistically signi-
      ficant over the whole range of items. These class
      effects are, nevertheless strongly significant
      ($p \leq .001$) in 56 per cent of the tests reported in
      Tables 1.5.1 and 1.5.2 and significant by conven-
      tional standards ($p \leq .05$) in 85 per cent of the
      tests.

(c)   This indication of the importance of class in the
      political culture is buttressed by the evidence

35

Table 1.5.1

Analysis of Variance Effects of
Region and Class on Political Attitudes

ITEM		Variance Explained by			
		REGION	CLASS	INTERACTION	TOTAL
1. Satisfaction with the federal government	1977	.040 xxx	.003	.018 xxx	.061
	1979	.020 xxx	.005	.013	.037
	1981	.058 xxx	.008 xx	.021 xxx	.085
2. Redistribution of powers between federal and provincial government	1977	.026 xxx	.006 xx	.026 xxx	.059
	1979	.048 xxx	.003	.024 xxx	.075
	1981	.078 xxx	.006 x	.025 xxx	.107
3. Political efficacy	1977	.005 xxx	.040 xxx	.019 xxx	.065
	1979	.003 x	.040 xxx	.015 x	.059
	1981	.003 xx	.058 xxx	.017 xx	.080
4. Extension of french language rights	1977	.370 xxx	.001 x	.010 xx	.382
	1979	.336 xxx	.004 x	.016 xxx	.351
	1981	.360 xxx	.005 xx	.008	.375
5. Civil rights of minorities	1977	.012 xxx	.010 xxx	.013 x	.033
	1979	.022 xxx	.003	.020 xxx	.045
	1981	.020 xxx	.008 xx	.015 x	.042

Table 1.5.2

Analysis of Variance Effects of
Region and Class on Political Attitudes

ITEM		Variance Explained by			
		REGION	CLASS	INTERACTION	TOTAL
6. Prejudice towards immigrants	1977	.032 xxx	.020 xxx	.013	.062
	1979	.036 xxx	.023 xxx	.016 x	.070
	1981	.063 xxx	.026 xxx	.012	.096
7. Approval of social welfare measures	1977	.048 xxx	.023 xxx	.008	.079
	1979	.084 xxx	.029 xxx	.019 xxx	.127
	1981	.078 xxx	.032 xxx	.018 xxx	.126
8. Support for labor rights	1977	.009 xxx	.018 xxx	.013 x	.040
	1979	.016 xxx	.015 xxx	.023 xxx	.055
	1981	.012 xxx	.014 xxx	.018 xxx	.047
9. Opposition to foreign investment	1977	.010 xxx	.006 xx	.014 x	.030
	1979	.020 xxx	.010 xxx	.016 x	.045
	1981	.008 xxx	.023 xxx	.016 x	.047

xxx $p \leq .001$; xx $p \leq .01$; x $p \leq .05$

1. Total variance explained differs from the sum of the unique variance explained by the main and interaction effects because of rounding and/or the inclusion of shared variance explained by region and class.

that the interaction of class and region has
statistically significant effects in over 85 per
cent of the tests, and that these effects are
highly significant in many of the tests where the
corresponding unique effect of class is not significant or of lower significance.

(d) As measured by the proportion of variance explained,
the unique effects of region substantially outweigh the unique effects of class--and the combination of the unique and interaction effects
involving class--on attitudes towards government
and linguistic rights. This reflects the strong
regional differences in partisanship, and in the
extent of the political confrontation between
different provincial governments and the federal
government--most notably, the opposition of the
Quebec government to Canadian federalism and
language policy.

(e) The unique effects of region are greater than the
unique effects of class on other issues of civil
liberties--the civil liberties of minorities and
prejudice towards immigrants--but they are not
greater than the sum of the unique and interaction effects involving class.

(f) The unique effects of region outweigh the unique
effects of class on attitudes towards social
welfare and opposition of foreign investment
(except in 1981), but they are outweighed by the
unique effect of class on attitudes towards
labour, and for all these latter dimensions of
ideology the unique effect of class plus the
interaction effect substantially outweighs the
unique effect of region. And

(g) The unique effects of class substantially outweigh
the unique effects of region, or the regional plus
the interaction effects, on attitudes towards
political efficacy.

On this evidence, it cannot be doubted that
regionalism is a fundamental aspect of Canadian political culture. However, the assumption that regionalism
is the dominant influence on Canadian political culture
can be questioned. Class has as important a direct
influence in a number of areas, and a significant
indirect influence in interaction with region in many
others. We cannot detail these interaction effects

wherever they are significant, but a few illustrations
will give the sense of the ways in which class is
important.

The interaction effect on satisfaction with the
federal government, for example, is particularly strong
in 1981. On inspection, this is mostly due to the
dramatically different position of houseworkers in
Quebec, whose average satisfaction score on the eleven
point scale is 7 as opposed to less than 6 for house-
workers in all other regions. This reflects both the
long-term pattern of particularly strong Liberal
identification of women in Quebec in the post-war era,
and the short-term effect of the mobilization of
Liberal/federal support among women after the contemptuous dismissal of "Yvettes" by a PQ cabinet
minister during the Quebec referendum. This is perhaps more an indication of the importance of gender
than of class, but the two aspects of the situation of
women are not unrelated, and the meaning and political
relevance of the interaction term is clear. Another
example is the interaction effect on attitudes towards
changes in the federal distribution of powers. Here
again, the interaction is largely due to the peculiar
behavior of a class in Quebec: the second group in our
class hierarchy, the middle class of small business,
technocrats and middle managers, takes a significantly
more favorable position to the increase in provincial
powers than does that class in other regions. There is
here confirmation of the thesis of the middle class
interest in provincial autonomy in Quebec. Finally, by
way of illustration, the substantial interaction effect
on attitudes towards the extension of French language
rights reveals that the upper three classes in the
peripheral regions--the Atlantic as well as the Western
regions--are substantially more anti-French than those
classes elsewhere. Since the upper classes are
slightly more anti-French everywhere, this indicates
the absence of a popular backlash against French
language rights and the particular resistance of middle
and upper classes attached to provincial states outside
of central Canada to any potential reallocation of
their states' resources to solve a problem of the
center's.

I come, then, to my final question in regard to
Tables 1.5.1 and 1.5.2: If region <u>and</u> class are both
necessary components of an adequate analysis of
Canadian political culture, have recent economic and
political changes increased the extent of regional or

class conflict, or both? If we examine the changes over time in the statistical explanation of each item, two generalizations respond to this question.

First, there are no more issues, or items, for which region's contribution to the variance explained increases over time relative to the contribution of class, than there are issues for which the relative effects of class increase over time. Regionalism has become more pronounced in these terms in attitudes towards the redistribution of powers in the Canadian federal system, and in attitudes towards immigrants. On the other hand, class effects have become proportionately more pronounced in attitudes towards political efficacy, attitudes towards social welfare, and attitudes towards foreign investment. In the last case, there has been a major shift over time in the relative dominance of the effects--class moving from the less dominant to the more dominant influence.

Second, on all but one of the items in Tables 1.5.1 and 1.5.2 there is an increase in the total variance explained by class and region between 1977 and 1981. That is to say, in every dimension of political culture, differences in public attitudes towards politics have become more strongly rooted in the different regional and class experience of individuals. Taken together, these two summary findings indicate that there is no consistent trend towards an increase in regional rather than class conflict or vice versa but that both kinds of division have become more intense in the political culture of Canada during a time of economic and political crisis.

iv) Conclusions

The findings summarized in the last section suggest a fairly definite answer to some of the questions raised in this chapter. Regionalism is a deeply entrenched feature of the political culture of Canada--there are significant regional differences in practically all dimensions of the political attitudes of the general public, but particularly in matters of identification with parties and governments. Regionalism does not, however, eliminate class cleavages in political culture--these are particularly visible in general ideological orientations towards the uses of party or state power, though not visible in identification with parties and governments. Moreover, in these latter areas as well as others there are important inter-

40

actions of class and region on political attitudes--on many issues, that is, the distribution of attitudes is peculiarly affected by the distinctive position of certain classes in certain regions. Finally, these additive and interactive effects of region and class have become generally stronger during the recent crisis--differences in attitudes between regions and between classes have become more clear-cut.

It is difficult, however, to move from this descriptive evidence in the Canadian case to an understanding of the larger questions raised in the chapter about the processes of regionalism and national integration in liberal states. What follows on this matter are rather speculative reflections on the survey analysis--reflections which, though not derived from the data, are, nevertheless, informed by them. The first point to make is simply a reiteration in context of the last point in the preceding paragraph: the recent economic crisis, and the Liberal government's campaign for national unity, have intensified regional and class cleavages in the Canadian political culture. Ironically, that is, a campaign explicitly designed to combat regionalism has intensified it. At the same time, increasing regionalism has been paralleled by increasing class cleavages--in other words, increasingly pronounced vertical (spatially or nationally disintegrative) cleavages have been accompanied by increasingly pronounced horizontal (spatially or nationally integrative) cleavages.

This "unity of opposites" is a happy conclusion for a chapter entitled "the dialectics of national unity." It does not, however, advance our explanatory as opposed to descriptive understanding of the problem. To do that we have to see the present in the historical context introduced earlier.

The national policy of the post-depression, post-war era in Canada followed the general outline of the post-war settlement between the parties of labor and capital in the European countries where the political class struggle was more clearly drawn. This policy rested upon the Keynesian theory of economic growth and stabilization, and social-democratic doctrines of redistributive incomes policy, social welfare services, and institutionalized labour relations. In Canada, the fact that this policy was introduced by a Liberal government rather than by a party of labour, as in most other Western countries, probably influenced the

41

relative invisibility of class politics in Canada. The
Canadian policy in the post-war era was thus more
easily cast in terms of the national interest and
technocratic wisdom than in terms of a settlement
between the opposing interests and political organizations of classes. In any event, the post-war settlement's initial successes furthered the political and
ideological mediation of class conflict. In Canada, as
in the rest of the advanced capitalist world, a
"collectivist" orthodoxy took shape according to which
a rational social contract was politically negotiated
for the distribution of shares of the assured economic
growth to competing interests. In Canada, however, the
success of this national policy reinforced regionalism
by accentuating regionally distorted patterns of
growth, and by inflating the budgetary powers of provincial governments.

The ideological consensus and regionalism so
engendered served to mute class politics, and the muted
class cleavages and swelling regional tensions
continued well after the collapse, nationally and
internationally, of post-war policy. In Europe, the
collapse has introduced a major ideological struggle
within social-democratic and conservative parties, and
a clarification of the ideological class struggle from
left to right. Although realignments in partisanship
suggest a decomposition of the class support for
different parties in many European countries, this is
arguably a temporary phenomenon, and one which in any
event does not obscure the very evident reappearance
of class-based issues and appeals in party politics.
In Canada, such developments have been slower to take
shape, but our data on the increasing salience of class
differences in political attitudes suggest that they
are nevertheless underway, or at least that there are
growing possibilities for a similar renewal of class
politics.

Such a conclusion, however, has to come to terms
with the concurrent increase in regionalism, which
might otherwise be expected to continue to override
tendencies toward class politics in Canada. In order
to come to a conclusion about the future dialectical
emergence of class politics and national unity out of
increasing regionalism, therefore, we have to
emphasize, and add to, our earlier qualifications about
the nature of regionalism in Canada. Three general
points summarizing our findings are relevant here.

First, although there are issues on which the
Maritimes, or the Prairies and British Columbia, differ
from Ontario, the regional differences within English
Canadian political culture are pronounced only in
attitudes toward party politics. The core of the
regionalism in Canadian political culture is the much
more marked differences between Quebec and the rest of
Canada. This regional cleavage is much less amenable
to political manipulation, and recent federal strategies show little promise (or intention) of compromising
with the distinctive cultural interests of Quebeckers.
Still, many observers indicate a decline in Quebec
nationalism in recent years, and our data suggest that
the peculiarities of Quebec are as much to be explained
by the greater clarity of a left-right cleavage on
class-related issues as by the distinctive emphasis
upon cultural issues. If greater security is achieved
in this latter area it may even be that the dynamism of
Quebec's politics and politicians may lead to the
invigoration of class politics in the rest of Canada as
they previously led to the invigoration of national
policy in the Trudeau era.

Second, the dominant theme in the national policy
of the Trudeau era--the emphasis upon expanding and
securing civil rights in the national political
community--has initially led to increased regional conflict over issues of civil rights, but the implications
for class-based national integration are not entirely
negative. The core of the problem--despite the current
nastiness of the resistance to the expansion of French
language rights in Manitoba--is not a resistance to the
expansion of French rights outside of Quebec. It is
rather the very different conception of these rights--
individual and collective--in Quebec and the rest of
Canada. This conflict can be expected to continue over
francisation policy in Quebec, but our data suggest that
there has otherwise been a growing national consensus
on the propriety of official and school bilingualism in
Canada. On other matters of the extension of civil
rights to women, native people, and immigrants, for
example, there is much less consensus. But such
regional cleavages as exist on these matters are again
largely due to the distinctive position of Quebec, and
disagreement on these matters shows some relationship
to class. Tenuous though this relationship may be, it
suggests the future possibilities of re-articulating
civil rights policy to create an alliance between
classes and the new social movements which currently
dominate the debate on these issues. The past emphasis

43

upon civil rights, that is, may have prepared for the renewal of class politics on a terrain different from the classic issues of economic growth and distribution--a terrain in which new generations of political activists in ambiguous class locations are most involved.

And third, other elements of the recent national policy of the Liberal government have interesting implications for the renewal of class politics and national integration of the post-war settlement have continued to be stressed, despite the difficulties imposed by the fiscal crisis. On issues of the desirability of such policy our data suggest a deepening of regional and class divisions. Although regional differences will persist as a result of provincial government disagreements over the funding and political control of social services, the deepening of the class differences over social welfare issues suggests that within provincial and national contexts the politics of the welfare state will in future have to take account of the potential for stimulating class conflict in this area. The current "no contest" between the major federal parties over medicare, for example, suggests that the official opposition is well aware of the dangers of otherwise promoting the appeal of the other parties to the Canadian working class on such issues.

The other issue on which recent national policy has been much more vigorously stated, and on which it departs from post-war Liberal policy, is economic nationalism. Here, more than elsewhere, the new national policy has been associated with an increase in class differences in public opinion. It is true that the "economic union" emphasis has been considerably moderated in recent Liberal government policy, and the ideological opposition to economic nationalism on the part of the federal Progressive Conservatives has been likewise deemphasized recently. However, the pressures of the international crisis which promote the need for new industrial policy and neo-mercantilist strategies of economic recovery make it difficult to keep such issues, and the latent class conflict they provoke, off the political agenda.

The preceding three paragraphs all emphasize the possibilities indicated in this analysis of a dialectical transition from regional to class politics in Canada. I must end, however, by stressing that such a transition is by no means automatic, and that there are indeed deeply institutionalized barriers to such transition. These barriers stem from the ideological and political emphasis in liberal states upon the separation of state and society, and the corresponding privatization or depoliticization of the mass public. The effects of this depoliticization are apperent from the widespread political alienation shown in our data. This alienation is itself a consequence of the failure of political parties to articulate systematically conflicting positions and class interests on matters of social welfare, economic nationalism, and labor relations, where our data show such conflict to exist. And this failure of the party system is reinforced by the fact that political alienation is, as our data show, strongly class-biased, depressing the level of activism and representation of working class interests. This reciprocal, feed-back chain from alienation to socially heterogeneous and ideologically similar political parties immunizes the political system against class politics. And the legacy of this immunity is a continuing vulnerability to virulent attacks of regionalism.

This then is the fundamental limit to the dialectical inversion of regionalism: liberal governments, though they campaign for national unity, avoid the issues which might mobilize a coalition with the working class on a nation-wide basis, or when they do raise them they face the active and organized opposition of already mobilized capital. This political incapacity is reinforced by deteriorating economic conditions, which belie the central promises of growth and redistribution made in the post-war settlement. In such conditions, public alienation from politics translates into rapidly escalating political discontent-- dissatisfaction with governments, or to a lesser degree with the system of government, and shifting party loyalties. As our data show, this political discontent is expressed in clearly regional terms.

Such discontent and its regional expression cannot be stemmed in the present crisis without new perspectives that respond to the collapse of the post-war settlement. Liberal nostalgia for Keynesian demand management and the social service state cannot now remedy the economic or political problems of the time. At best, therefore, the paralysis of liberalism and the weakness of social democracy in Canada will simply reproduce the futile politics of regionalism. The weaknesses of the left and center in Canada may, how-

45

ever, as in other liberal states, open the way for a
populist new right to capitalize on the public discontent and ideological discord that I have examined in
this chapter.

Chapter Two

Protecting the French Language in Canada.
From Neurophysiology to Geography to Politics:
the regional imperative

J. A. Laponce

When languages come into geographical contact, they
enter a variety of cooperative and/or conflictual
relationships. The relationship is predominantly collaborative when each language is used to express a
different social role; it is predominantly conflictual
when the languages in contact cover the same social
roles and are used within the same contexts. An
example of collaborative relationship is in the use
of English and Shona in contemporary Zimbabwe, or Latin
and French in 14th century France; one language is that
of everyday life while the other is that of international scientific communication. Collaboration may also
result from the desire to separate neatly the secular
from the profane as, for example, when 19th century
Polish Jews used both yiddish and hebrew. But, when
languages in contact are not segregated by roles, when
they are not socially specialized, then, one language
seeks dominance over the other; it seeks, eventually,
to eliminate the weaker language altogether.1

Bilingualism is frequent--if only because of the
need to communicate with foreigners and because of the
size of geographical migrations across language borders--
but it is not natural: we are born with the need to
speak a language, any language, not with the need to
speak more than one. Bilingualism is thus, typically,
a transition phenomenon that leads toward unilingualism, either by the merging of the languages in contact, or by the exclusion of the weaker language.

To reduce the cost of communication, languages
tend to reduce their overlaps and to give themselves
exclusive geographical niches. That tendency is not
limited to languages: people who have in common the
same ethnic origin, the same race, or the same religion,
sometimes even simply the same tastes, exhibit a similar geographical groupishness that may well be
rooted, as van den Berghe (1981) suggests,

47

in the combination of the biological and cultural
phenomena to which we give the name of "bonding".2
The preference for associating with the 'like me' or
the 'like my mother' may indeed be the result of
early childhood experiences. That there be such a
universal tendency would be sufficient reason for
considering the biological correlates of the distinction between mother and foreign languages and considering the conflicts that result from their overlaps;
but, in the case of language, as distinct from race,
religion or ethnic origin, there is an additional
reason for considering the neurophysiological correlates of bilingualism. That reason rests in the fact
that language, unlike religion or race, is a universal,
an every-day means of communication. I can ignore my
neighbours' race, my neighbours' religion; I cannot
as easily ignore my neighbours' speech. In matters
of religion or race, one can pretend to be blind,
but in matters of language, as Zolberg puts it,
one cannot as easily pretend to be deaf.3

i)   Neurophysiological and neuropsychological findings

    He who moves from his discipline to that of
another in search for data, risks, like the one-day
tourist, to attach undue importance to the bizarre,
the unusual, to what cannot easily be assessed as
either trivial or essential, for lack of having seen
the whole landscape. To guard, at least partially,
against that danger I will use three tests that will
help locate the findings encountered in my "travels"
on "foreign" grounds. These tests are in the simple
questions: How fascinating? How well established?
How relevant is the finding?

    The last two questions are standard, but why the
first? Why should the fascination exercised by a
particularly unusual finding be retained as a
criteria for inclusion? In traditional 'good' logic
it should not. But good logic is not always the best
criterion for discovering interesting connections.
Both de Bonno and Koestler advise the researcher not
to resist the temptation of what the one calls
'lateral' and the other 'diagonal' thinking, that
kind of reasoning which seeks connections between
seemingly unrelated factors that happen both to be
interesting in their own rights.4

    There follows, variously located on our three
dimensional test, some findings, encountered during a

48

journey to neurophysiology and psychology, a journey
prompted by an interest in bilingualism and regionalism.

A fascinating, weakly established but potentially very important finding: the Tsunoda study of the "Japanese" brain

Tadanobu Tsunoda, the author of the Japanese
Brain5 found, as expected, that the Japanese, like
people of other nationalities, have their speech
functions normally concentrated in the left hemisphere of the brain; but he found also, to his sur-
rpise, that the left hemisphere of his Japanese subjects received a wider range of sounds than the left
hemisphere of Westerners. The Japanese brain,
according to his findings, processes not only
linguistic sounds but also non-linguistic natural
sounds such as animal cries, the rustling of leaves,
the rolling of waves, and the chirping of crickets.
Further studies led him to note that, in this greater
involvement of the left hemisphere, the Japanese
were different not only from Westerners, but also from
Chinese and Koreans as well. Indeed, he could find
only one other linguistic group with characteristics
similar to those of his Japanese subjects, the natives
of the Polynesian Islands, at least those who spoke
Polynesian languages. Tsunoda explains the Japanese
and Polynesian deviation from the norm by the unusual
sound-meanings that characterize both Japanese and
Polynesian tongues, the only ones to make an extensive use of steady vowel-sounds. In those languages,
a vowel can, by itself, have a conceptual meaning of
its own and a combination of vowels (in the absence
of any consonnants) can also have a specific semantic
significance.

Tsunoda concludes that the Japanese mind is,
in part at least, shaped by the Japanese brain which
is itself shaped by the Japanese language. Consequently, says he, one can speak of a distinctive Japanese
psychology since a Japanese, unlike a Westerner, does
not separate, in his brain, verbal reasoning from
intuition, at least not to the same extent.

The most obvious cultural implication of this
yet insecure finding is that if two languages, such
as Japanese and English, affect so differently the
way of reasoning, then bilingualism implies bi-
culturalism; one could not, in some cases, shift

language without shifting culture as well. Thus, the mind might not be the only one to object to the shift from one language to another, the brain also might 'object' because of the way it is wired in one's dominant language. Tsunoda reports of his own efforts to learn English in the United States:

> As I was struggling to learn English
> my ability to think creatively
> seemed to dry up. When I returned
> to Japan I stopped all efforts to
> learn English, suspecting that
> thinking in English was unhealthy;
> and then I began to produce a stream
> of creative original ideas. I was
> convinced at the time that learning
> a foreign language has serious
> demerits for a Japanese.6

Tsunoda's experiments and his own experience support Albert and Obler's assertion, in their study of the Bilingual Brain, that knowledge of multiple languages has anatomical consequences and leads one to assume that these anatomical consequences, in as much as they take the form of physiological rigidities, have, in turn, cultural consequences of their own.7

A common, fairly secure and highly relevant finding: dismissing the single switch theory; language storage and language retrieval in the bilingual brain

It is a common observation that languages are intolerant of synonymy. The so-called synonyms of a typical thesaurus are, in fact, words whose meanings are close rather than similar; indeed, why should a language have two significants for only one signified? It would be uneconomical. Typically, a given term is "surrounded" by a varying number of other terms that express each a distinctive nuance, as if a variety of significants 'looked at' the same concept from different vantage points. We increase our vocabulary, from early childhood on, not by piling up significants on top of the same signifieds, but by adding, simultaneously, new significants and the corresponding new signifieds. However, when we learn a foreign language, the process is different. The reason for acquiring a foreign terminology is not to add a new signified (cat and chat should be the same animal) but to be able to communicate with

someone who happens to use significants that are
different from ours. For a mind that 'dislikes'
synonymy, is the piling up of significants on the
same signified a natural phenomenon? If not, what
happens? We can answer that question psycho-socio-
logically as well as neuro-physiologically. The
socio-psychological answer consists in noting that in
a closed, well-integrated social system, where two
languages coexist at time 1, given a long enough lapse
of time, we shall find, with few exceptions, that,
at time 2, the languages will have merged or that one
will have eliminated the other.

We know of very few individuals who have created
a second language for the sole purpose of duplication.
The many artificial languages such as esperanto,
interlingua, or solresol do not fall in the pure
duplication category since their purpose is to create
a new language that will facilitate communication
among existing natural languages. The normal
individual does not seek redundancy for the sake
of redundancy. Thus the question: what happens to
that individual when redundancy is forced on the self
by the social necessity of acquiring a second language?
How do we store different languages? In different or
in the same mental compartments? If two languages
are stored in separate compartments, so separate
that there is no mixing, no interference, then the
problems posed by synonymy and redundancy are not
as serious as if the languages are stored in a single,
common container.

The neurophysiologist Penfield proposed in the
1950's a single-switch explanation of bilingual
mental storing.8 According to his theory, the
bilingual brain has a single-switch mechanism that
blocks access to one language when the other is
either encoded or decoded. If so, the cost of
bilingualism is to be measured solely in terms of
learning time and storage capacity but not in terms
of interferences or delayed reaction times. Learning
two languages would be the equivalent of learning two
different sports, or learning to drive both a car and
a bicycle. Subsequent experiments on the bilingual
memory indicate however that interferences are
frequent even among so-called fluent bilinguals. The
single-switch mechanism explanation has now taken
second rank to the so-called tag-theory according to
which concepts are classified not primarily by
language but by meaning, the meaning resulting from

the specificities that distinguish a concept from another.9 The image of a cat would be 'surrounded' by a cluster of words such as 'cat', 'she-cat', 'chat', 'matou', etc. each word being tagged for its distinguishing characteristics, for example 'male' 'female' 'French' or 'English'. The tag-single-container theory explains better than the single-switch why bilinguals are affected by interferences, and why they are affected by slower encoding and decoding times than unilinguals. The tag-theory implies that it is not only the mind that rejects bilingualism as inefficient, it implies that the brain itself contributes to the rejection. In other words, the tag-theory leads one to assume that bilingualism is mentally inefficient and that the brain, in the absence of societal demands to the contrary, strives toward the greater efficiency of unilingualism.

A well-established, highly relevant and secure finding: the Dornic experiment

        Between balanced bilingualism and unilingualism, between fluency in two languages and fluency in only one, nearly all bilinguals stand at an intermediate position; so-called perfect bilingualism is an ideal that appears reached only by those who are better bilinguals than those who judge them. So-called fluent bilinguals know their limitations and have no difficulty in identifying their dominant language. That one reacts more quickly, that one is more at ease in one language than in another, is verified by a series of simple experiments conducted by Dornic who asked so-called fluent Swedish-English bilinguals to perform arithmetic tasks in both of their languages, tasks that ranked from very simple to complex.10 Dornic verified and measured precisely what common observation had led him to predict: the reaction time curves are not parallel in the two languages. The more complicated the task, the greater the difference in reaction time between the dominant and the second language. On simple tasks there is hardly any difference; on very complicated tasks the differences become extreme.

ii) From Neurophysiology to Geography

        These various findings point in the same direction. From a neurophysiological point of view, bilingualism is inefficient and unnatural; it is costly, it causes interferences, and it may, in some cases, alienate the self from one's own culture, from one's familiar ways of thinking and reasoning.

Considering only the more secure of these findings, the Dornic experiments, should be sufficient to explain why individuals tend to form homogenous linguistic groupings in physical space. They do so as a result of the addition of the many individual decisions represented by the choice of mates, doctors, teachers, grocers or politicians who shall all preferably speak one's dominant language and who should be, also, within easy reach. The grouping of people according to their dominant language minimizes the cost of communicating and maximizes the likelihood of communicating effectively. The equally relevant if slightly less-firmly-established tag-theory points to the same conclusion and suggests that the greater efficacity of operating in only one language finds its explanation not only in the conservatism of the mind but also in the wiring of the brain. Finally, the less secure but fascinating findings of Tsunoda, like those of Rogers and Ten Houten10 on the greater involvement of the right brain hemisphere of Hopi children, suggest that a change of language may involve a change of personality, not only because of the varied cultural contents of the languages used (the Whorf and Sapir hypothesis) but, also, in some cases, because of the different 'wiring' required for the processing of different languages.

The 3000 to 7000 languages spoken today in the world are very unevenly distributed on the surface of the earth, but, whether large or small, they all have clearly identifiable geographical niches. They are, typically, more geographically concentrated than are races or religions, whether they be languages covering a single and small geographical area - the 700-odd languages of Papua New Guinea for example - or whether they have, like English, many large geographical homes distributed over more than one continent. Of the many examples one could give of the relative distribution of language and religion, let us take only two, those of Switzerland and Canada. But why, it might be asked, choose to compare religion to language? For the reason that ethno-religious and ethno-linguistic cleavages are, mistakenly, often not considered separately in the analysis of dominant group-minority relations although the two types of cleavages have markedly different geographical correlates due, in part - a large part - to different biological underpinings.

In Switzerland, there are obvious areas of catholic or protestant concentrations - the cantons of
Valais, Obwalden and Appenzell (I), are over 95%
catholic while Bern and Appenzell (A) are predominantly protestant (80% and 76% respectively), but the
dominant characteristic of the spatial distribution
of the two major religions is that they do not form
contiguous areas.12 If there is catholic concentration
in the South, there are also catholic islands in the
center and the North, and, in some cantons, such
as Geneva, the two religions are territorially mixed.
By contrast, the linguistic boundaries are geographically clear, even when they run through a canton such
as that of Fribourg or Valais - the West is French,
the extreme South is Italian, and the rest is German
(with the minor exception caused by the mixing of
German and the declining Romanche in the South-East).
One can argue that the difference in the spatial
behaviour or religion and language is, in Switzerland,
the result of legislation, a legislation that does
not set any obstacle to the mobility of religion but
restricts language use by giving to the cantons the
possibility of enforcing unilingualism in government
operations and in the schools. Indeed, but it is
nevertheless significant that in a country whose civil
war was fought not between linguistic but between
religious factions, the religions have tended to
merge territorially, while the languages, with the
help of a restrictive legislation, have reinforced
their territorial exclusiveness. The same phenomena
characterizes Canada, if we compare, as does figure 1,
the spatial distribution of Catholics and francophones.
As in Switzerland, language is concentrated geographically; religion, by contrast, tends to spread throughout the whole political system.13 Furthermore, as
indicated by tables 1 and 2, the Canadian minority
languages that resist best the assimilation pressure
of English are those that have a high level of
territorial concentration (french) as well as isolation
(esquimo).

But the tendency of languages to concentrate
geographically, a tendency that could have been
illustrated by many other examples, is contradicted
by at least two centrifugal factors, a) the migration
of individuals in search of benefits other than
linguistic, in search of work wealth, freedom, congenial landscapes, or better climates, and b) the need

of all societies, if not all individuals, to communicate, to exchange information with their neighbours. The result of the first tendency is that languages become mixed territorially; the result of the second is that all societies develop a group of bi- or multilinguals (the size of that group varies considerably from society to society) able to provide links with other linguistic groups. In other words, while neurophysiology leads to the geographical concentration of languages, politics, economics, and culture will always, to some extent, work in the opposite direction. Consequently, languages are in a situation of flux - in some respect similar to that of animal species - that makes them expand or contract depending upon how much territory and how many minds they control. How do political systems respond to these situations of language overlap? The problem is typically one of border setting and border control. Indeed, in as much as languages in contact create territorial borders and border conflicts, they create problems that politics cannot ignore: the politics of regionalism.

iii) <u>From Geography to Politics</u>

To the problems posed by bilingualism, governments have had a variety of responses that can be grouped under the three categories of "laissez-faire", "personalism" and "territorialism".14

The laissez-faire formula consists in preventing that territorial borders be created that would restrict the flow of languages over space. In the animal world, this laissez-faire leads either to the elimination of some species by others or to the stable equilibrium of different species that share the resources of the environment and sometimes feed on one another. Languages are much more likely to experience the first rather than the other solution. The continued co-existence of two languages within the same populations will occasionally result, as already noted in the introduction, from different languages being used to separate more clearly the roles than one desires to separate. Standard German is used by the Swiss germanophones to communicate and operate within the larger international community of German speakers, while the Swiss local patois is used to maintain one's distinctiveness not only from non-Swiss Germans, but also from other Swiss. In Bolivia, in the early decades of colonization, the Spanish settlers - who

had decided that the Indians were unworthy of the
Castillian tongue - used Quechua or Aymara to communicate with the natives, reserving Spanish for communication among themselves. In societies that seggre-
gate roles and groups, the languages that have become
mixed territorially may, under a laissez-faire policy,
continue to coexist, notwithstanding the added cost
and the inefficiency of storing and using two or
more languages, because this coexistence helps in
maintaining the social or psychological segregation
desired. In equalitarian societies, on the contrary,
the mixing of languages at the territorial level will
typically result in the fusion of languages in contact
or in the elimination of the socially weaker by that
of the dominant group, or still, in the elimination of
the numerically small by the numerically superior.
In the equation of linguistic assimilation both
quality (being associated with the ruling ethnicity
or group) and number (being the more numerous language)
may well work in opposite directions -- with the result
that, sometimes, a conqueror will adopt the language
of the conquered -- but may also work in unison.
In the latter case the destructive pressure of the
language of the dominant group over those of minorities
is overwhelming.

A state interventionist policy may range from a)
imposing a single language in the schools and in
public life (the French policy following the Revolution
of 1789); to b) maintaining the minority languages alive
at the geographical and institutional peripheries
of the political system while imposing a single
language at the center (the present policy of the USSR);
and to c) attempting to give an equal share of both
the peripheries and the center to more than one official language, as in modern Belgium.

Among those varied policies, let us consider
two types of solutions intended to maintain linguistic
diversity - the so-called 'personal' and the so-called
'territorial' or 'regional' solutions. The first
takes into account, the other ignores the neurophysiological and geographical correlates of multi-
lingualism. Broadly speaking, the personal solution
seeks to make language as territorially transportable
as possible; it gives the individual the right to
obtain government services and schools (for example)
not only within the language's territorial niche,
but on the 'ground' of the other languages as well.
It seeks to mix the languages, as much as possible,

both in the minds of the state's subjects and on the
territory of that state. The ideal is a bilingualism
by superposition. If everybody speaks the two
(or more) state languages, then, it is argued, the
speakers of those languages will be at home everywhere.
The territorial solution, on the contrary, provides
a geographical translation of consociationalism. It
seeks to separate the languages in contact by giving
them each exclusive geographical areas, tied together,
at the level of political elites, by a small amount
of individual and territorial bilingualism.

   Let us consider the effect of these two policies
in a state such as Canada where the languages in contact are used to express the same social roles, rather
than in a diglossic system where the languages would
be used to segregate roles. Let us imagine a
hypothetical encounter between two Canadians, both
bilingual, but belonging to two different linguistic
communities - the latter being defined by one's
mother and preferred language. Let us further imagine
that this encounter will take place in either of
three settings: a) the home territory of the dominant language, b) the home territory of the minority
language, and c) a neutral territory. The question
is: what language shall be used in the encounter?
If the two languages were known equally well, the
problem could easily be solved - you speak my language on my home ground, I speak yours on your home
ground, and we speak either or alternate in the case
of a neutral context. But that solution would ignore
the findings of Dornic and others: bilinguals are not,
except on trivial matters, equally at ease in either
of their two languages. The language that will prevail will be that with the highest common denominator
of communication effectiveness. It will be, typically,
the language of the politically dominant group, since
that group uses its very dominance to shift the cost
of second language acquisition from itself onto the
minority. An English Canadian is less likely to be
competent in French than a French Canadian to be
competent in English (36% of French Canadians are
bilingual french/english compared to only 7% among
anglophone). Consequently, the likelihood of our
hypothetical encounter taking place in the language
of the dominant group will be overwhelming on the
home territory of that group as well as on neutral
ground of the minority language. The policy of
'personalism' does not diverge markedly from that of
'laissez-faire'. It facilitates the penetration of the

57

minority language by the dominant group and invites
the minority to disperse itself territorially, hence
to weaken its power of resistance to assimilation
pressures.

Such is the policy of the Canadian federal
government. The declared intentions of that policy
are to protect the French language in English Canada
but, since a reciprocal right is given to English in
Quebec, the effect will likely be to faciliate the
dispersal of French, hence the weakening of its
power of resistance to assimilation (see figure 2.2)
while helping the penetration of English into Quebec,
into the French language core-area. Until 1982 the
federal policy was successfully counteracted by that
of the Quebec government who sought to transform
Quebec into a kind of Swiss unilingual canton. But
the constitutional revision of 1982 has given the
central government the upper hand by making it
responsibile for the protection of an individual's
linguistic rights, the right in particular to be
educated in the language of one's choice (either
French or English).

Let us now consider more closely the likely
effects of an encounter among bilinguals that would
take place in the language of the dominant group on
the territory of the minority language. The Dornic
findings tell us that the more complex the linguistic
message, (hence, probably, the higher the individual
in the social hierarchy) the greater the gap between
the performance in one's second language compared to
what it would have been in one's first. Furthermore,
the tag-theory leads us to expect a greater amount
of interference, delay, and imprecision on the part
of the individual forced to operate in his lesser
known language. Finally, the Tsunoda hypothesis calls
for the possibility that the sense of inferiority
and relative inadequacy forced on the minority
individual be not simply of an instrumental nature;
it might be as disturbing, emotionally, as would be
an unwanted change of personality. In short, the
policy of personalism, that which favors the mixing
of languages territorially, has the likely effect
of upsetting the minority by alienating it on its
own territory, hence leading either to the acceptance
of assimilation to the dominant group or to separatist
movements that seek to gain control of a linguistic
border that would provide a defense against 'foreign'
intrusions.

The 'territorial' and 'regional' solution, by contrast, uses borders to separate the languages in contact and to establish the rules governing the linguistic hierarchy, a hierarchy that may vary geographically as one crosses the linguistic border. Switzerland stipulates clearly where the linguistic borders run that separate German from French from Italian. The Swiss citizen who moves from Luzern to Geneva knows that he will not, in Geneva, find German public schools and that his dealings with the Geneva public authorities will have to be in French; and vice versa for the Genevese who moves to Luzern. The estrangement, the sense of inferiority resulting from having to operate in one's second language is thus systematically shifted on those who cross the linguistic boundary. The negative and distressing effects of having to operate in a second language are not eliminated, they could not be, but they are clearly advertized by the linguistic border and they are shared equally - at least as nearly equally as possible - between the dominant and the minority ethnicity. Such a territorial solution eliminates, or at least reduces considerably the political tensions that result from an individual having to use his second language against his wish, on what he considers to be his home ground. The Swiss Supreme Court recognized the need for very rigid linguistic borders when it ruled against a German businessman who wanted to use German in an Italian canton. The court argued

> The internal linguistic borders of
> our country, once established should
> be considered unchangeable; the assur-
> ance given to each of the original
> founding (ethnic) groups, of the
> integrity of the territory where its
> language is spoken and over which
> its culture is spread, constitutes
> the guarantee of good relations among
> the various sections of the country;
> each must be given the right to
> prevent any encroachment.15

In short, assuming the policy of a state to be the survival of a minority language, the territorial solutions of the Swiss and Belgian type appear neurophysiologically and geographically functional while, by contrast, the Canadian solution that denies the possibility of permanent linguistic borders appears dysfunctional. A policy of linguistic regionalism is imperative to the survival of a minority language.

Notes

1. See V. Weinreich, Languages in Contact (The Hague: Mouton, 1968); W.F. Mackey Le bilinguisme: phenomene mondial (Montreal: Harvest, 1966); J.A. Laponce "Relating linguistic to political conflicts" in J.G. Savard and R. Vigneault (eds) Multilingual Political Systems: problems and solutions (Quebec: Laval University Press, 1975) 185-207; J.A. Laponce "Le comportement spatial des groupes linguistiques" International Political Science Review, 1(4), 1980, 478-494.

2. Van den Berghe The Ethnic Phenomena (New York: Elsevier, 1981).

3. A. Zolberg, "Splitting the difference: federalization without federalism in Belgium" in M. Esman (ed) Ethnic Conflict in the Western World (Cornell: Cornell University Press, 1977) 103-142

4. E. De Bono Newthink: the use of lateral thinking (New York: Basic Books, 1968); A. Koestler, The Act of Creation (London: Hutchinson, 1964).

5. T. Tsunoda The Japanese Brain (Tokyo; Taischuukan, 1978) (in Japanese).

6. Ibid.

7. See M. Albert and L. Obler The Bilingual Brain: neurophysiological and neurolinguistic aspects of bilingualism (New York: Academic Press, 1978).

8. W. Penfield and L. Roberts Speech and Brain Mechanisms (Princeton: Princeton University Press, 1959).

9. See a review of these findings in S. Dornic, Human Information Processing and Bilingualism (Stockholm: Institute of Applied Psychology, 1975).

10. Ibid.

11. L. Rogers, W. Ten Houten, C. Kaplan and M. Gardiner "Hemisphere Specialization of Language: an EEG study of bilingual Hopi Indian children"

International Journal of Neuro-Science 1, 1977, 1-6.

12.   P. Vidal-Lablache, <u>Atlas historique et geographique</u>, (Paris: Colin, 1951).

13.   J. A. Laponce, "Le compartement spatial des groupes linguistiques".

14.   D. McRae, "The principle of territoriality and the principle of personality in multilingual states", <u>Linguistics</u>, 33-54.

15.   G. Heraud, <u>L'Europe des ethnies</u> (Nice: Presses d'Europe, 1974).

Figure 2.1

Relative concentration of Catholics and people who speak French at home in Canada, in the 109 major urban constituencies, 1971.

Catholics

West

			X	X	X	X	X	X	
	X	X	X		X	X	X	X	X
X	X	X	X	X		X	X	X	X
X	X		X	X		X	X	X	X
X		X		X	X	X	X	X	X
X	X	X		X	X	X	X	X	X
X	X	X	X	X	X	X	X	X	X
	X	X	X	X	X	X	X	X	X
	X	X	X	X	X	X	X	X	X
	X	X		X	X	X	X	X	X

West x … x East

Language spoken at home

West

						X	X	X	
						X	X	X	
						X	X	X	
						X	X	X	
						X	X	X	East
						X	X	X	
						X	X	X	
						X	X	X	X
				X	X	X	X		
				X	X	X	X	X	

West … East

| x | districts in which the percentage of either Catholics or Francophones is above half the national average |

63

Figure 2.2

Effect of the Linguistic Environment (at the city
level) on the Retention of One's Mother Tongue as the
Language Spoken at Home. For Canadian Cities over
25,000

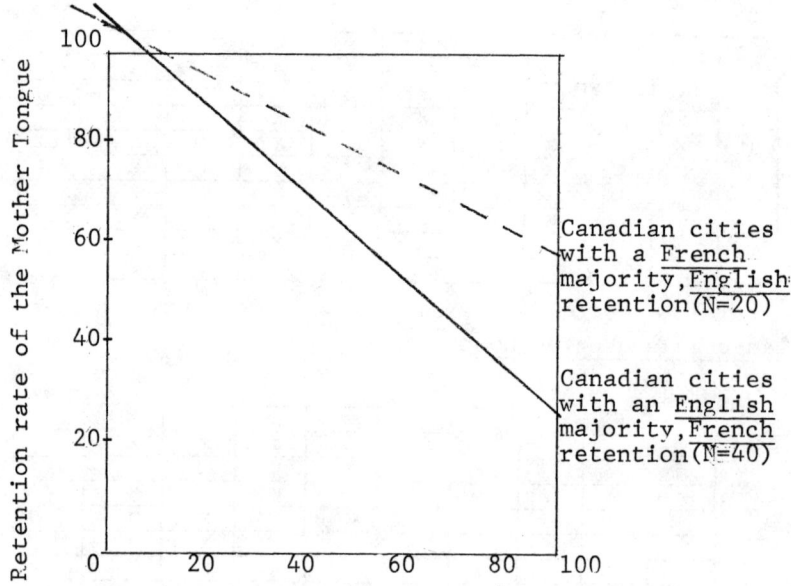

— % of population that speaks English at home
(100% = anglophones and francophones). Canadian
cities over 25,000

-- % of population that speaks French at home (100%
= anglophones and francophones). Canadian cities
over 25,000

Table 2.1

Percent of people who speak habitually at home the
language they learned as a mother tongue.   Canadian
census 1971*

Fnglish	98.8
French	93.8
Fsquimo	90.7
Portuguese	79.9
Italian	74.1
Chinese	73.8
Native Indian	69.2
Spanish	61.1
Swedish	61.0
Estonian	61.0
Lettish	58.4
Lithuanian	54.3
Japanese	50.6
Hungarian	50.1
Czeck	45.9
Finish	45.4
Slovak	45.0
Polish	43.8
Ukrainien	41.9
German	35.1
Arabic	35.0
Russian	34.1
Serbian	32.7
Rumanian	26.7
Dutch	21.2
Yiddish	19.8
Flemish	19.0
Danish	14.1
Croatian	12.7
Greek	7.6
Norvegian	6.4
Indo. Pakistani	5.9
Slovene	5.0
Welsh	4.6
Gaelic	.3

*Source: Canadian census, Catalogue 92.776, Bulletin
          S.P.6 (Ottawa: Government printer, 1976).

Table 2.2

Percentage 'French' of the total population of each Canadian province and territory

	NWT	Yuk-on	BC	Alb	Sas	Man	Ont	Que	NB	NS	PEI	Nfld
					1971 Census							
French mother tongue	3.3	2.4	1.7	2.8	3.4	6.1	6.2	80.7	33.9	4.9	6.5	.6
French home language	1.6	.0	.5	1.3	1.7	4.0	4.5	80.7	31.3	3.4	3.8	.4 .4
French only official language	.2	.0	.0	.2	.2	.5	1.2	60.8	15.9	.5	.6	.1
French mother tongue	2.2	2.7	1.6	2.7	2.6	5.1	5.4	82.4	33.6	4.2	4.8	.4
					1981 Census							
French home language	.9	1.3	.5	1.3	1.0	3.0	3.9	82.5	31.4	2.9	3.0	.3
French only official language	.0	.1	.0	.1	.0	.2	.7	60.0	12.9	.2	.1	.0

Chapter Three

The Creation of States:

theoretical and practical problems

Okwudiba Nnoli

There is in Nigeria today--1983--a groundswell
movement for the creation of new states from the component parts of the Nigerian federation. In fact, the
movement is so popular that practically every politician
publicly supports it. How is this apparently popular
movement to be understood scientifically? And since
the purpose of understanding is to inform correct practice, what should be the attitude of progressive forces
to the demand for the creation of states in Nigeria?
This chapter seeks to answer these questions.

Historically, the movement for the creation of
states in Nigeria has been associated with the politics
of Nigerian federalism. This politics concerns the
correct relationship among various precapitalist
societies which were brought together within the Nigerian
state by colonialism, and between them and the Nigerian
state. The issue has created various practical and
theoretical problems in the body politic of the country.

For example, the federated states have become,
among other things, instruments for securing preferences
and privileges for their indigenes to the exclusion of
others, even at the expense of universally accepted
norms and criteria in the field of employment and the
enjoyment of social, economic and political amenities.
Such state exclusionism, chauvinism and discrimination
often violate the right of the individual to freedom of
movement within the borders of the federation, rights
to housing and work, choice of employment, just and
favorable conditions of work, protection against
unemployment, and adequate remuneration.

Futhermore, problems arise because the process of
the creation of states--and their discriminatory activities once they are created--tend to disunite the will,
sympathies and ambitions of the various classes and
sections of the various communal groups within the

67

country. It becomes not only more difficult to generate and sustain national awareness but also to be able to direct such awareness into the channel of combined eforts to build a new society. The existence of chauvinistic states creates difficulties not only for the task of mobilizing and moulding the various communal groups in accordance with progressive principles, but also for the task of ending as quickly as possible such phenomena as alienation and distrust among communal groups fostered by the antagonistic nature of capitalist society. A situation is fast developing in which most Nigerians will be born, attend primary and secondary schools in their own local government areas, attend universities and other institutions of higher learning in their own states, and then work in the public service of only their own states. This will be an intolerable situation.

Nevertheless, the movement for the creation of states is popular precisely because it responds to certain aspirations of the people. What are those aspirations? One of them is the desire to eliminate privileges along communal lines. This is a desire of democracy. Consistent democracy is opposed to any form of privilege. However, the high incidence of nepotism in Nigeria contradicts this democratic aspiration.

The tendency of the peripheral capitalist system to preserve and encapsulate such pre-capitalist institutions as the extended family system, its high propensity for the uneven development of the various communities and regions of the country, its neglect of integrative links among various communities, the domination of the society by the petty-bourgeoisie and comprador bourgeoisie oriented towards distribution rather than production, the ideological bankruptcy of these classes and the pervasive poverty of the population have contributed to the granting of privileges along kinship and communal lines.

Historically, the Nigerian response to a colonial and neocolonial society in which occupational differentiation and consequently class consciousness is low and the incidence of destructive competition for scarce valuable resources is high, has been to build a system of preferences based on communal groups such as the nuclear family, extended family, clan and linguistic group. This system creates ingroup-outgroup boundaries which serve to exclude other individuals and groups from the enjoyment of privileges. Such a discriminatory

system of privileges and preferences is further
entrenched by the orientation, opportunism and indiscip-
line of the ruling petty-bourgeois and comprador
bourgeois classes. Unable to play a creative role in
production they are not oriented to the growth of production as a basis for their share of the national
wealth. Instead, they thrive on the exclusion of one
another.

Inevitably, the pattern of exclusion which they
adopt runs along racial and other communal lines.
First, foreigners are excluded. Then various domestic
communal groups such as linguistic groups, regional
formations, clans, and families are excluded in that
order as the size of the cake being shared diminishes.
Often this intra-class struggle of the ruling classes
for power and wealth is presented to the masses as a
general struggle of the communal groups for survival
and well-being.

Another aspiration of the people in the demand for
the creation of states concerns the democratization of
the society's decision-making process. It is part of
the overall desire of the masses to be the subject
rather than the object of government. It is part of
their search for a structure of government which provides them with an unfettered initiative and democracy
in the functioning and development of their society,
and gives scope to their creative initiative. The movement for new states embodies and articulates the
people's protest against the remoteness of the government from their local conditions, their powerlessness
in publicly expressing their views and having such views
incorporated into public policy, their dissatisfaction
with the extent of their, and local, participation in
politics, as well as the effects of such participation.
The movement expresses part of the hopes of the masses
to be able to exact accountability from their representatives in the various decision-making bodies of the
country. Under conditions in which the national leadership is oriented toward foreign models, the use of
foreign resources including personnel, importation of
foreign goods and ideas, and excessive concern with
external markets and other conditions, the people wish
to reassert the priority and primacy of local desires,
resources, aspirations, involvement, and peculiarities.

Thus, there are two contradictory streams in the
movement for the creation of states. One of the streams
is identified with the ruling petty-bourgeoisie and

69

comprador bourgeoisie. It is the stream of petty-bourgeoisie opportunism, narrow mindedness, prejudice, chauvinism, particularism, discrimination and exclusiveness. In this stream, the selfish ambitions of reactionary sections of society are palmed off as communal interests. Deceived in this way, various communities are set against one another. They are told that to perform their communal duty and defend their community rights, they should be mindless of the needs of the other people, seize whatever privileges they can, and hold smaller communities in reign.

People are made to believe that the backwardness of communities and strife among them arise from inherent differences among them. But it is well-known that the causes of such strife are not rooted in communal distinctions between peoples. They stem from the antagonistic nature of capitalist society in general and peripheral capitalist society in particular. The economic interests of the exploiting and ruling classes give rise to conflicts among peoples as well as between representatives of one and the same community. The proletariat is split into communal camps corrupted by the crumbs that fall from the table of their respective petty-bourgeoisie and comprador bourgeoisie. And when the proletariat of one camp supports the privileges of its petty bourgeoisie it inevitably arouses distrust among the proletariat of another camp thereby weakening the class solidarity of the workers.

The other stream in the movement for more states is identified with the mass political line. It embodies a genuine desire to surmount as quickly as possible conflicts among communal groups. This desire is expressed in the demand for the abolition of all privileges including those of the advantaged and disadvantaged communities alike. The goals here are genuine equality of rights and real equality in all spheres of social life. This stream is opposed to communal chauvinism and exclusiveness of any kind, even of the most just, pure, refined and civilized brand. Instead, it advocates the strict application of the common laws, rights and obligations of citizenship.

Such a stream contraposes the wranglings and divisiveness among the various communal factions of the ruling classes to the demand for the unconditional unity of the various peoples of the country. It demands the development and growing frequency of intercourse among communal groups in every form, the breakdown of communal

70

barriers, and the creation of the national unity of
capital, labor, economic life in general, politics and
science. But it demands a unity in which the various
communities fully participate in local and national
life, a unity that sweeps away all the old precapitalist, caste, parochial, religious and other particular-
istic barriers to progress.

How should the contraditon between these two
streams in the movement for more states be resolved?
This is the significant question which theory and
practice must answer in the present politics of Nigerian
federalism. An adequate answer must at the same time
resolve a related contradiction between the right of the
individual and that of the community. The 1979 Nigerian
Constitution provides for the guarantee of fundamental
rights to all Nigerian citizens.2 Such rights include
the right to life, dignity of human person, personal
liberty, and personal property, freedom of thought,
conscience and religion, freedom of movement, freedom
of expression, peaceful assembly and association, and
freedom from discrimination.

At the same time, the constitution practically
sanctions the right of communities in its "federal
character" provisions.3 One of the implications of
these provisions is the inadvertent creation of three
types of citizens in Nigeria. The most privileged are
those citizens who belong to the indigenous communities
of a state in which they reside. Those citizens who
are indigenes of states other than those in which they
reside are less favoured. In order to fully enjoy
their human rights they have to move back and forth to
their "states of origin." The least privileged are
those citizens who are unable to prove that they belong
to a community indigenous to any of the states of
Nigeria.4 Such a discriminatory system of citizenship
inevitably engenders discrimination in jobs, land
purchase, housing, admission into educational institutions, marriages, business transactions and the distribution of social welfare services. Associated with
these provisions is the right of each state not only to
organise its affairs in its own way and develop at its
own pace but also its right to "catch up" with the
other states, if necessary, by excluding indigenes of
these other states from full participation in its
activities, and discriminating against them in its
distribution of resources.

Motivated by the desire to remedy the imbalance in the levels of socio-economic development of the various communal groups and thereby "promote national unity, foster national loyalty and give every citizen of Nigeria a sense of belonging to the nation notwithstanding the diversities of ethnic origin, culture, language or religion,"4 these "federal character" provisions confer certain privileges on some communities and not on others. Since no time-frame is associated with these privileges in order to indicate that they are short-term in nature and should be phased out as soon as the necessary national cohesion is achieved, they have assumed the character of permanent rights of communities. In the process, they have turned the relationship among communal groups into a permanent political issue in a manner that clearly contradicts provisions of the constitution regarding residence and other human rights and even completely undermined the development of a national citizenry, a basic requirement for national cohesion.5

The idea of human rights implies the protection of the individual from a community or communities. Since the law which protects also restricts, human rights imply restrictions on communities from violating these rights. This is incompatible with community rights which imply among other things the protection of the community from the individual of a different community within the same state, including the restriction of the latter in the enjoyment of human rights. Thus, when a member state of the federation of Nigeria implements a discriminatory employment policy designed to protect the interests of its indigenes by requiring fellow citizens who are non-indigenes to work on contract bases, even for a limited time, while its indigenes work on a permanant basis, it clearly violates human rights provisions. A similar violation occurs when its secondary and other institutions of learning operate discriminatory admission quotas for children of non-indigenes.

In fact', such policies violate the International Convention on the Elimination of All Forms of Racial Discrimination of 21 December 1965.6 In its Article I the Convention defines racial discrimination as "any distinction, exclusion, restriction or preference based on colour, descent or national or ethnic origin with the purpose or the effect of nullifying or impairing the recognition, enjoyment and exercise, on a equal footing, of human rights and fundamental freedoms in the political, economic, social, cultural or any other field of public life."7 Similarly, this convention rejects the argument that inherited or basic differences in the cultural, educational and other spheres provide a justification for a policy of separate development or one of discriminatory development of the type sanctioned by "federal character" policies.

i)   National or Ethnic Question in the Creation of State?

In seeking to answer correctly the theoretical and practical questions raised by the movement for new states in Nigeria, it is necessary first to scientifically identify the phenomenon under discussion. Is it a national question? Or is it an ethnic question? Analytical problems arise when a facile comparison is made with a similar phenomenon in the Soviet Union. Today, the politics of federalism in the Soviet Union has given rise to federated states in the form of 15 Union Republics, 20 Autonomous Republics, 8 Autonomous Regions and 10 Autonomous Areas enjoying varying degrees of autonomy.8

The emergence of these federated states in the Soviet Union was the culmination of the movements which dated back to early twentieth century Russia and which were clearly recognized as national movements. The political issue at stake was the national question. In a number of respects these movements were similar to those which have been involved in the demand for more federated states in Nigeria. They have both campaigned against the oppression of one communal group by another, run along communal-linguistic lines, been desirous of taking political charge of their own affairs, and been intent on using the political instrument to end their relative backwardness. Therefore, it has been quite tempting, particularly for those not familiar with the scientific methodology of social analysis, to view the movement for the creation of states in Nigeria, and the relationship between language groups in African countries, as similarly involved with the national question. This is wrong.

The categorical requirement of social theory in investigating any social question is that the issue be examined within definite historical limits and, if it refers to a particular country, that account be taken of the specific features distinguishing that country from others in the same historical epoch.9 Answers should not be sought in abstract definitions deduced from all sorts of comparisons across time and space. Rather they should be sought in a historico-economic study of the issue.10

This was the basis on which Lenin severely criticized Rosa Luxembourg's attack on the Russian social-democrats for their program on the national question. "But does Rosa Luxambourg raise the question as to what historical period Russia is passing through, or what are the concrete features of the national equation and the national movements of that particular country in that particular period? No she does not!"11 "If one interprets the Marxist programme on the national question in a Marxist and not a childish way, one will quickly grasp that it refers to bourgeois-democratic national movements. The programme refers only to cases where such a movement is actually in existence."12 The national question can only be understood through an analysis of concrete national movements.

Such an analysis would reveal that throughout the world, the emergence of capitalism from the womb of feudalism has been characterized by the development of national movements. This is because such movements were a progressive force seeking to provide a most congenial environment for the development of capitalism. The spread of commodity production to all corners of a territory signifies the victory of capitalism over feudalism. And this is most easily accomplished in a politically united territory whose population speaks a single language with all obstacles to the development of that language and to its consolidation in literature eliminated.13

Language is the most important means of human intercourse. Unity and the unimpeded development of language are among the most important conditions for genuinely free and extensive commerce on a scale commensurate with capitalism, for a free and broad grouping of the population in all its various classes, and lastly, for the establishment of a close connection between the market and each and every proprietor, and between buyer and seller.14 Free rein is given to capitalism once an indigenous bourgeoisie captures this linguistic-territorial home market.

Thus national movements arose in Europe during the period between 1789 and 1871 in response to this capitalist imperative and against the reactionary

74

oppression, parochialism, chauvinism and communal
inequality of feudalism and absolutism. The tendency
of each national movement was toward the formation of a
national state in which the population spoke the same
language. At that time, the national state was the
form most suited to the prevailing demand for capitalist
and economically progressive relations as distinct from
medieval precapitalist relations. It was the form
through whith the freest, widest and speediest development of capitalism could be secured.

Therefore, for the whole of Western Europe, the
national (linguistic) state was typical and normal for
that period of capitalism. Consequently, from an
historico-economic analysis of these national
movements, an understanding of the national question
must inevitably reach the conclusion that it means the
political separation of linguistic groups from one
another, and their constitution into independent
national states. Similarly, the concept of self-
determination which was very closely associated with the
national question cannot, from a scientific point of
view, have any meaning other than political self-
determination, state independence, and the formation of
a national state.

This period in the history of the national question
was the period of the collapse of feudalism and
absolutism in Europe and the formation of the bourgeois-
democratic society and state when the national movements
became mass movements for the first time and in one way
or another drew all classes of the population into
politics through the press and the practice of representative government. The typical features of this period
were the awakening of national consciousness and the
drawing of the workers and peasants into these movements
in connection with the struggle for political liberty
in general and the right of the national in particular.
By the time that this period drew to a close most of
Western Europe had been transformed into a settled
system of bourgeois states.

In Eastern Europe and Asia on the other hand, the
period of the bourgeois-democratic revolutions did not
begin until 1905. These revolutions in Russia and the
Balkans awakened a whole series of bourgeois-democratic
national movements seeking to resolve the national
question by creating nationally independent and
nationally uniform states. It was this specific concrete historical feature of the national question in

these countries that made the recognition of the right
of nations to self-determination relevant and urgent to
their linguistic groups.

Finally, there are the semi-colonial countries
such as China, Persia and Turkey, and all the colonies
of Asia and Africa whose national movements grew, not
out of the womb of feudalism and absolutism, but out of
the specific concrete conditions of imperialism and
colonialism. The demands of the nationalist leaders of
these movements were for the unconditional liberation
of the colonies and the right to self-determination in
national states free from oppression by foreign nations.
These demands also responded to the imperatives of the
development of capitalism in the colonies and semicolonies. In a commodity-producing society, no
independent development or development of any sort is
possible without capital. In Europe during the period
of the national movements the oppressed and dependent
nations had their own capital, their own bourgeoisie,
and an easy access to capital on a wide range of terms.
The colonies, on the other hand, had no capital, no
bourgeoise of their own. And under the hegemony of
finance-capital no colony could obtain any capital
except on terms of political submission.

Once the financial oligarchy took a dominant position in the imperalist countries, it negated the basis
for a national bourgeoisie in the colonies and semicolonies. By reserving the market of the oppressed
countries for its own capital and commodities, finance
capital made it impossible for the national bourgeoisie
of these countries to accumulate capital and to complete
the bourgeois-democratic revolution. Thus, under
imperialism the national question concerned the rights
of the oppressed colonies and semicolonies to political
and economic independence under bourgeois-democratic
constitutions. It was a struggle that involved all the
communal groups of the dominated territories irrespective
of linguistic differences because all of them were
subjected to imperialist oppression, and colonialism
had established a new linguistic basis (the metropolitan
language) for the development of capitalism. It
endeavoured to create in each colony a politically
united territory whose population spoke the metropolitan
language as the political and economic medium of intercourse with all obstacles to the hegemony of this
language being progressively eliminated.

Thus the national question in the colonies concerned the anti-imperialist struggle of these colonies for political and economic emancipation from foreign domination. The attainment of political independence from colonialism achieved the political objective of this struggle and transformed the colonies into neocolonies where the anti-imperialist struggle was transformed to that for economic liberation, the creation of indigenous capital, a national bourgeoisie. An aspect of the national question associated with the nationalist struggle for independence was the demand for the implementation of bourgeois-democratic norms, values and principles in the political life of the colonies. This demand was realized when, just prior to political independence, the colonialists introduced bourgeois-democratic constitutions in the colonies insisting on them as a precondition for the granting of independence.

However, very few concrete demands emerged over that aspect of the national question concerning economic independence without which newly-won political independence would be ephemeral. All indications are that the petty-bourgeoisies which now dominate the neocolonies of Africa can neither articulate concretely this demand nor be willing or able to accomplish it. Therefore, in Nigeria and the other neocolonies of Africa the national question has not been fully resolved. The remaining task is the anti-imperialist struggle for national economic independence.

This task has nothing whatsoever to do with the various movements for the creation of states in Nigeria. The movements cannot, therefore, be in any way involved with the national question. In fact, the demand for states may serve to divert attention away from the national question, and confuse the exploited masses of Nigeria at the ideological level. Thus confused they cannot face the imperialist enemy resolutely. Sentiments arising from backward communal precapitalist relations have been utilized in every situation since the rise of capital under feudalism. With the crisis of modern imperialism, with the pressing national question in the colonies and neocolonies, these have been utilized by the imperialists to disorganize the colonies.15 Because of the narrowness of the material interest of the ruling petty-bourgeoisie and comprador-bourgeoise such sentiments are exploited in advancing their narrow interests against each other and against the working people.16

Underlying the movement for the creation of states in Nigeria is the ethnic question. This is clear from an historico-economic analysis of the movements. They arose out of the frustrations of the petty-bourgeois factions of the minority ethnic groups in their socio-economic and political competition with equivalent factions from the dominant ethnic groups. In Nigeria, imperialism created conditions in which (foreign) capital could not breakdown communal barriers, obliterate communal distinctions and assimilate language-cultural groups into a new capitalist culture, in the way that capitalism operated in the imperialist countries where it acted as the greatest driving force transforming the parochial, feudal and precapitalist societies into the cosmopolitan capitalist societies of today.

The capitalist mode of production tends to disintegrate the precapitalist modes when interaction between the two is unrestricted and limited to the economic level. In Nigeria, imperialism provided the necessary restrictions and limitations because the capitalist mode which it introduced was exogenous and governed at the economic level by a restrictive division of labor imposed from outside, and at the political level by the imperatives of the need to subdue a conquered population and guarantee social, economic and other privileges to foreigners from the colonizing power. Consequently, the capitalist mode became dominant without destroying the precapitalist modes and therefore precapitalist social and cultural relations throughout the country. These relations survived as important social forces as far as the further development capitalism was concerned and in a subservient manner to the dominant capitalist economic, social and cultural relations. Nevertheless, they retained enough strength, particularly at the sociocultural levels, to provide an occasional rallying point for the population. Thus, sentiments associated with the precolonial communal societies abound, ready to be exploited by those who wish to do so.

The petty-bourgeois leaders of the various communities in the country exploited these parochial sentiments. Against competition from other members of their class who came from different linguistic groups they invoked the myth of ethnic identity along lines previously fabricated by the colonialists in their calculated policy of divide-and-rule. In their search for the crumbs from colonial production, contending communal factions of this class emphasized the exclusion of their rivals from the other communal groups. And

when they got into positions of political power they
used the government to exclude them.. Unable historically to increase production because of their parasitic
role in the production process, members of this class
depend on this device of exclusion to increase their
benefits from society. Thoroughly diffident about
their ability to survive and prosper under a system of
merit in hiring, promotion, trade and business they
prefer the security of at least being able to rely on
exploiting ethnic and other communal preferences where-
ever and whenvever they can. Each gives preferences to
members of his group as a means of ensuring that they
may return the gesture sometime when he may need it.
The whole system is rationalized in terms of ethnic
diversity and the need to accord to each group a say
and a share in national life.

    Such conditions were conducive to the use of the
ethnic group as a political base. The struggle for
power became equallly interpreted in ethnic terms. It
became a struggle for the hegemony of the various
communal factions of the petty-bourgeoisie, first in the
regional enclave, and then in the country as a whole.
And the masses were fully mobilized in this ethno-
political struggle. As political parties inevitably
became ethnic in character they created the false
impression that they were the champions of the interest
of the various ethnic groups, and that the struggles
among them for political power in the country represented the struggles of the various ethnic groups for
political ascendancy in the society. They covertly and
sometimes overtly and openly used emotive ethnic
symbols in politics, and preyed on alleged ethnic conflicts of interests as a means of mobilizing mass
support for the selfish class interests of their
leaders.

    The strategy of the various political parties for
winning political power and using it revolved around
the ethnic group. This included the mobilization of the
ethnic group for overwhelming electoral support,
expanding the political base through winning over the
political support of the neighboring ethnic groups,
winning elections in that part of the federation in
which the ethnic homeland exists and consequently controlling its government. Furthermore, it emphasized
the use of this governmental power to coerce all the
recalcitrant ethnic groups in the area into support for
the major ethnic group, the encouragement of agitations
by minority ethnic groups against governments controlled

by rival political parties, and to control the federal government by the most viable alliance of ethnic groups. Also, the strategy involved using both the sub-federal government and/or the federal government under its control to divert resources and give preferential treatment to members of the dominant ethnic group.

Under these conditions of ethnic consciousness and the struggle for political power as well as economic and social resources, the minor (language) ethnic groups lost out. The petty-bourgeoises of these groups were unable to achieve or retain political and economic leadership in the existing sub-federal systems. Therefore, they opted for leadership of smaller units to be carved out of these units. Only such leadership guaranteed to them the enormous power and socio-economic benefits accruing from the public service, trade and business. They perceived their opportunities for political leadership, contracts, senior positions in the public service, import and trading licences and loans for business activities frustrated by the tendency of the more numerous ethnic groups to secure these benefits for their own section of the petty-bourgeoisie. By leading minority group agitation against "domination" and for new federal states under the control of their own ethnic group these "minority" leaders hoped to carve out a place in the Nigerian political and economic sun for themselves.

However, in each newly-created state there were usually majority and minority ethnic groups with the dominant (formerly in the forefront of the minority agitation for separate state) proceeding to divert most of the resources to its own petty bourgeoisie. Inevitably this behavior generated agitation for the further splitting of the new states. The process goes on ad infinitum, even taking place now within the same ethnic group as a result of similar dynamics among those different communal groups within it. It has even become advantageous in the competition among ethnic groups for resources controlled by the federal government to have as many states as possible created within the same group. This would enable more members of the petty bourgeosie of that group to benefit from the distribution of the nation's resources.

These ethnic dynamics in the creation of states in Nigeria are reinforced by the uneven development inherent in Nigeria's peripheral capitalism and by the disarticulation of the country's economy. The activi-

ties of imperialist capital affected the various ethnic
homelands differentially depending on their role within
the imperialist scheme of things. Development was
attracted only to those homelands of gainful economic
activity for the colonialists. Others remained relatively backward. this created antipathies between these
two groups of homelands and a feeling by the latter
that it would not be able to catch up with the rest
unless it controlled its own affairs and enjoyed certain
privileges above the others. Also, in the colonial
economy there was virtually no unity across the
communal homelands of the country. Its dominant sector
was import-export oriented and, therefore, externally
oriented rather than being internally oriented toward
the integration of the various communal homelands. A
consequence of this disarticulated economy is that it
could be broken up into microeconomies without any
serious danger to overall national economic life. The
weakness of national consciousness and national cohesion
and, therefore, the absence of any restraint in the
desire to splinter the country into innumerable
federated states is a reflection of this disarticulation.

Thus, the movement for the creation of states in
Nigeria is ethnic in origin and character. The problem
is to solve the ethnic question: the contradition among
the various linguistic groups within the country. Over
the years, this ethnic problem has not only persisted
but has intensified, leading to an uncontrollable
demand for the creation of states. Obviously, this
escalation creates serious difficulties for the social
order and the political process in the country. The
intensified polarization of the society into
subnational ethnic and subethnic cultures widely
seperated in terms of identity and loyalty encourages
further hostility rather than greater cooperation in
relations among communal groups in the country. Therefore, the necesssity to find a solution to the ethnic
question has become even more urgent.

This ethnic movement does not demand separate,
independent and sovereign statehood. The only exception
was the demand for Biafra by the Igbo petty-
bourgeoisie. However, this demand was made under
exceptional conditions of widespread massacre and untold
humiliation of the Igbo masses and leaders alike in
1966. The widespread insecurity of the people and
their frustration and anger at the inability or
unwillingness of the federal authorities to put a halt

to these atrocities caused this demand to go beyond the normal limits of agitation for states. The Biafran experiment failed becuse it was not praticable. The consensus of the African states as reflected in numerous resolutions of the Organization of African Unity and supported by the world community at large is against the creation of independent sovereign states out of the component parts of existing African states. Hence, most African and other countries of the world opposed Biafra, even though they widely condemned the massacres that precipitated seccession.

The ethnic question involved in the movement for the creation of federated states in Nigeria contrasts in a fundamental way with the national question whose resolution gave rise to the prevailing sovereign nation states. The awakening of the masses from feudal lethargy and imperialist obscurantism by the national question, and their struggle against all national oppression and for the sovereignty of the people are progressive. They conformed with the imperatives not only of the further transformation of capitalism in the direction of greater release of productive forces but also the creation of a politically large enough territory in which the proletariat's struggle against the bourgeoisie can develop on a broad basis. Capitalism's broad and rapid development of the productive forces calls for large, politically compact and united territories since only under such conditions can the bourgeois class together with its inevitable antipode--the proletariat--unite and sweep away all the old medieval, caste, parochial, petty national and subnational, religious an other backward barriers to progress.

On the other hand, the fragmentation of the internal space of the territorial unit and the decentralization of state power to subnational but federated units are antithetical to the progressive development of capitalism, particularly if as in the case of Nigeria, these subfederal units persistently hinder the free flow of capitalist market forces. Capitalism requires for its development the largest and most centralized possible states. Other conditions being equal, the class conscious proletariat will always fight against precapitalist particularism, and always encourage the closest possible economic amalgamation of large territories. The great democratically centralized state is a tremendous step forward from medieval and precapitalist disunity to the future socialist unity of the whole world.

Although it is inexusable for the democratically centralized state to preclude local self-government with a certain measure of autonomy to areas with special conditions, it is ridiculous to talk about the conditions and demands of modern capitalism while at the same time taking not the modern nor the capitalist, but the medieval, feudal, precapitalist and ethnic or other communal criteria as the basis of administration or constitutional engineering. Nigeria will not make progress until these federated ethnic states are superseded by those based on a really modern division that meets the requirements of capitalism.

ii) The Creation of States and the Struggle for Progress

At the same time as the conflict among the ethnic groups of Nigeria for the creation of states takes place, the struggle to accomplish the remaining task of the national question goes on, as does the struggle to abolish capitalism and usher in socialism. The proletariat is generally and correctly regarded as the leading force in the struggle against capitalism and for socialism. What is not so widely known is that the proletariat is also the leading force in the struggle for national economic independence, the surviving task of the national question.

In the final analysis local petty-bourgeois economic nationalism merely seeks promotion within the hierarchical income, status and power structure of the imperialist system, rather than national economic independence as such. In fact petty-bourgeois power and privilege derive ultimately from the center of this system located in the imperialist countries. Local capitalists cannot successfully challenge these countries because they cannot compete with the large and powerful aggregate capital from the center. They are prisoners of the taste patterns and consumption habits set by the advanced countries and must depend on foreign capitalist institutions for access to international markets, technical advice, capital, political ideas and, when necessary, military support.

In Nigeria, the interests of the local capitalists contradict those of the working class and peasantry. In the resultant struggle, the capitalists often shrink back from self-reliant and independent capitalist development well before the complete resolution of the national question. Instead, they enter into an alliance with imperialism through partnerships in economic enterprises

83

and military aid in political relations. This provides some security for, and benefits from, the system based on capitalist ownership but it does not show any way forward to economic independence. It is increasingly evident that Nigerian capitalists do not have an over-riding interest in ending economic dependence on imperialism. They cannot be expected to do so unless they misjudge their interests. These are not deeply antagonistic to the interests of imperialist capital and, therefore, cannot generate the kind of politico-economic momentum required to break economic dependence.

Only the underprivileged classes--the working class and the peasantry--have an objective interest in ending both economic dependence and the hegemony of capital. Their interests are deeply antagonistic to those of imperialist capital. Foreign capitalist enterprises represent the unjust exploitation of their labor and the neglect of their basic needs and tradi-tional consumption habits. The poor classes have a class interest in overthrowing these enterprises and replacing them with others more attuned to their own and the local interest. And of the two classes, leadership devolves naturally on the working class. It is the more cosmopolitan, more modern, better organised and better able to understand the workings of capitalism and imperialism. Historically, therefore, it has always and everywhere led the struggle against capital in capitalist societies, and for economic independence in countries at the periphery of the imperialist system.

Thus the Nigerian proletariat is simultaneously involved in the ethnic question and the labor question. The former is reflected in the movement for the creation of states, and the latter in the struggles against capitalism and for economic independence. It should be immediately clear that in the resolution of these struggles and problems the ethnic question must take a subordinate position to the labor question. Marx had no doubt as to the subordinate position of even the national question to the labor question. Successful struggle against exploitation in Nigeria requires that the proletariat be free of ethnic chauvinism and absolutely neutral in the fight for supremacy among the petty-bourgeois of the various ethnic groups. If the proleteriat of one ethnic or communal group gives the slightest support to the privileges of its own ethnic petty-bourgeoisie, that will inevitably arouse distrust among the proletariat of other ethnic or communal groups. This will weaken proletarian class

84

solidarity or even prevent it from forming, to the detriment of the fight against capitalism and imperialism. The interests of the working class and of its struggles to resolve the labor question demand complete solidarity and the closest unity of the workers of all ethnic groups. They demand fierce resistance to the ethnic slogans and policies of the petty-bourgeoisie of every ethnic group.

On the question of the demands of ethnic groups, as on every other question, the proletariat must be interested first and foremost in its self-interest. The petty-bourgeoisie always places its ethnic demands in the forefront. With the proletariat, however, the ethnic demands must be subordinated to the imperatives of the class struggle against capitalism and for economic independence. The most important immediate objective in this class struggle is for the proletariat to ensure the development of its class. This is hampered by the tendency of the petty-bourgeoisie to subordinate working class interests to petty-bourgeois objectives in ethnic politics. Therefore, a major task of the proletariat on the ethnic question is to strengthen its class against the petty-bourgeoisie and the imperialists, and to educate the masses in the spirit of consistent democracy. Without the latter the oppression of one ethnic group by another cannot end.

On the ethnic question, consistent democracy on the part of the proletariat is imperative because every ethnic faction of the petty-bourgeoisie is out for privilege for itself. Under cover of "federal character," quotas in institutions of higher learning, disadvantaged areas, socioeconomic imbalance, ethnic self-determination, indigeneity, and such concoctions, the petty-bourgeoisies haggle with one another for privileges. Even progressive elements of both the major and minor ethnic groups, advantaged and disadvantaged areas, advanced and backward areas alike fall prey to the accompanying ethnic prejudices essentially because they are beneficiaries or potential beneficiaries of these privileges, or victims of the ethnic system of resource distribution.

Under the present system of ethnic competition this haggling for privileges is regarded as practical. Progressives are urged to face the reality of Nigerian politics; a reality which is not based on principles that promote democracy, liberty and proletarian unity. Sheer opportunism prevails. It is reflected in the persistent inability of the petty-bourgeoisie to establish any principles for the creation of states in the country. Opportunism has remained the hallmark of the exercise. The proletariat must be opposed to all privileges, to all exclusiveness, to all opportunism.

This opposition may not be realistic in the short-run but it is in effect the best guarantee for the achievement of the most democratic of all possible solutions to the ethnic question. The proletariat needs only such universal guarantees, whereas the petty bourgeoisie of every ethnic group requires guarantees for its own interest regardless of the position of, or possible disadvantages to, other ethnic groups. This call to face reality is in fact merely a call for the uncritical acceptance of petty-bourgeois aspirations. The proletariat must oppose such "realistic" thinking. While recognizing the equal rights of all ethnic and communal groups it must value above all the place in the forefront the alliance of the proletarians of all communal groups and assess any ethnic demand from the angle of the worker's struggle for progress. It must fight against the privilege and nepotism of the dominant or advantaged ethnic groups, but must not support or condone in any way the striving for privileges and nepotism on the part of the minor or disadvantaged ethnic groups.

Only a policy that is based on clear, consistent, democratic and proletarian principles is realistic in the search for solutions to the ethnic problem. Such a policy must appraise each concrete ethnic question from the point of view of removing all inequality, all privileges, all exclusiveness. The principal task of the proletariat under such a policy is that of day-by-day agitation and propaganda against all ethnic and communal privileges, and for the equal right of all communities and ethnic grops to a share of national life. Only in this way can all progressive forces defend the interest of democracy or forge a powerful alignment of the proletarians of all ethnic groups on an equal footing.

A policy of consistent democracy on the ethnic question was even recognized by the Willink Commission appointed in 1958 by the colonialists to look into the demands for more states. In the view of the Commission, the entrenchment of fundamental human rights in the constitution and the successful implementation of demo-cratic practices were the major requirements for allay-

86

ing the fears of ethnic minorities. These fears, as expressed to the Commission, concerned the maintenance of public order, with the ethnic minorities complaining that the instruments of law and order were and would be arbitrarily used against them by governments controlled by the majority ethnic groups. Fears were also expressed about the nepotic distribution of public service jobs and social amenities. These fears could very well be allayed by the consistent application of democratic principles. Hence the Commission recommended against the creation of states.

Under the slogan of ethnic heterogeneity and cultural diversity the petty-bourgeoisie of all the ethnic groups in Nigeria, through the movements for new states and the divisive and exclusive activities of the existing states, are in fact splitting the peoples, emasculating democracy and haggling with all reactionary forces over the sale of the people's rights and liberties. The slogan of cultural diversity is a petty-bourgeois fraud which sows the seed of corruption among the masses and causes immense harm to the struggle for freedom and progress. The place of those who advocate the slogan of cultural diversity is among the petty-bourgeoisie and not among the people. All those who seek to serve the proletariat must unite the workers of all ethnic groups, and unswervingly fight petty-bourgeois ethnic chauvinism and even genuine nationalism, domestic and foreign.

For the class-conscious workers there is only one solution to the ethnic problem in Nigeria insofar as it can in general be solved in the capitalist world of profit, squabbling and exploitation: and that solution is consistent working-class democracy. Under it there are absolutely no privileges for any one ethnic group. It contraposes the ethnic wrangling of the petty-bourgeoisies with the demand for the unconditional unity and amalgamation of the workers of all ethnic groups and nation states. Only this kind of unity and amalgamation can uphold democracy and defend the interests of the workers against capital. All advocacy of the segregation of the workers of one ethnic group from another as expressed by the federated states of Nigeria in their policies on admission to schools, hiring and promotion in the public service, the enjoyment of medical and other social amenities, and active participation in political and cultural life, or an attempt to contrapose on ethnic culture as a whole to another ethnic culture represents petty-bourgeois chauvinism, particularism and exclusiveness against which it is essential to wage a ruthless struggle.

Similarly, any movement for ethnic cultural autonomy is petty-bourgeois because it converts petty particularism into an absolute category, exalts it as the acme of perfection, and purges it of violence, backwardness and injustice. The proletariat cannot support any consecration of ethnicity and parochial particularism. On the contrary, it supports every policy that helps to obliterate ethnic distinctions and remove ethnic barriers in human relations, and supports all activities that tend to cement ties among peoples and merge ethnic groups. To act differently means siding with petty-bourgeois reaction. Furthermore, advocacy of ethnic cultural autonomy not only divides peoples but in fact draws the proletariat and bourgeoisie of one ethnic group closer together.

On the other hand, there are two sides to the resolution of the ethnic question as expressed in the movement for federated states in Nigeria. One of these concerns the right of each ethnic group to be treated equally with all the others, for its members to be secure in their life and property, from arbitrary arrest and punishment, and for them to enjoy equal opportunities in trade, business, employment, schooling and the enjoyment of social amenities. This is the democratic side of the movement. By awakening the masses from political lethargy and launching them into the struggle against oppression, inequality and injustice the movement for states is progressive. Hence progressives must support all of these aspects of the movement.

This task is largely a negative one--to eliminate oppression, arbitrariness, injustice and nepotism. But this is the limit to which the proletariat should go in supporting ethnic demands, for beyond that begins the "positive" activity of the petty-bourgeoisie striving to fortify ethnicity. To throw off all ethnic oppression and privilege is the imperative duty of the proletariat as a democratic force. It is also in the interest of the proletarian class struggle, which is obscured and retarded by ethnic conflicts and distrust. But to go beyond these strictly limited historical objectives and help ethnic movements means betraying the proletariat and siding with reactionary forces. Thus it is necessary to recognize fully the historical reality of ethnic movements. But to prevent this recognition does not lead to bourgeois ideology obscuring proletarian consciousness.

The other side of the movement for states is the unambiguous demand for the national and international unity of the workers in their class struggle. The petty-bourgeois movement of an oppressed ethnic group has a general democratic content that is directed against oppression. It is this content that Marxists should support. At the same time, they must strictly distinguish it from the tendency toward ethnic exclusiveness. Any overexaggeration of this ethnic side may lead to the complete neglect of the national and international aspect and an underestimation of the urge to create a national state and carry on the proletarian struggle in cooperation with workers living across state boundaries. The aim of socialism is not only to end the division of mankind into compartments within states and the isolation of states from one another but to bring peoples together within and across states and to integrate them. International unity of the working class is the major instrument of this world-wide task.

It is the duty of Marxists to teach the workers not only to be indifferent to ethnic and even national distinctions but also to be internationalist. The proletariat must not think only of their community, ethnic group or state but must place above these the interests of all communities, ethnic groups and states: common liberty, equality and progress. This is precisely because the international unity of the working class is the surest guarantee for the creation and consolidation of the working class state in any part of the world. And without this socialist unity of the workers short-term privileges obtained for them by their petty-bourgeoisie will surely evaporate. Under socialism the working people will not consent to seclusion, isolation and narrow egoism for purely economic motives. They will seek the drawing together of peoples and integrate all sections of the world population at an even faster pace under the banner of proletarian internationalism. Therefore, Marxists must always fight against ethnic and national narrow-mindedness, seclusion, exclusiveness and isolation, and subordinate the particularity of ethnic demands to the general interest of the proletarian revolution.

iii) Conclusion

In conclusion, then, a correct approach to the demand for the creation of states in Nigeria must stem from an integration of these two sides of the ethnic question: the full right of all ethnic groups to equality, justice, and progress on the one hand, and the unambiguous demand for the interethnic unity of the working class on the other. It is clear that we must subordinate the demand for most states--an expression of the ethnic question--to the labor question. Nevertheless, one cannot and must not ignore these apparently popular movements for more states or dismiss them out of hand. To brush them aside once they have started and to refuse to support what is progressive in them will mean in effect recognizing one's own ethnic group as a model. An essential aspect of their existence is the demand for democracy, and against injustice and oppression. And there can be no victorious socialism that does not practise full democracy. The proletariat cannot prepare for its victory over the domestic and foreign capitalists without an all-round consistent and revolutionary struggle including but not limited to the progressive democratic demands of the ethnic movements.

Rejection of all the demands of these movements would only play into the hands of petty-bourgeois and other reactionary forces. Rather, Marxists should formulate these demands and put them through in a revolutionary and not in a reformist manner, going beyond the bounds of bourgeois legality, breaking down legal, social and cultural barriers against these democratic demands, and drawing the masses into decisive action in a way that extends and intensifies the struggles for every fundamental democratic demand up to those involved in the direct proletarian onslaught on local and foreign capital. The proletariat should make use of the conflicts that arise over the ethnic movement for more states as grounds for mass action and for revolutionary attacks on capitalism and imperialism.

The petty-bourgeois leaders of the state movements persistently utilize the slogans of ethnic liberation to deceive the workers. There is not one of these democratic demands which cannot serve and has not served under certain circumstances, as an instrument in the hands of the petty-bourgeoisie for deceiving the people. However, in contrast to the petty-bourgeois democrats, Marx regarded every democratic demand, without exception, not as an absolute, but as an historical expression of the struggle of the masses led by the bourgeoisie, against precapitalist backwardness. Therefore, the proletariat can overcome the machinations of the bourgeoisie in their use of democratic demands only by subordinating its struggle for all democratic rights, including the demands for inter-ethnic equality and justice, to its revolutionary struggle for the overthrow of the bourgeoisie.

In practical terms Marxists may support the demand for more states at the abstract level without supporting the demand for any specific state. It must do so on the basis of the slogan--no ethnic inequality, no ethnic privilege--and through country-wide laws promulgated in a consistently democratic manner that do not depart from the principle of equality. In addition, Marxists must engineer the movement for states in the direction of agitation for a revolutionary development policy that satisfies the basic needs and traditional consumption habits of the population through the use of local resources; the transformation of the economy in such a way that the various ethnic homelands are linked together making it difficult for one ethnic group to prosper without inputs from the others; a shift in orientation of the masses from distribution of resources along ethnic lines to distribution at the workplace.

Such agitation should also focus on the creation and strengthening of local political and governmental decision centers which enable the masses of the people to have a day-to-day influence on their affairs; and the strict application of democratic rules and regulations in the intraclass relations among the petty-bourgeoisie. Finally, inherited political, economic and social differences across communal and ethnic lines should be vigorously combated by the strict implementation of identical rules, norms and values throughout the country on the basis of no privilege for the advantaged and disadvantaged groups alike. This must be accompanied by the liquidation of the inherited socioeconomic imbalance in the achievements of the various ethnic groups.

This imbalance can be corrected by extending employment facilities, educational institutions of all types, and health and other welfare services on a disproportionate scale to the disadvantaged areas. Special development authorities should be established for these areas to implement this policy rapidly. Nevertheless,

all citizens of the country, and not just the indigenes
of these areas must be equally eligible to benefit from
the activities of these authorities. Furthermore, such
authorities must be viewed and constituted as a stop-
gap measure and, therefore, must have a built-in
mechanism for phasing themselves out as soon as their
mission is accomplished. They must not become permanent
institutions of national life, capable of turning these
areas into privileged communities of the future. In
these ways consistent democracy can prevail without
damaging the imperatives of proletarian unity.

Notes

1. It is regretable that Marxists in Nigeria and
    Africa find it fashionable to deal only with
    questions of capital acumulation, economic capital-
    ist nations, and the character of the state. Very
    litle effort is devoted to the analysis of social
    movements and political processes. This is
    unfortunate. Marxists must be concerned with any
    and all social phenomena in their society and take
    positions on any and all political struggles in
    it. Otherwise they are bound to become irrelevant
    to the cause of the history of their people and
    incapable of effecting any change in their
    affairs.

2. Federal Republic of Nigeria, The Constitution of
    the Federal Republic of Nigeria, 1979 (Lagos:
    Federal Ministry of Information, 1979), Chapter
    IV, Section 30-42.

3. Ibid., Section 14 (3) and (4); Section 135 (3);
    Section 203 (1) (b) and (2) (b).

4. Yusuf Bala Usman, "Democracy and National
    Cohesion: the bankruptcy of the C. D. C.
    Majority Draft", National Union of Gongola Students
    at the Murtala Mohammed College, Yola, January
    1977, 8 - 10.

5. Constitution of the Federal Republic of Nigeria,
    1979.

6. United Nations General Assembly Resolution 1904
    (XVIII) of 20 November 1963, (New York: United
    Nations).

7. Ibid., Article I.

8. Edward Bagramov, One Hundred Nationalities--One
    People (Moscow: Progress, 1982). 27.

9. V. I. Lenin, Critical Remarks on the National
    Question. The Right of Nations to Self-
    Determination, (Moscow: Progress, 1974. 6th
    edition), 44.

10. Ibid., 39.

11. Ibid., 46

12. Ibid., 48.

13. Ibid., 40.

14. Ibid.

15. D. Wadada Nabudere, "Imperialism, the National
     Question and the Politics of 'Class Formation' in
     Uganda. A Critical Review of M. Mamdani's Politics
     and Class Formation in Uganda", Utafiti, 3 (1),
     1978, 167.

16. Ibid.

Chapter Four

Regional Development in the Age of High Technology

Marcel Leroy

i)   Introduction

    Comparisons are never easy. Especially when
attempting to compare and generalize between situations
as different as those of Canada and Africa, caution is
advised. Yet, unless we are satisfied to stay on an
abstract theoretical level, hard evidence from different cases has to be considered. More often than not,
similarities do appear; insights gathered by analyzing
one case may shed light on another; and, perhaps more
importantly, looking at two different cases in success-
ion, one gains a grasp of the broader issues that could
not have been obtained by making only one case study.

    It is in this spirit that I proceed to compare the
prospects for economic development in marginal areas of
Canada and of African countries. While the information
presented here is heavily biased toward Canada, nevertheless I hope my discussion will be of some use to all
readers.

ii)   The Nature of Regional Disparities

    In many industrialized countries, some regions are
lagging behind the level of economic development for
the country as a whole. This has always been apparent
and resulted in the use of terms such as "heartland" and
"hinterland" or "core" and "periphery". In trying to
define these differences, we can see discrepancies for
both income and employment levels.

a)   In Canada, personal income levels in the Atlantic
region (provinces of Newfoundland, Nova Scotia, New
Brunswick, and PEI) average about 70% of the overall
Canadian figures (actual figures go from 67 to 79%).
Some provinces are obviously above the national
average (Ontario, British Columbia, Alberta), so that
personal income levls in the "wealthy" provinces are
about 50% above those of the "poor" provinces.

For business income, the discrepancy is greater:

Atlantic regions are at about 40% of the national average
(personal income includes a substantial proportion of
federal transfer payments; business income does not).

For natural resource revenue, Alberta is far ahead of
the national average, and the Atlantic provinces are
again in the poorest, this time at only about 10% of
the national figures. (Canada. Department of Finance.
Estimates, various years).

b)   Employment levels are also lower; unemployment in
the Atlantic region has consistently been about 50%
above the national average for the past twenty-five
years. Also, labor participation rates are lower (5 to
10% below national levels).

    The Canadaian situation is not unique. In fact,
regional disparity also exists in the United Kingdom,
Ireland, Norway, etc. The ranges of disparity for
income and employment levels are similar to those for
Canada. In some countries (like Yugoslavia) regional
differences are even greater.

    Political pressures have led to the adoption of
consistent policies to further the development of the
regions through:

a)   reducing unemployment levels in the marginal
regions;

b)   reducing discrepancy in income levels by raising
productivity and employment; and

c)   increasing labor participation rates to national
levels. (For similar analyses, see Francis, 1974 and
Brewis, 1976).

iii) Approaches to Regional Development

    There are many ways in which the federal govern-
ment in Canada has tried to raise the level of economic
development of the poorer provinces. The level of
federal transfer payments is very high and contributes
greatly to personal incomes in the poorer provinces.
For 1976, the per capita share of Nova Scotia for
federal transfer payments was 1.65 times the Canadian
average, although Nova Scotia only provides 84% of its
share of total revenues (Pinfold, 1979). Expressed
differently, federal spending constituted 38% of the
Nova Scotia provincial GDP in 1961, but grew to 48% by

1976. (Nova Scotia Department of Development, 1978).
Only a small portion of these federal monies has as its
express goal the development of the poorer provinces.
Most payments are to individuals (pensions, unemployment insurance) or to governments (equalization payments and grants of various types and description, for
health care, post-secondary education etc.). Less than
2% of federal expenditures in the poorer provinces has
for explicit purpose the stimulation of economic
activity (during the 1970's channelled through the
Department of Regional Economic Expansion, now through
other departments).

Because of 'the nature of the Canadian economy, encouragement of private investors is the major tool used
to stimulate the economic development of the poorer
provinces. Direct government control is not seen as
ideologicaly acceptable unless it is done to rescue
activities that might otherwise disappear (for instance,
underground coal mining in the 1960's). The incentives
have been mainly capital grants to companies investing
in designated areas (normally 25 to 50% of capital),
with some tax advantages and sometimes employment
grants. It should be mentioned that the capital grants
quickly leak out of the poorer areas for which they are
targeted, for they are usually used to purchase equipment manufactured in the more wealthy provinces, so
that these grants often are a subsidy for the industrial
core.

The effectiveness of these development policies is
hard to assess. Regional disparities have been
reduced, but not by very much. One of the consequences
that can be observed, however, is that the policies
have resulted in shifting jobs from the marginal to the
central work worlds (more capital, more skill, more
permanent jobs) (Clairmont, 1978, and Lazar, 1977).
Given the dualistic nature of economies in developing
countries, this way of looking at economic development
should be valid here, too.

Given the fact that most regional development
money was and is given in the form of capital grants,
there may have been a tendency to overcapitalize, and
to substitute capital for labour (Woodward, 1974 and
1975). Development efforts in developing countries can
fall into the same trap. Small-scale labour-intensive
technologies are often more technically and economically efficient than large-scale capital intensive
approaches (for a study on Tanzania along such lines,

97

see Perkins, 1983). There has been some support for developing service activities in poorer provinces in the last few years. In some respects, this may be a cheaper way to create employment. If one could offer incentives to an insurance company to locate its head-quarters in a small town, it might create a thousand jobs or so, but the company may be wealthy enough not to want any incentive. In Canada, the federal government has given the example of moving some of its services from Ottawa to the Atlantic region (Department of Veteran's Affairs to Charlottetown, Prince Edward Island, Citizenship Branch to Sydney, Nova Scotia etc).

Offering support for new services, however, may be harmful to the development of small communities. Support to shopping centers has destroyed small local stores, and in the long run might reduce the quality of life in small communities. It is interesting to note that in Norway, grocery stores in small settlements are eligible for subsidies if travel in excess of 4 kilometres would otherwise be necessary to have access to such a store (Kirby, et al, 1981). This maintains services that keep population in small settlements, and increases the quality of life there.

Many possible approaches to stimulate growth in lagging areas have not been tried in Canada. Imposing limits to growth in urban centers might have been such an approach. It is used in Norway to limit location of new offices and industries in the cities of Bergen and Oslo, and also to control expansion of existing firms. This is coupled with incentives to steer the companies toward desired locations (Hofstad, 1973). Monetary policy has not been used in Canada to promote growth of lagging areas, even though theoretical studies show there is promise in such an approach (Dow, 1979).

Essentially, the impact of development policies (see Leroy, 1980; see also Matthews, 1983) has been to:

a)   stimulate production mildly;

b)   increase regional income marginally; and

c)   shift manpower, again in small numbers, from the marginal to the central work world.

iv)   Economic and Technological Changes and their
      Impact on Regional Development

The continuing recession brought with it a drop in
demand for consumer goods, leading to excess industrial
capacity. Demand for some manufactured items and even
raw material may never pick up as the decline in demand
for copper, for example, is structural, not cyclical.
Much the same is true for the decline in demand for
steel. There can be no growth in the periphery for
sectors in which there is vast excess of productive
capacity in the core. Major United States steel companies are now making their cutbacks of a couple of
years ago permanent and are closing down large parts of
their operations. Under the circumstances, Third World
steel production can hardly be expected to expand.

Technological changes introduced another set of
innovations: micro-processing, bio-technology, and
computer-based communication. We might start this
discussion with a note of caution: the production and
development of computer hardware is likely to have much
less economic impact than the application of such
technology to existing economic activities.

Many economic aspects of the new technologies
appear unfavourable for the less developed areas of
industrialized countries, and in some ways for the
export potential of developing countries:

a)   If robotics eliminate the advantage of cheap
labour, this will reduce the advantage of the less
developed countries toward the industrialized world.
Textiles, etc., might then move back to the economic
core areas (this has already happened to a limited
extent).

b)   Micro-processor induced automation in the core
will reduce the demand for migrant labour (Atlantic
Canada has traditionally exported labour, first to the
Boston area of the United States, and since the 1920's
to Ontario and later Alberta). This will lead to diminishing income in marginal regions, and increase
unemployment.

c)   High technology requires levels of investment, and
yet employs few people in relation to the value of its
output. It may not be worth attracting industries
producing high-tech equipment, and perhaps even those
utilizing it, to developing regions in the industrial-

ized or the Third World, unless one can assume they
will create substantial spin-offs (either through other
high-tech industries or through related expansion). An
employment multiplier for these industries has not yet
been established.

d)   Some people have claimed there is no specific
advantage to concentration in high-tech based activities. This may be so, but in practice they exhibit
little tendency to regionalize. Why?

-    Management control and marketing are important
     reasons for centralizing production.

-    Large corporations capable of funding product
     development are likely to develop and control
     the most profitable application for the new
     technologies.

-    Conglomeration of high-tech industries is partly
     a matter of social preference. They can go where
     they want, but that means California (Silicon
     Valley) or, in Canada, the Ottawa Valley.

-    "Software" may originate in decentralized loca-
     tions but in practice usually orginates in the
     centre, because of the faster flow of ideas and
     easier contacts there.

-    To the extent that the application of high-tech
     by existing industries may have greater employ-
     ment effects, this may again be concentratred in
     the industrial centres because of existing infra-
     structure and know-how.

e)   The impact of the application of high-tech on
scale is interesting:

-    the optimum size of companies may decline;

-    shorter production runs become possible, as it
     is easier to reprogram machines; and

-    greater diversity in production results.

In many ways, these consequences are esthetically and
socially appealing, but they are unlikely to spread
production to less developed areas or countries.

Traditionally, it has been assumed that large

factories, with lots of products to be transported, would be most suited for the center and enjoy the greatest scale advantage there. It has also been assumed that small- and medium-size enterprises can more easily operate from the periphery, but a Swedish study (Fredriksson and Lindmark, 1979), shows that small and medium firms need more contact with suppliers and markets. A standarized, mass-produced item can be marketed at a distance. Less standarized items require more contact with the customer; and the firms producing them can most easily operate near the buyer. Subcontractors are most often located near the buying firm (Steed, 1982). An example of this is the auto parts manufacturers that supply the major automobile producers and assembly plants in the Detroit-Windsor area. Virtually all Canadian suppliers of parts to the North American automobile industry are located in Southern Ontario, close to the larger plants. Again, we are forced to conclude that the smaller size of companies, or at least of plants, induced by technological change, may not be an advantage to marginal regions.

The outlook is thus rather gloomy for the less developed parts of industrialized countries, but one may still hope that the periphery can partake in whatever expansion occurs in the core.

Limiting myself to industrialized contries, if such expansion is to take place, in which sectors will it occur?

a)   In manufacturing, very few could predict growth in employment--some would predict growth through productivity increases and others no growth at all.

b)   Demand in areas such as housing, infrastructure and general construction may be limited. Increased demand in those areas would necessitate considerable government expenditure, that may not be forthcoming unless social expenditures are curtailed in favor of stimuli for construction or public works.

c)   In recent decades, most growth in employment for industrialized countries took place in service industries. Yet the impact of micro-electronic technology in offices is likely to curtail employment. A Canadian study (Menzies, 1981) concludes, on the basis of technological forerunners in compterization (a corporate head office, an insurance company, a bank and some supermarkets), that technological change in each

101

case reduced employment.

v)   A Look into the Future: relevance of Canadian and
     African experience

     In industrialized countries, while there might be
growth in output value in both manufacturing and
services, there is not likely to be any growth in
employment. This raises a serious question of social
policy: when technological change eliminates jobs,
will the remaining work be divided? Especially in
countries where the labor force is still growing, how
can anything approximating full employment be maintained?

     Interesting in this respect is the discussion in
Europe (Jallade, 1981) that favors splitting up
employment policy into two sectors, a new kind of
dualistic economy:

a)   In manufacturing, labor efficiency and productivity are to be maintained; and

b)   In the service sector, new jobs are to be created,
especially in the "quarternary" sector (non-commerical
service sector).

This is already practised in Norway: about 20% of the
jobs are considered to be in the internationally
competitive sector.   In these activities, where efficiency is needed, high investment and technological
change are mandatory. But in the service sector, there
is more flexibility and jobs can be stretched (reduced
working hours etc) to achieve fuller employment.

     Any region, however, needs a economic backbone,
some product or service for export (the one-fifth of
Norwegian employment in the internationally competitive sector is the crucial portion).   What can be done
in marginal regions in the light of our discussion on
the impact of technological change?

a)   Even though some new conglomerates have formed in
the United States (Boston area plus two or three
others), there isn't enough critical mass in marginal
regions to spawn new Silicon Valleys.

b)   If one looks at "high-tech" application in the
development of new products, consumer goods and
services, there are opportunities for marginal regions.

These require identifying new needs and developing new products to fill them.

c)   Another possible approach is "integrated innovation"; application of new technologies to traditional production and services. This is the main hope for marginal regions of industrialized states, and for the Third World (Wad, 1983).

This suggests some avenues for development for both marginal regions in Canada and the Third World:

a)   If growth is to be based in traditional sectors, the rural areas deserve most interest. Bio-technology holds great potential for both food production and market crops and is suitable for small scale applications. However, there has to be a serious effort at rural development before innovations can be introduced.

b)   Growth centers should then be seen as service centers for a hinterland, rather than on their own. By concentrating on large cities alone, the markets are being further fragmented (Taylor, 1970).

c)   Import substitution is advisable when costs permit. This applies to marginal regions of industrialized states (such as Atlantic Canada) because many items are shipped thousands of kilometres and yet could easily be made or at least assembled locally (such as refrigerators: molded plastics, metal and foam insulation, can be handled locally while the electrical parts are imported). This goal is similar to self-reliance, though not at any cost. "Regional Selective Self-Reliance" (Stöhr and Palme, 1977) is the best term I found to indicate that some moderation is required in import substitution to prevent escalation of costs.

d)   Finally, some products for export from the region or Third World country have to be identified. In view of the preceding discussion, we would almost have to conclude that most marginal regions and developing countries will have to concentrate on some resource-based activity but apply modern technology to it, update their market information on what is in demand and perhaps apply their own marketing efforts (this is done in industrialized countries through co-operatives or local entrepreneurs, as in Norway).

103

BIBLIOGRAPHY

Brewis, T. N. "Regional Economic Policy. The federal role". Regional Poverty and Change. compiled by Gunther Schramm. (Ottawa: Canadian Council on Rural Development, 1976).

Clairmont, Donald H. et al "A Segmentation Approach to Poverty and Low-Wage Work in the Maritimes". Marginal Work World Programme, Institute of Public Affairs, Dalhousie University, December 1978.

Dow, Sheila C. "Regional Demand for Money: an application for Canada". Canadian Economics Association, Saskatoon, May 1979.

Francis, J. P. "Regional Development Policies" in O. J. Firestone (ed.), Regional Economic Development. (Ottawa: University of Ottawa Press, 1974).

Fredriksson, C. and Lindmark, L. "From Firms to Systems of Firms", in F. E. I. Hamilton and G. Linge, (eds.) in Spatial Analysis, Industry and the Industrial Environment, Vol. 1, (Chichester: Wiley, 1979).

Hofstad, Svein. "Regional Policy in Norway", Norwegian Commercial Banks, 47 (3), September 1973.

Jallade, Jean-Pierre. "The Employment Problem in Western Europe: an examination of basic issues", in Jean-Pierre Jallade, (ed.), Shirley Williams Introduces Employment and Unemployment in Europe, (Trentham: Trentham Books, 1981).

Kirby, Av D., J. A. Olsen, P. Sjoholt, J. Stolen. The Norwegian Aid Programme to Shops in Sparsely Populated Areas. (Oslo: Norwegian Fund for Market and Distribution Research, 1981).

Lazar, Fred. "Regional Unemployment Rate Disparities in Canada: some possible explanations". Canadian Journal of Economics, 10 (1), February 1977.

Leroy, Marcel. "The Impact of Federal Development Policies in Atlantic Canada". (October 1980).

Matthews, Ralph. The Creation of Regional Dependency (Toronto: University of Toronto Press, 1983).

Menzies, Heather. Women and the Chip: case studies of the effects of informatics on employment in Canada. (Montreal: Institute for Research on Public Policy, 1981).

Nova Scotia Department of Development. "The Future Economic Environment Facing Nova Scotia: trends and influence", Halifax, 1978.

Perkins, F. C. "Technology Choice, Industrialization and Development Experiences in Tanzania", The Journal of Development Studies, 19, (January 1983).

Pinfold, Thomas. "Some Aspects of Federal Resource Flows in the Nova Scotia Economy". Canadian Economics Association, Saskatoon, May 1979.

Steed, Guy P. F. Threshold Firms: backing Canada's winners. Minister of Supply and Services, Science Council of Canada, Ottawa, 1982.

Stöhr, W. and H. Palme. "Centre-Periphery Development Alternatives and their Applicability to Rural Areas in Developing Countries", as quoted in D. R. F. Taylor, "Some Observations on Theory and Practice in Regional Development in Africa" in Regional Economic Development: the river basin approach in Mexico, edited by D. Barkin and T. King, (eds.), (Cambridge: Cambridge Unversity Press, 1970).

Wad, Atul. "Limitations and Opportunities for Developing Countries of Emerging Microelectronics Technologies" in New Frontiers in Technology Application by E. U. von Weizsäcker, M. S. Swaminathan, and Aklilu Lemma (eds.), (Dublin: Tycooly International Publishing, 1983).

Woodward, Robert S. "The Effectiveness of DREE's New Location Subsidies", Canadian Public Policy, 1 (2), Spring 1975.

_____, "The Capital Bias of DREE Incentives", Canadian Journal of Economics, 5 (1 & 2), May 1974.

Chapter Five

Limites Systémiques au Développement Régional au Canada

Edmond Orban

i) Asymétrie et disparité des ressources régionales internes

Quand on parle de développement économique, on fait appel à des éléments d'ordre quantitatif nécessairement reliés au processus de production tels que, notamment, les ressources naturelles, la main-d'oeuvre et les capitaux.

Les deux premiers éléments se retrouvent en partie sur place dans chacune des regionsl du Canada, bien qu'à des degrés très variables. Par contre, les capitaux investis dans les régions proviennent généralement en majeure partie de l'étranger, du moins pour les secteurs clefs de l'économie. Mais ici aussi il y a de profondes différences d'une province à l'autre en ce que concerne le degré et la nature de la dépendance à l'égard des investissements étrangers.

Si l'on considère maintenant la qualité des facteurs de production et leur développement dans un cadre regional (ou provincial) les constatations varient également d'une région à l'autre en ce qui concerne la capacité d'organisation des ressources naturelles et humaines, que ce soit au niveau de l'Etat provincial avec son systèmed'éducation, ses organismes de recherche, ses subsides à l'entreprise privée ou dans la cadre de l'enterprise elle-même qui constitute souvent le principal moteur des innovations d'ordre technlogique.

On observe donc une forte disparité et asymétrie dans le potentiel interne et externe des dix provinces. Plusieurs études sur le fédéralisme nous montrent que dans la majorité des Etats fédéraux dans le monde ce type d'inégalité est beaucoup plus prononcé et risque de saper les fondements même du système politique concerné. Et ce, tout d'abord dans une relation horizontale (des provinces ou régions entre elles), parce que l'inégalité des possibilités et des réalisations concrètes en matière de développement est un phénomène particulièrement visible d'une province riche à une province moins nantie. Cette dernière, en général moins industrialisée, sera souvent tentée d'imputer en partie son retard ou sa faiblesse relative au fait que la ou les provinces plus riches se sont développées dans une certaine mesure à ses dépens.

D'un autre côté, le gouvernement central est perçu par les provinces, tour à tour, comme un élément moteur d'intégration ou désintégration fédérale selon la façon dont on aborde ses politiques en matière de développement régional. On juge que celles-ci sont trop centralisatrices lorsqu'elles ne contribuent pas directement au développement des régions concernées. Mais dès qu'un subside ou des prêts substantiels ont été accordés à une région donnée, rares sont les provinces bénéficiaires que protesteront au non du principe de la décentralisation, même si dans certains cas (comme en matière de recherche et d'éducation) de tels avantages, conditionnels ou pas, peuvent, à plus ou moins long terme, limiter les pouvoirs des dites provinces. Quoiqu'il en soit une des causes de tension réside engalement dans le fait que plusieurs provinces estiment que le gouvernement central a davantage favorisé le dévelopment des régions dites centrales, c'est-à-dire l'Ontario et le Québec si l'on se place au point de vue des provinces des prairies (et des provinces maritimes). Par contre le Québec aura souvent tendance à se considérer comme lésé par rapport à son voisin ontarien qui, dans le domaine économique, lui sert souvent de base de référence.

Pour un observateur étranger vivant dans le cadre d'un système fédéral centralisé (majorité des cas) ou à plus forte raison dans un Etat unitaire, comme la France et la Belgique par exemple, il est évident que les provinces canadiennes avec le sous-système politique que constitue un Etat provincial, disposent d'un outil remarquable pour la formulation et l'application de politiques de développement régional. Ceci est vrai dans une certaine mesure, surtout dans une perspective comparative, lorsque l'on voit à quel point les régions dites périphériques sont démunies de moyens de défense politique (au sein du système politique lui-même) dans la majorité des Etats contemporains. Souvent ce sera le gouvernement central lui-même que prétendra (en exclusivité, faute de véritable gouvernement intermédiaire) remédier aux inégalités du développement régional. Etant donné le vide institutionnel précité, ses politiques ne partent pas de la base. Et, au nom

108

de l'intérêt national, elles contribuent à accentuer
une tendance à la centralization à laquelle le système
politique tout entier sert de support et d'infrastructure. A ce point de vue, les tentatives récentes de
développement régional en France sont partriculièrement
révélatrices des limites politiques d'ordre systémique
que présente un tel pays, souvent à la pointe du progrès
dans d'autres domaines pourtant.

Ceci dit, il n'en reste pas moins vrai que la
marge de manoeuvre de l'Etat provincial canadien reste
fort limitée (surtout dans le cas des petites provinces)
par des facteurs internes et externes qui risquent de
perdurer malgré les changements à première vue rapides
et profonds que nous sommes en train de connaître au
Canada. Voir, à cet égard, les cas de région où l'on
passe d'un régionalisme de nature principalement
défensive à un régionalisme plus agressif2 caractérisé
par un accroissement de l'appareil étatique provincial.
Ce type de régionalisme coïncide (dans le cas québécois
notamment) avec un nationalisme tourné de plus vers la
région, au point de remettre en question les structures
mêmes de l'Etat fédéral. L'actuel gouvernement du Québec
constitue un exemple tangible de ce passage du régionalisme "expansionniste" au nationalisme tout court. En
l'occurrence, les symboles eux-mêmes ont une significa-
tion profonde et des implications pour le genre de
système politique que l'on préconise. Car, en
l'occurrence, quand on parle de nation québécoise, cela
signifie que l'allégeance première est due à une région
et non à l'ensemble du pays et à l'Etat fédéral qui lui
sert de cadre. Or, fait à signaler, cette escalade
dans les revendications politiques coïncide dans une
large mesure avec un accroissement des possibilités
internes de développement de la dite région.3

Dans les autres provinces mais encore une fois avec
des degrés très variables, on observe le rôle croissant
joué par l'Etat provincial dans les domaines clairement
de sa juridiction tels que la culture et les services
sociaux (santé, éducation, Welfare en général) mais
également dans des secteurs relevant plus directement
du développement économique régional (transport, commu-
ication, exploitation des ressources naturelles, indus-
trialisation, etc.). L'Etat provincial est amené à
intervenir de plus en plus sous forme de réglementation
des activités économiques mais aussi dans le cadre de
subsidies, de prêts plus ou moins conditionnels,
d'exemptions de taxe, d'aide diverse a l'exportation,
etc., entrant ainsi en concurrence avec le gouvernement
central lui-même lorsqu'il s'agit de

109

développement économique. Le développement régional
est devenu une priorité pour les deux niveaux de
gouvernement mais on ne s'entend guère sur les modalités
de collaboration et les priorités. Dans plusieurs cas
le governement central est plus soucieux de maintenir
ou plutôt d'acquérir un minimum d'indépendance économique à l'égard de l'étranger, alors que certaines
provinces sont tentées d'accepter des investissements
avec moins de conditions et se soucient davantage du
profit à court terme lorsqu'il s'agit de l'exploitation
étrangère de leurs ressources naturelles ou même de la
mainmise sur les entreprises régionales.4

Parallèlement à ce double mouvement d'expansion
économique et politique régionale on observe enfin un
autre phénomène interne, lourd de conséquence pour les
relations des provinces entre elles et surtout des
provinces avec le gouvernement central, à savoir: le
développement de l'appareil bureaucratique des provinces les plus importantes. Ces dernières ont connu, au
cours des dernières décades, une expansion que tradui-
sent bien les courbes ascendantes en matière d'utilisa-
tion quantitative et qualitative de personnel et plus
généralement les augementations des recettes et des
dépenses. Le développement accéléré des institutions
d'enseignement, notamment au niveau collégial et
universitaire (majoritairement financé par l'Etat provincial) ont contribué (dans le cas québécois surtout)
à renforcer une prise de conscience régionale. La loi
de Parkinson jouant, il va sans dire que l'appareil
bureaucratique étatique ou para-étatique a "fonction-
nellement" intérêt à voir s'accroître ses possibilités d'intervention en matière de développement
régional. Ceci est vrai également pour la catégorie de
professeurs, de chercheurs et de diplômés universitaires
qui pour des raisons diverses (souvent culturelles dans
le case québécois) veulent limiter leur activité au
marché du travail de leur région voire même de leur
ville. Leur conception du développement régional
dépendra évidemment de bien d'autres facteurs. En ce
qui concerne plus particulierement les diplômés, leur
place et leur rôle dans le système de production représente une variable importante. "Un cadre" canadien
d'une firme multinationale ne verra pas le développement
régional dans la même optique meme si parfois les
intérêts à court terme peuvent converger. Le centre de
gravité des dits intérêts se situe à des endroits très
différents et dans des rapports de force souvent très
inégaux dépendant de l'importance des organismes qu'ils
représentent et défendent.

Et nous abordons ici la limite principale au
développement régional5, elle relève du système économique
international.

ii) Facteur Systémique Externe

Plus haut nous avons noté que certaines provinces
canadiennes disposaient de ressources physiques et
humaines leur permettant de participer à des politiques
de développement régional.

Mais, généralement jusqu'ici et a des degrés
variables, plusieurs provinces manquent d'au moins
plusieurs des éléments suivants: technologie, capitaux,
main-d'oeuvre spécialisée, ressources naturelles
(énergétiques notamment), possibilités d'écoulement des
surplus de production, etc. Plusieurs d'entre elles
connaissent un degré de dépendance très élevé. A tel
point que l'on peut parler dans leur cas d'une relation
Centre-périphérie. La littérature sur ce thème est
d'ailleurs variée et abondante, qu'elle soit canadienne
ou d'origine étrangere, précise ou générale.6

Comme le démontre fort bien la Rapport Gray
(Foreign Direct Investment in Canada, 1972), le
développement économique du Canada et de ses régions a
été déterminé en grande partie par le flot des
investissements étrangers. Contrairement aux capitaux
d'origine britannique dont l'emprise sur l'economie
canadienne était relativement limitée, les
investissements américains se sont révelés beaucoup
plus envahissants, à la fois dans le domaine des
matières premières (pétrole, minerais, etc.) mais
également dans les secteurs secondaires et primaires,
prenant le contrôle de firmes locales et créant des
succursales dirigées à partir de sièges sociaux, la
plupart du temps situés aux Etats-Unis. Dans le cas de
l'Ontario et du Québec les investissements directs se
sont concentrés notamment dans des secteurs de pointe
tels que l'industrie pétro-chimique, l'électronique,
l'industrie automobile, etc. Dans le cas des provinces
plus petites le contrôle de l'économie générale est
d'autant plus fort que bien souvent ces provinces
dépendent seulement de quelques firmes multinationales
pour leur développement ou tout simplement leur survie.

Disposant de secteurs de production moins diversi-
fiés et souvent de secteurs "mous" (textile, chaussure,
etc.) le développement de ces régions, serait des plus
précaires s'il ne s'en remettait qu'aux lois dites du

marché. Des auteurs tels que Singer et Baran ont souligné également l'extrême dépendance des régions dites de la périphérie, productrices de matières premières pour des marchés externes et incapables d'influencer le processus de transformation de celles-ci dans un cadre ne fut-ce que partiellement régional.

D'autre part, au niveau de gouvernement central et dans les provinces ou l'Etat provincial s'est suffisamment développé, on observe des réactions d'une ampleur certes très variable mais ayant au moins comme dénominateur commun d'exiger plus de retombées économiques pour les régions. C'est dans cette foulée que l'on peut commencer à parler de développement régional.

Il est évident que les firmes multinationales représentent l'acteur principal du développement régional. Face à ce dernier, le gouvernement fédéral et les provinces peuvent être divisés (voir paragraphe 3, limites systémiques internes d'ordre politique). Le Gouvernement central peut prétendre contrôler les investissements étrangers de façon à pouvoir reprendre à plus ou moins long terme une partie du contrôle l'économie du pays. Certaines provinces, par contre, répétons-le, peuvent se montrer plus soucieuses des retombées immédiates de ces investissements, que ce soit dans une phase de démarrage ou d'expansion de leur économie.

Dans la mesure où l'état fédéral ou provincial s'avère capable de garder une autonomie suffisante à l'égard des F.M.N. (Firmes Multinationales), il peut, du moins théoriquement, acquérir un certain pouvoir de marchandage et intervenir au niveau des décisions. Tout dépend du rapport de force dans lequel on se situe à un moment donné et dans un secteur donné. Mais c'est là une mission d'autant plus difficile que les F.M.N. ne se contentent pas d'investir, elles déterminent en grande partie la nature et l'orientation des développements régionaux parce qu'elles disposent en outre d'un élément clef: la maîtrise des technologies de pointe. En conséquence les décisions sur l'allocation des ressources locales relèvent de celles-ci et de la "maison mère." Or, la grande majorité de ses cadres formés d'étrangers, souvent peu sensibles aux besoins strictement régionaux sont pénétrés d'une rationalité où le profit de l'entreprise joue un rôle sans contrepoids organique jusqu'ici.

Quant à l'élite régionale à la tête des unités de production sur le terrain, de par les exigences de l'organisation qu'elle sert, elle a tendance également à s'identifier à celle-ci. C'est d'ailleurs une condition de réussite que de s'identifier clairement au mode d'organisation, au style, aux objectifs de l'unité que l'on sert. Le type de socialisation (formation universitaire, contacts sociaux) en même temps que les intérêts matériels de cette élite concourrent trop souvent à la couper de la masse des simples producteurs et consommateurs de la région. Si elle est forcée de faire un choix entre les intérêts de la région et ceux de l'entreprise qu'elle sert, cette élite ne peut guère être considérée comme une alliée du développement régional. Il y a des conflits de ce genre notamment lors de la fermeture ou du déménagement des entreprises à l'étranger. En résumé, on ne peut nier qu'il y ait des intérêts communs nombreux entre les F.M.N. et les régions mais il serait absurde de considérer que l'intérêt de ces entreprises coincide avec celui de la région, selon l'application régionale du slogan "ce qui est bon pour G.M. est bon pour les Etats-Unis." L'élite précitée, étant donné l'importance des intérêts qu'elle représente, sera forcément impliquée dans un programme de développement régional. Mais il ne faut pas se dissimuler les limites systémiques que cela implique, quelle que soit la bonne volonté individuelle.

D'autre part, dans certaines provinces, une partie importante du personnel politique peut lui-même vivre plus ou moins en symbiose avec cette élite, partageant ses valeurs, ses intérêts, en raison notamment des rebombées économiques qu'elle envisage pour la région.7 A cet égard, il suffit d'observer les divisions régnant au sein du P.Q. (Parti québécois) actuel, pour se convaincre que l'unanimité est loin de régner (même chez les éléments les plus nationalistes) quant au rôle que devraient jouer les F.M.N. au Québec et ce, malgré la clarté apparente d'un programme dit "social-démocrate."

Notons cependent que le personnel politique provincial a parfois pris des initiatives assez audacieuses, entraînant un conflit plus ou moins larvé avec des entreprises dépendant au moins en partie de l'étranger. Les nationalisations de la potasse et de l'électricité constituent des exemples typiques. Néanmoins, de telles mesures, même si elles ont un impact considérable pour le développement régional (voir notamment le rôle moteur joué par Hydro-Quebec) ne sont que des exceptions dans le contexte nord-américain. Au niveau fédéral on a également observé à quelle opposition interne et externe s'est heurté le gouvernement dans sa tentative de "canadianiser" une partie de l'industrie pétrolière dominée par les intérêts américains.

Il n'est pas étonnant d'ailleurs que l'on parle de plus en plus d'intégration croissante de l'économie des régions canadiennes dans l'économie des Etats-Unis. Chacune des régions, prises séparément (à plus forte raison les simples provinces), constituent autant de fragments d'une périphérie par rapport aux grands centres de décision américains. De plus, ces derniers ont tendance à se déplacer vers l'ouest et le sud, accroissant encore davantage le degré de "périphérisation" décrit plus haut.

Face aux divisions des provinces entre elles (voir la concurrence à laquelle elles se livrent pour obtenir des investissements) et face aux divisions opposant les provinces au gouvernement central, on retrouve des entreprises étrangères transcendant les limites des régions et des pays et connaissant un degré d'intégration très poussé dans la poursuite d'objectifs manifestement plus clairs, plus précis et d'ordre purement matériel. Le caractère centralisateur de leurs prises de décisions offre un contraste saisissant par rapport aux principes de base d'un régime qui se veut fédéral. Cette centralisation dissimule parfois son visage sous des étiquettes nouvelles, changement d'appellation, régionalisation des unités de production, etc. mais son influence n'en reste pas moins grande, surtout face aux provinces les plus démunies.

Bénéficiant en outre d'une énorme marge de manoeuvre en raison de la diversité de ses investissements et possibilités d'investissement à travers le monde, pareil acteur s'avère difficilement implicable dans un développement régional qui ne cadrerait pas avec l'essentiel de ses intérêts.

A partir du moment ou le gouvernement central ou les sous-systèmes politiques que sont les provinces, tentent d'acquérir un minimum de contrôle dans certains secteurs stratégiques pour orienter ou réorienter leur dévelopment économique, ils risquent (corrélation en sens direct) de se heurter à ce type d'entreprises. Ces dernières peuvent d'ailleurs conjuguer leurs efforts et, comme si ce n'etait pas encore suffisant, elles pourront plus ou moins ouvertement faire appel à l'aide du gouvernement des Etats-Unis, via ses

différents départements et agences. Il est un fait
notoire que ce gouvernement et ses ambassadeurs en
première ligne sont devenus plus que jamais de fermes
protecteurs des F.M.N., fer de lance de l'économie
américaine à l'intérieur et à l'étranger.

Au nom du libéralisme international, de l'efficacité et du progrès, il est facile de condamner de haut
les "régionalismes étroits et dépassés" au même titre
que les nationalismes légitimes ou pas. Malheureusement
le libéralisme et l' "intégration économique" ne profit-
ent pas à tous les citoyens et à toutes les régions.
Certains s'enrichissent plus et plus vite que d'autres.
Or, les disparités et asymétries (signalées dans le
paragraphe 1) ne se corrigeront pas d'elles-mêmes, en
fonction des lois du marché.

En d'autres termes il faut des contre-poids8, des
mécanismes de réajustement. Où se logeront-ils? Au
sein du gouvernement central en coopération avec les
provinces? Au niveau des provinces lorsqu'elles
s'estiment sufficamment fortes pour négocier? Dans le
cadre de regroupements régionaux (provinces maritimes,
Prairies, etc)? Où tout cela à la fois?

Ici encore une fois on touche une autre limite
d'ordre systémique mais essentiellement politique car
elle concerne directement la distribution du pouvoir
etatique.

iii) <u>Limites Systémiques d'Ordre Politique Interne</u>

Dans une économie dont l'infrastructure est aussi
dépendante des facteurs externes, on pourrait
s'attendre, du moins en logique, à un regroupement des
forces internes du pays pour assurer un meilleur
développement des différentes régions. Pour un auteur
comme Harold Laski et plusieurs de ses disciples
travaillistes, ce regroupement ne peut se faire que
dans le cadre et sous l'égide d'un Etat fort central-
isé.9 Seul contre-poids possible, selon lui, aux
tendances hégémoniques des grandes entreprises.

Ce type de socialiste s'oppose donc diamétralement
aux théories d'un Proudhon pour qui, au contraire, la
souveraineté doit appartenir aux régions. Les régions
dans ce cas sont la base même du développement bien
qu'elles se doivent de coopérer entre elles dans un
réseau de liens de plus en plus nombreux et intenses.
Ici le gouvernement central voit ses attributions et ses

pouvoirs réduits au plus strict minimum. On peut même parler dans ce cas de quasi extinction de l'Etat. Le modèle canadien rejette ces deux approches mais il est tiraillé entre deux tendances: l'une le poussant à la centralisation que l'on retrouve dans un Etat unitaire classique, l'autre (centrifuge) l'attirant au contraire vers un type de confédération d'un genre nouveau et où en tout cas le gouvernement central verrait ses pouvoirs sensiblement diminués au profit des provinces ou régions nouvelles. Quoiqu'il en soit, au départ, le gouvernement central semble particulièrement favorisé par la constitution pour s'occuper de développement économique. Tout comme dans les autres Etats fédéraux des pays développés (et à plus forte raison dans les Etats fédéraux moins nantis mais plus centralisés), le gouvernement central dispose de l'essentiel des pouvoirs économiques10 (monnaie, commerce extérieur et interprovincial, etc). Ces pouvoirs se sont d'ailleurs renforcés au cours de la révolution industrielle et des deux grandes guerres.

Avec la division du travail entraînée par le développement industriel on assiste en même temps à une spécialisation croissante des activités économiques au sein d'un marché de plus en plus vaste. Ce dernier exige une libre circulation des biens, des personnes et des services. Les forces du marché adressent donc au pouvoir politique supérieur des demandes qui vont dans le sens de ce libéralisme. Ce qui, entre parenthèses, n'empêchera pas les mêmes entreprises de réclamer des mesures protectionnistes et autres faveurs aux gouvernements provinciaux.

Mais ce que nous voulons souligner ici c'est que pour une firme multinationale le gouvernement central est "l'interlocuteur le plus valable," celui qui est le mieux armé pour favoriser ou limiter leur action. De toute façon les dites entreprises exercent également des pressions sur les gouvernements provinciaux, dont certains sont plus perméables à celles-ci mais il n'en reste pas moins vrai que le gouvernement central tend à devenir un "manager" de l'économie, en ce sens qu'il tente de régulariser les demandes et d'assurer un minimum de stabilité de prix pour les entreprises du secteur privé. Dans la même foulée, le gouvernement central est amené à collaborer avec les entreprises dans le domaine de la technologie et, par conséquent, de l'éducation et de la recherche (domaines relevant des provinces également).

Quel que soit le degré de dépendance du gouvernement central à l'égard des forces dominant le marché
canadien, on ne peut que constater un phénomène commun
à beaucoup d'Etats modernes, à savoir que ses fonctions
et ses pouvoirs tendent à s'accroître en réponse aux
exigences d'un développement que, jusqu'ici, les régions
livrées à leurs seuls moyens n'ont pas été capables de
conduire harmonieusement. Dans cette perspective les
exigences à l'égard du gouvernement central croissent
en intensité. Elles partent de l'ensemble des citoyens,
émanent des entreprises et des provinces elles-mêmes.
Le tout pêle-mêle dans un entrecroisement d'intérêts
qui sont souvent loin de coïncider.

Les pouvoirs du gouvernement central augmentent
mais avec eux augmentent également les tensions et les
occasions de conflit. Ce gouvernement est perçu comme
étant l'arbitre du développement des régions mais en
cas d'échec (réel ou supposé) il devient rapidement un
bouc émissaire et une cible facile pour les provinces
frustrées.

On observe alors plusieurs comportements paradox-
aux, les régions les moins développées se plaignant que
le gouvernement central a trop favorisé les régions les
plus riches, demandent une intervention accrue du dit
gouvernement en leur faveur mais acceptent par conséquent implicitement une limitation de leurs pouvoirs.
Cette attitude renforce le processus de centralisation,
quels que soient les mécanismes utilisés dans cette
aide au développement régional (subsides, prêts, péré-
quations, etc). Par contre, une région centrale telle
que l'Ontario pourra davantage jouer sur deux tableaux
à la fois. Son gouvernement dispose de ressources
physiques et humaines de nature à assurer (au moins en
partie) un développement régional axé sur les intérêts
de la région. Mais en même temps il continue de
recevoir une aide considérable du gouvernement central.

Ici aussi le phénomène de perception (qui ne coïncide pas nécessairement avec la réalité objective) joue
un rôle considérable. Il est un fait qu'aux yeux des
différentes provinces l'Ontario a été privilégié par
les politiques de développement du gouvernement central.
Cette perception tend évidemment à sous-estimer le jeu
d'autres facteurs notamment d'ordre externe.12 Si l'on
suit ce raisonnement jusqu'au bout, une province comme
l'Ontario ne s'opposera pas aux politiques de développement à la fois régionales et nationales du gouvernement central parce qu'elle en est la principale béné-

ficiaire. De là à dire qu'elle approuve les tendances
centralisatrices du dit gouvernement il n'y a plus qu'un
pas à franchir. Mais on risque alors d'escamoter une
réalité infiniment plus complexe que les perceptions
précitées.

Les provinces de l'ouest, quant à elles, vont
jusqu'à étendre cette perception a la province de Québec
principale bénéficiaire avec l'Ontario des politiques
gouvernementales d'Ottawa. Il est vrai que la domination actuelle de l'appareil politique et bureaucratique
fédéral par les représentants des deux "régions centrales" ne facilite guère les choses. La sous-
représentation des régions de l'ouest au sein du
gouvernement central entraîne donc un manque de
confiance a l'égard de celui-ci et par conséquent tend
a accentuer un phénomène de repli sur soi-même. Simultanément, le gouvernement central étant considéré comme
un frein au développement régional, certains seront
tentés de chercher des alliés ailleurs, accentuant
l'action des forces centrifuges, voir désintégratives.

Meme des interventions du gouvernement central,
que l'on pourrait ailleurs considérer comme positives du
point de vue fédéraliste, seront jugées défavorablement
par les provinces concernées.13 En d'autres termes les
provinces s'opposent aux politiques de centralisation
lorsqu'elles touchent plus ou moins leurs intérêts
strictement régionaux. Dans le cas inverse, elles les
acceptent au moins tacitement tout en récoltant les
bénéfices immédiats.

Dans le cas des gouvernements provinciaux anglophones ce n'est pas le régime fédéral en tant que tel
que l'on remet en question mais bien les politiques d'un
parti au pouvoir et plus précisément de ses conceptions
concernant le développement des régions. Ces critiques
sont d'autant plus virulentes (de la part des provinces
des prairies et de la Colombie britannique) que l'axe
du développement économique se déplace de plus en plus
vers l'ouest. Et ici on assiste a un phénomène relativement disfonctionnel ou le centre de gravité politique
coïncide de moins en moins avec le centre de la dynamique du développement. Une véritable représentation
des intérêts de l'ouest au sein de l'appareil fédéral
pourrait leur assurer une meilleure participation aux
politiques de développement. Mais ici on touche à
une des limites du système politique canadien, aux
carences des partis politiques qui ont perdu leurs
dimensions nationales, au mode de scrutin lui-même qui

gagnerait à être pondéré par un minimum de "proportionnelle," etc. Si nous soulignons ces aspects, c'est parce que pour l'ensemble des provinces anglophones, malgré tous leurs desiderata et contradictions, elles atteignent un degré de consensus à l'égard du fédéralisme que l'on ne retrouve certes pas au Québec. Dans ce dernier cas ce ne sont pas seulement les politiques de développement qui sont concernées mais bien l'infrastructure même du système fédéral et son fonctionnement tout entier.

Pour les partisans d'une plus grande autonomie provinciale en matière de développement et pour un nombre croissant de personnes, il existe un autre phénomène particulièrement visible et objet de critique, à savoir: la bureaucratie du gouvernement central. Quels que soient les services rendus par celle-ci, elle est perçue comme étant souvent un obstacle à un développement régional collant aux nécessités locales. Selon certains, l'expansion de cette bureaucratie s'effectuerait en quelque sorte en vase clos, axé prioritairement sur les besoins professionnels des décideurs de la fonction publique. Plusieurs auteurs soulignent le fait que les "technocrates public" ont tendance à développer un gouvernement parallèle, de plus en plus indépendant du système politique dans la poursuite de leur carrière et de leurs intérêts.

On mentionne aussi le fait que les départements et agences gouvernementaux et "parastataux" ont tendance à s'étendre quantitativement et qualitativement, avec cette circonstance aggravante que ceci se fait aux dépens des institutions provinciales. Ce que l'un gagne les autres le perdent. Ce processus faisant boule de neige, on ne voit guère comment l'enrayer dans le cadre des procédures habituelles.

Le vaste mouvement en faveur de la "déréglementation" observé au Canada également constitute ici aussi un indicateur significatif des réactions du public et des régions face à une centralisation jugée excessive.15 Encore une fois, ce phénomène n'est pas spécifique au Canada et tout comme aux Etats-Unis la réaction anti-Etat vise essentiellement le gouvernement central. S. H. Beer écrivait d'ailleurs à ce sujet ce qui suit: "The public sector has become such a large proportion of the total society that it generates within itself powerful forces leading to further government action. Centralization, in short, breeds further centralization."16

Autre aspect, la centralisation technocratique a
comme caractéristique de se réclamer de valeurs telles
que la rationalité, l'efficacité, le souci de l'égalité,
voire de l'uniformité dans le cadre du creuset dit
national. Ceci peut l'amener à sous-estimer la
diversité et la spécificité des besoins régionaux et en
tout cas à vouloir réduire les différences (légitimes
ou pas) au profit d'une standarisation qui coïncide
avec les objectifs et les valeurs précitées.

Chez les représentants de cette tendance on est
donc enclin à considérer comme "disfonctionnel" le comportement des provinces qui "dépassent la mesure"
lorsqu'elles prétendent vouloir jouer un rôle moteur
dans leur propre développement et formulent leurs exigences en conséquence. Ce qui, bien entendu, enlève
une partie des pouvoirs aux agents en question.

Cette tendance est encore plus nette lorsque ces
personnes et leurs organisations se heurtent à des
exigences venant d'une province où le gouvernement leur
donne l'impression de vouloir désintégrer l'ensemble du
pays. Dans ce cas ils peuvent arguer davantage du
principe de la légitimité nationale face à des visées
sécessionnistes.

En résumé, si en matière de développement régional
il y a de nombreux exemples de coopération entre
départements et agences des deux niveaux de gouvernement, il n'empêche que, perçus dans l'optique précitée,
les dits rapports peuvent facilement dégénérer en conflit ouvert. Dans le cas précédent il y a actuellement
(dans une mesure qu'il ne faut cepedant pas dramatiser)
un affrontement (d'intensité d'ailleurs très variable)
entre deux types de bureaucratie. L'une tendant à maintenir, voir à augmenter ses prérogatives. L'autre
désirant assumer sur son propre territoire un certain
nombre de pouvoirs exercés par la première, soutenu en
cela par le gouvernement provincial au pouvoir.

Pour les tenants de l'"option souverainiste" il va
sans dire que c'est alors tout le système bureaucratique
fédéral qui constitue un obstacle au développement
régional. Une telle vue n'est pas partagée par les
gouvernements des autres provinces. Le Québec s'en
différencie non pas par un degré de mécontentement plus
poussé mais bien d'une façon fondamentale, dans la
méthode de réaménagement de l'ensemble du système
politique et en particulier la redistribution des pouvoirs économiques du central vers la région.

iv) Conclusions

Certains croient que le gouvernement central à pu,
a un moment donné, être un obstacle au développement
économique d'une région ou l'autre par des interventions
inadéquates. D'autres pensent qu'il devait intervenir
mais en se souciant réellement des besoins spécifique-
ment régionaux. C'est la thèse de W. Y. Smith, par
exemple, lorsqu'il écrit:

> except for the proposals relating
> to federal-provincial finance, the
> economic problems of provinces and
> regions are ignored...
>
> Federal policy makers have largely
> ignored the fact that Canada con-
> sists of economically disparate
> regions, etc.[17]

D'autres opinions sont plus nuancées et présentent
minutieusement le pour et le contre en fonction de
critères variables.

Quant à nous, ce qui nous a le plus frappé c'est
le danger de polarisation que peut constituer un
problème de cette nature. En d'autres termes, par une
sorte de simplification ou de réductionisme, une région
ou une province peut en arriver à cristalliser ses
revendications au développement dans une relation unidi-
mensionnelle, c'est-à-dire province contre gouvernement
central, sans suffisamment tenir compte du poids énorme
des facteurs externes (relevés dans le premier paragraphe). Dans une telle optique on est porté à mettre
l'accent sur la faiblesse des moyens de défense actuels
de la province et sa dépendance forcée à l'égard
d'"Ottawa." Mais, en même temps, et c'est là un aspect
non négligeable au point de vue dynamique, on insiste
sur le potentiel humain et physique de la région.
Potentiel[18] qui devrait pouvoir se mobiliser et se
développer plus harmonieusement si l'on sortait du
"carcan de l'Etat fédéral centralisé."

Lorsqu'une telle prise de conscience (et ici la
psychologie joue un rôle aussi important que les faits
objectifs) se combine avec une nette discontinuité ou
disparité dans le développement de la région par
rapport à une ou plusieurs autres régions (celles que
l'on veut bien voir), le degré de frustration augmente.
Si, en outre, les causes de ce "développement inégal"

peuvent être principalement attribuées au gouvernement
central, la quantité de responsables diminue et
l'adversaire n'en apparaît que plus visible et plus
menaçant. Lorsque, par dessus tout cela, les facteurs
culturels viennent renforcer le particularisme régional
par rapport aux autres régions anglophones (considérées
souvent en partie à tort comme monolithiques), on a
alors une accumalation et une conjugaison de facteurs
de nature désintégrative. Si de tels facteurs contin-
uent à jouer simultanément et avec intensité, ils
risquent fort d'amener un nombre croissant de citoyens
de la dite région à exiger un transfert du contrôle du
développement du "centre politique" à la région devenue
à son tour Etat national.

Dans cette analyse, nous n'avons pas voulu étudier
les politiques de développement régional telles que
réalisées par le "fédéral" ou les provinces ou régions.
Le bilan que l'on pourrait faire s'avère très difficile.
Il serait en outre l'objet d'interprétations fort
variables selon les conceptions que l'on se fait des
avantages de la centralisation et de la décentralisation, selon aussi la place que l'on désire accorder aux
entreprises privées en distinguant les petites, moyennes
et grandes enterprises, les entreprises régionales,
nationales, internationales, etc.

L'objectif ici était de mettre en relief, avec
suffisamment de recul, deux limites d'ordre économique
et politique à un développement axé sur les régions.
Le régionalisme tout comme le nationalisme en tant que
phénomène politique et social coïncide souvent avec une
nette identification des intérêts régionaux. C'est
pourquoi un simple compromis entre la centralisation
économique et la régionalisation culturelle ne constitue pas (ou plus) une politique valable pour
l'avenir. R. Watts a fort bien exprimé ce constat
lorsqu'il écrit:

> regional, linguistic, or cultural
> groups have developed a deep-rooted
> anxiety that, because of the per-
> vasive impact of public economic
> policy upon all aspects of society,
> centralized fiscal and economic
> policies aiming at the rapid deve-
> lopment of an integrated economy
> will undermine their cultural

distinctiveness and opportunities for
employment in culturally congenial
conditions.19

Ceci nous amène immanquablement à nous poser au
moins la question à savoir dans quel type de système
politique le développement régional aurait le plus de
chance d'être assuré? Il y a certes tout éventail de
systèmes dont les pôles extrêmes sont relativement bien
connus. On ne manque pas, en effet, de modèle d'Etat
unitaire très centralisé. Par contre on a eu quelques
expériences confédérales aux liens fort lâches qui
peuvent servir de laboratoire au moins partiel pour une
réflexion. Entre les deux s'échelonnent une série de
solutions mixtes en mouvement continuel plus difficiles
à saisir. Alors qu'au Canada, jusqu'ici, on a surtout
parlé d'intégration interne,20 en Europe occidentale et
en Afrique également, on observe des expériences
relevant d'un processus d'intégration externe. Les deux
procèdent à partir d'une même dynamique dont les forces
à première vue contradictoires sont au fonds complémen-
taires si le systèmepolitique parvient à les équilibrer.
La première de ces forces (appelée trop vite centrifuge)
pousse à une certaine identification ou enracinement
regional parfaitement légitime et l'autre, faite
d'ouverture, aspire à participer aux avantages et res-
ponsabilités d'une communauté élargie.

Tout système politique qui ne tiendra pas vérit-
ablement compte de ces forces "vitales," comme dirait
Bergson, est forcément voué à l'échec à plus ou moins
long terme.

L'historie du monde est un cimetière de systèmes
politiques éclates, trop souvent parce qu'ils ont été
incapables, pour toute sorte de raisons, d'opération-
naliser deux principes de base aussi élémentaires.
Mais, que d'obstacles entre la théorie et la pratique!
Aussi, quel asynchronisme entre le développement techno-
logique ultra accéléré que nous connaissons et le peu
d'évolution des structures mentales des principaux
acteurs (internes et externes) impliqués dans le débat
crucial du développement régional et du développement
tout court sur l'ensemble de notre planète!

Notes

1. Dans le cas de provinces telles que l'Ontario et le Québec il s'agit incontestablement de régions au sens habituel du terme. Pour la clarté de l'exposé et vu les aspects politiques du sujet traité nous considérerons les provinces comme des régions.

2. Raymond Breton parle quant à lui de régionalisme "expansionniste" ou "entrepreneurial" qui se caractérise notamment par le développement du secteur public au niveau provincial. Larry Pratt utilise l'expression "State and province building" à propos des stratégies de développement de l'Alberta.

3. Et ce malgré la crise actuelle qui risque de renforcer ce mouvement dans la mesure où une partie de la population en arrive à croire que son développement est bloqué par le système politique.

4. Les positions prises à l'occasion du fonctionnement de l'Agence de "tamisage" des investissements étrangers (créée par le gouvernement Trudeau) consistent un cas intéressant à analyser. Voir également le fonctionnement du MEER (ministère de l'Expansion économique régionale).

5. Quand nous parlons des limites économiques et politiques du dévelopment régional c'est dans la perspective d'une autonomie régionale par rapport aux agents économiques signalés plus loin.

6. A titre documentaire, pour la première catégorie signalons par exemple: les groupes Waffle et W. Gordon, Kari Levitt, Ch. Taylor, Watkins, Rotstein, plut tout un courant de pensée socialiste ou non qui se développe principalement en Ontario et au Québec.
Les auteurs étrangers de référence assez récente sont entre autres: Samir Amin, Rokkan, Magdoff, Th. H. Moran, Baran, Vernon, Miliband, Galtung, Sweezy, etc.

7. Phénomène apparenté à ce que certains auteurs qualifient de "pénétration" au sens à la fois économique, politique et culturel.

8. C'est un concept auquel les fondateurs du fédéral-
    isme aux Etats-Unis étaient particulièrement
    attachés, du moins au moment de leur lutte "anti-
    coloniale".

9. Voir le texte court mais célèbre "The obsolescence
    of federalism".

10. E. Orban, "Fragmentation des économies nation-
    ales", Policy Options, 2(3), 1981, 23. Voir
    egalement La centralisation dans l'Etat
    fédéral: un processus irreversible? (Montreal:
    Ed. Québec-Amérique, 1984).

11. Par développement harmonieux, nous voulons dire
    un développement produisant des effets équitables
    pour l'ensemble des citoyens de la région mais
    aussi en tenant compte dans une certaine mesure
    des besoins de l'ensemble du pays.

12. Les étrangers ont eu tendance à investir dans cette
    région privilégiée à plusieurs points de vue avec
    les effets d'entraînement que cela suppose. Le
    gouvernement central a contribué à accélérer ce
    mouvement mais dans quelle mesure?

13. Voir notamment les politiques du gouvernement
    central concernant l'approvisionnement et les prix
    du pétrole et la recherche de formules de péré-
    quation permettant une meilleure redistribution
    des ressources à travers les régions.

14. Même un document aussi modéré que le "livre beige"
    du P. L. Q. implique des transformations pro-
    fondes. Quant au "livre blanc" du P. Q., il pré-
    conise un système n'ayant guère de points communs
    avec un régime fédéral.

15. Voir l'ouvrage, P. Aucoin (ed.), The Politics and
    Management of Restraint in Government, (Montreal:
    Institut de recherches politiques, 1981).

16. Centralisation aux dépens des régions également
    faut-il ajouter. Voir S. M. Beer, The moderni-
    zation of American Federalism, (Publius, 1973),
    53.

17. L'auteur, ancien président du Conseil de développe-
    ment de la région de l'Atlantique (provinces
    maritimes) analyse les conséquences désastreuses,

selon lui, de cette politique ou absence de politique pour les provinces maritimes et le Québec. Voir: "Recognition of Regional Balance" Policy Options, 2(5), 1981, 43.

18. Nous utilisons ce concept dans le sens conféré par Aristote, c'est-à-dire "en Puissance", par opposition à "en Acte" au réalisé.

19. David Cameron, (ed.) Federalism, Regionalism and Political Integration in Regionalism and Supranationalism, (Montréal: Institut de recherches politiques, 1981).

20. Pour une définition des concepts d'intégration interne (exemple le fédéralisme) et d'intégration externe (exemple la Communauté économique européenne). Voir Barréa.

Chapter Six

Regional Development in Canada:

the case of the provincial North

Geoffrey R. Weller

i)   Introduction: the Canadian provincial North

The vast region of Canada between the populated
south and the far north of the Yukon and Northwest
Territories has been labelled many things. It has
been called the Canadian Shield, the mid-north, the
near-north, Mid-Canada and the Boreal Zone. These
terms result from defining the boundaries of the
region on the basis of climatic, geological and social
factors rather than on political factors.1 The region
is, in fact, made up of the northern portions of
various provinces and most of these provinces have
defined their own northern regions for purposes of
public administration. Thus the provincial north from
a public administration and political viewpoint is
comprised of the various provincial norths as defined
by the provinces themselves.

Thus I define the provincial north in the Prairies
as the boundaries of the Northern Alberta Development
Council,2 the Department of Northern Saskatchewan 3
and the Manitoba Ministry of Northern Affairs.4   In
Ontario the boundaries of the Ministry of Northern
Affairs constitute that province's northern region.5
In Quebec the area that constitutes the provincial
north is that covered by the James Bay and Northern
Quebec Agreement6 and the most relevant agency is
the Secretariat des Activites Gouvernementales en
Mileau Amerindien et Inuit (SAGMAI).   In Newfoundland
the provincial north is generally considered to be
Labrador and the most relevant agency the Department
of Rural, Agricultural and Northern Development.7
There is no commonly accepted definition of a northern
region in an agency with primarily northern responsibilities in the manner of most of the other provinces.
The government of British Columbia does, however, send
a representative to the Interprovincial Conference of
Ministers Responsible for Northern Development.

All of the provincial norths cover huge land
areas. Each one of the provincial norths is bigger

than all the Maritime provinces (New Brunswick, Nova
Scotia and Prince Edward Island) put together.
Labrador constitutes nearly one third of the total
area of Newfoundland with an area of 115,830 square
miles and all of the other provincial norths are
larger and constitute a greater percentage of the
total area of their respective provinces. Northern
Quebec comprises roughly 70% of Quebec and covers
410,000 square miles and is the largest percentage
of the provincial norths. Northern Ontario comprises
the largest percentage of a provincial territory as
it encompasses approximately 80% of the total area of
Ontario. Northern Ontario and northern Quebec are
each nearly three times the size of Zimbabwe.

Because of the huge size of the provincial norths
most of the cities and towns located in them are
situated a long way away from their provincial capitals
and from the national capital. Sudbury, on the southern edge of the north in Ontario, is 300 miles from
Toronto and Kenora, on the Ontario-Manitoba border,
is 1,200 miles from Toronto. The residents of Kenora,
in fact, tend to orient toward Winnipeg, Manitoba's
provincial capital, which is only one hundred miles
away. Many of the far northern communities are still
innaccessible by road and can only be reached by water
or by air. Labrador is located on the main north
American land mass and is actually physically separated from the rest of the province of Newfoundland by
the Strait of Belle Isle.

The geology of the provincial norths is much
the same for they are all located largely on the
Canadian Shield. This formation is rich in mineral
resources but it has few areas with even passable soil
conditions. This makes agriculture difficult if not
impossible on any significant scale, a fact only
really learned after mainly unsuccessful attempts to
settle the little agricultural land that is available.
The climate of the provincial norths is uniformly
harsh. Winters are cold, extremely cold in the far
north, and summers are short and cool. This, of
course, further restricts agriculture. Most of the
area is, in fact, covered by coniferous forests
except in the part around Hudson Bay which consists
largely of swampy lowlands. The very far northern
parts of Quebec and Labrador extend above the tree
line.

The populations of all the provincial norths

constitute only a very small percentage of the totals
in their respective provinces. The population of
northern Saskatchewan, for example, is approximately
27,000 out of a provincial total of one million.
Northern Alberta has a population of 115,000, northern
Manitoba 96,000, northern Quebec 83,290 and Labrador
36,500. Northern Ontario has a much larger population
(805,000) than all the others combined but the total
population of Ontario is 8.5 million so the percentage
of the provincial population total is still small.
None of the northern regions have more than 10% of the
total population of their respective provinces.

Not only are the populations of the provincial
norths very small they are widely scattered and there
are, therefore, relatively few large population
centres. In most of the provincial norths the
largest centres are rarely bigger than 20,000-30,000
and most are very considerably smaller. Only in
northern Ontario are there cities with populations
of over 100,000 and even then there are only two
of them - Thunder Bay (115,000) and Sudbury (150,000).
Most of the provincial norths are experiencing out-
migration, especially of the young. The populations
of most cities and towns have gone up and down with
the boom and bust cycle of the primary industries
upon which most are dependent. Some, like Elliot
Lake in northern Ontario, have gone through boom and
bust and back to boom again just in the period since
the end of World War Two.

The population of the provincial north is racially
and ethnically very mixed. It is divided between
whites and indigenous peoples with a far larger
proportion of indigenous peoples to whites than in
the south. The white population, which is usually
located in the larger centres, is ethnically mixed.
The indigenous peoples, which are usually located
in small scattered communities are very fragmented.
There are status Indians, non-status Indians, Metis
and Inuit. The population lives in widely scattered
pockets because of the nature of the Canadian Shield
rather than in the more evenly spread pattern associated with agriculture. This scattered nature of the
population tends to weaken regional consciousness
and cohesiveness.

The relatively small populations of the provincial
norths has meant they lack political clout in terms
of the number of seats they possess federally and
at the provincial level. Northern Ontario, the

largest of the regions, returns only 16 provincial MPP's out of a total of 125 and 11 federal MP's out of 282. The level of representation has been declining proportionately and is likely to continue to do so as the regions are either experiencing population decline or only very slow growth compared with provincial rates, so reapportionment is bound to affect them adversely.

The economies of the provincial norths are essentially resource based. The three big employers in all of them are the forest industries, mining and tourism. Because of the need to export bulk commodities from the regions, the transportation industry is also of importance in most of the provincial norths, although especially so in northern Ontario because this region straddles Canada's East-West transportation corridor. The power generation industry is also of significance because of the abundance of hydro-electric resources, especially in northern Quebec and northern Manitoba. There are few secondary manufacturing industries in any of the provincial norths and, as has been noted, the geography and climate is not conducive to a significant agricultural sector. The nature of the economies is partly what determines the scattered nature and low total size of the populations for not only are they partial economies but resource industries are notoriously capital intensive and becoming increasingly so. The few major centres of population that have already developed do not have very diversified economies and this promotes out-migration.

The geography of the regions and the nature of their economies have combined to create a lack of cohesiveness throughout the provincial norths; that is, they are not integrated, reasonably reliant regional economies. Their economies have, essentially, been structured on the basis of the needs of other regions as is reflected in the transportation networks which have historically been, and largely still are, structured to facilitate the movement of bulk commodities out of the regions and not for the purposes of intraregional communications. The lack of integration in the regional economies is partly due to the fact that most of the major industries are owned and controlled by groups headquartered outside the regions with, thereby, little interest in developing regional economies.

130

Although the economies of the provincial norths are essentially resource based the traditional economy of hunting, fishing and trapping is significant. The traditional and resource economies are, in fact, quite distinct with the resource economy being largely associated with the white north of the larger communities and the traditional economy being largely associated with the native north of the smaller more remote communities. This further fragments the economy and population of the regions and makes for a general lack of cohesiveness and integration.8

The structure of the economies of the provincial norths has meant that on the whole their populations are less well off than the residents of the southern parts of their respective provinces. In addition, there is a vast gulf between the standard of living of the white population and that of the indigenous population. For many people the general conditions of life in the more remote areas of the provincial norths are very poor. Apart from the difficulties presented by the harsh climate, the populations remain isolated, often extremely so, as a result of the huge distances combined with poor transportation and communication facilities. Poverty, remoteness and neglect by government means truncated or non-existent local government structures and relatively poor servicing in all respects. In the more remote areas there are still communities with no clean water supplies, no roads, no sewers and no proper garbage collection and disposal facilities. Moreover, health, educational and other social services are poor in comparison with southern regions.

The nature of the economies of the provincial norths, population characteristics and lack of cohesiveness all clearly indicate they are hinterland regions of their respective provinces. Many of the residents of the two regions are alienated and aggrieved because they feel the regions are being exploited by their respective southern centres. They see their natural resources, money and people being extracted to serve the interests of the southern regions which in their view do not help create balanced development in their north or properly protect their northern environments. The sense of alienation may originate merely from the fact that the products of those who labour in the

region are seen as going elsewhere. Many of the
industries are owned by corporations headquartered
outside the regions and the wealth created by the
regions is seen as being taken for use elsewhere.
Moreover, many of the industries import their managerial staff, pollute the environment, establish
company towns and leave when resources are exhausted.
The narrow existing economic bases of the two regions
adds to the sense of alienation. This is perhaps
mainly because the regions' young have to think of
leaving the north and breaking family ties if they
wish to enter white collar occupations. The existence
of the tourist industry does little to change perceptions because it is low wage and seasonal and also
leads to local residents perceiving their regions as
being largely playgrounds for those from the south.

There is, therefore, an atmosphere in all of
the provincial norths in which the local populations
feel exploited, underprivileged, alienated and unable
to control their own destinies or that of their
regions. This has led to political reactions of many
different types which will be detailed later.

ii) Perceptions and Approaches

While the provincial north has been neglected
historically by both the federal and provincial
governments and, partly as a consequence, suffers
from a great many problems it is, curiously enough,
the region of the country which largely defines the
image of the nation both at home and abroad. Certainly the image of Canada abroad is defined by the
shield terrain, the log cabin, snow and the RCMP
officer on a dog sled rather than the industrial
suburbs of Montreal, Toronto and other cities in
which the vast majority of the population lives in
a narrow strip clinging to the American border.
Much as with Australia the image of the country is
defined by the vast sparsely populated interior of
the nation rather than its true heartland and this
leads to misperceptions which have unfortunate
consequences.

The provincial north has been important in
defining a distinctive Canadian consciousness. The
region has been Canada's 'frontier' for many decades
and pride is taken in surviving the rigours of winter
and the manner in which frontier existence develops
a rugged self reliance and strength of character.

Many have argued that Canada's destiny lies in exploiting the regions' resources which have usually been regarded as inexhaustible. The most recent and most grandiose of these schemes was the Mid-Canada corridor concept put forward by Richard Rohmer and Acres-Bechtel Corporation.9 Essentially the idea was to populate the provincial north (mid-Canada as Rohmer called the region) with millions of new residents, construct an integrated nation-wide transportation network at a higher latitude than those currently in existence, enlarge key towns, rapidly expand the resource industries and add secondary manufacturing industries. Such a project would have required enormous amounts of capital and a concerted national effort. Neither was forthcoming and indeed Canada is most unlikely to have its equivalent of Brasilia and the efforts to develop and settle the vast interior of Brazil.

The reality is that the provincial north has largely been ignored and neglected by all governments for decades, that most Canadians are astonishingly ignorant of even the most basic facts about the region and that most Canadians have no desire to go there for anything but hunting and tourist purposes. The region is, and always has been, a vast hinterland rich in natural resources which as been dominated by and exploited by the metropolitan centres of Canada and the United States. Moreover, it is almost certainly likely to remain an exploited hinterland in the foreseeable future.

The vast area which in large part defines Canada's national image at home and abroad and which contributes very significantly to the nation's balance of trade and industrial system via the exploitation of its natural resources has been woefully neglected. This neglect has created a wide range of problems that it will be very difficult to tackle. These problems range from a deeply divided society, especially between whites and the indigenous peoples, to an economy divided between the resource based and the traditional which only exacerbates the racial divisions. In addition, both economies are partial, unstable and form an inadequate base for the delivery of the normal services southern populations expect. Thus there are problems of poverty, poor health, poor educational and other social services, inadequate local government services and the lack, in many areas, of the basic skills needed to develop local self-government.

The provincial north, even though it has, as we shall see, attained somewhat increased significance and attention in recent years is still neglected in southern policy making centres. The agencies responsible for administering the north, many of them of very recent origin, have difficulty getting their points accepted. Moreover, they tend to be regarded as bureaucratic dumping grounds and generally treated as poor relations.10 There is no great mission to rectify conditions in the provincial north let alone develop it on a major scale. The area is still treated as a remote fringe rather than the great interior of the nation.

It is hardly surprising, therefore, that most discussions of the provincial north tend to use the metropolis - hinterland or centre - periphery modes of analysis. This approach has a respected and indigenous exponent in the form of Harold Innis.11 He recognised that Canada's economy largely depended upon the export of staple resources and that the nature of their production and export depended on a long term relationship of metropolitan dominance over the hinterland areas. Indeed this dependence on hinterland natural resources continues to this day. As time has passed furs, then forests, then minerals and then hydroelectricity have all formed important or leading sectors of the national economy. The major questions of concern here are why regions with abundant natural resources have remained economic backwaters and what should be done to transform the situation.

The answers to these questions vary considerably depending upon ones point of view. The staples theory has been modified by Watkins 12 from a purely economic theory to one linked with social and structural conditions which determine who and where resources are developed. Then there are those who explain regional disparities by saying some regions lack certain social, economic, political or cultural factors and this prevents them from developing. This is usually labelled the development approach and in Canada the element usually lacking is identified as something rather vaguely labelled 'entrepreneurship'.13 The neo-classical argument is that certain regions remain undeveloped because governments have interfered in the operation of the free market in them. Usually

they criticise government attempts to help develop
regions in this form as interference especially
minimum wage rates and transfer payments.14

Of increasing popularity in Canada are Marxist
explanations of regional disparities. This
perspective regards regional disparity as a
variation on the general pattern of class exploitation
in a capitalist society and is as much linked to
social and political factors as to economic ones.
Wallace Clement15, Carl Cuneo16 and Henry Veltmeyer17
are among those who have adapted this approach to the
Canadian context though not specifically to the case
of the provincial norths.

The dominant approach in Canada, the one that
has mainly determined policy outputs, has been what
can be termed the Keynsian approach. This approach
views regional disparities in much the same light
as fluctuations in the business cycle and advocates
treating them in much the same way, that is, by
government intervention to smooth out the variations.
This theory has been linked in Canada with the growth
pole approach, especially throughout much of the life-
time of the Department of Regional Economic Expansion
(DREE), and has provided much of the justification for
most of Canada's regional development policy.18   It
has been closely linked with an incentives approach
of grants, tax concessions and cheap access to
resources and an infrastructure development approach
intended to attract industry to a region. Before
detailing some of the specifics of this approach
as applied in the context of the provincial norths,
this chapter will discuss the development of industrial
and governmental interest in the region and take a
look at the policy making framework that has developed.

iii) The Growth of Interest in the Canadian Provincial
      North

Before the Second World War the provincial norths
were essentially forgotten backwaters. The resource
industries had not penetrated very far north at that
time and so the economies of the provincial norths
were based on the traditional pursuits of hunting,
fishing and trapping. There was some tourism, largely
based on hunting and fishing, but this was a seasonal
and low wage industry that did not employ large
numbers of people. The income from the traditional
pursuits was insignificant and a great deal of

poverty, often extreme poverty, resulted. Most of
the population became dependent upon government
handouts.   In fact, the provincial north at this time
could not be described as being part of the normal
wage economy of the country.

The federal government became interested in the
provincial norths before the provincial governments
whose territory it was.   This was largely because
defence concerns, which are a responsibility of the
federal government, affected the provincial norths
before resource development concerns, which are
a responsibility of the provincial governments.   The
Federal governments concern for the provincial north
began largely during the Second World War, but
continued throughout the cold war era and to the
present, mainly as a result of the need for the
construction and maintenance of defence sites of
various types across the north.   This was followed
by a general concern for the basic health and welfare
of northern residents which derived largely from the
federal government's responsibility for status Indians
and its decision to treat Inuit in the same manner
as status Indians.   This led to a much more visible
federal rather than provincial presence in the
provincial norths.   The Medical Services Branch
nursing stations, the federal schools, the Department
of Transport, Department of National Defence and
RCMP establishments were all symbolic of this.   In
many ways the provincial norths, especially northern
Quebec, were more like extensions of the Northwest
Territories than parts of their respective provinces.19

In the 1950's and 1960's the natural resources
of the provincial north began to be exploited on a
significant scale.   This produced a new, second,
economy alongside the traditional economy and also
sparked the interest of the provinces in their own
northern areas.   As the provinces began to project
their authority northwards they increasingly came
into conflict with the already established federal
authorities.   Nowhere was the problem more acute
than in Quebec where Rene Levesque, Minister of
Natural Resources in the 1960's was shocked to
discover that there had been so little provincial
interest in northern Quebec that it was essentially
English speaking (English was the second language
of the Cree and Inuit, not French) and dominated by
the federal authorities.   This led to an effort,
which continues to this day, to bring the area firmly

under provincial control and reorient its population
toward identification with provincial authorities
rather than federal authorities and the French rather
than English Canadian milieu.

The development of the newer second economy in
the provincial norths and the growth of federal-
provincial conflict led to pressures which in the late
1970's led to new bureaucratic initiatives on the
part of the provinces in the form of the establishment of agencies to deal specifically with the provincial norths. Especially by the 1960's the provinces
began to realise that the natural resources of their
northern regions could contribute significantly to
their revenue positions and they, therefore, began
to wish to develop the areas, often on a grand scale.
As this occurred or was planned the Indians and Metis
became increasingly resentful as it robbed them, or
would rob them, of their traditional means of liveli-
hood.20 Moreover, environmental concerns became
important as it became clear that large scale development of the resource sector brought with it significant
environmental costs. The 'mining' of the forests
concerned many, as did the serious cases of air and
water pollution and the flooding of huge tracts of
land that occurred.21 As development picked up speed
many of the smaller communities discovered they were
left out of the process and that a dual economy
was being created. This, of course, created a great
deal of bitterness and pressure for change, especially
as the nature of the dual economies reinforced governmental rivalries and racial divisions. Those left
out of the white, essentially urban, resource economy
were mainly the indigenous peoples (although by no
means always) who felt they deserved a fairer share
of the economic benefits resulting from the development
of the resource sector. This attitude, but at a
different level, also began to affect the white,
resource north as it became conscious of the difference
between its interests and those of the southern
regions. The new resource based towns and cities
began to strenuously pressure for industrial diversification so they could avoid the boom and bust cycle
and stem the outmigration of the young.22 Discontent
in the northern regions reached the point by the 1970's
where there were increasing calls for the creation of
new provinces.23 None of these calls were very serious
or threatening but the very fact they occurred at
all was of concern to the provincial governments.

137

The provincial governments responded to the new saliency of the provincial north and the need to deal with a wide variety of problems in very different ways.24 British Columbia decided not to establish a special or separate agency whereas Alberta, Quebec and Newfoundland all created specialised agencies but ones with relatively limited mandates. Alberta established the Northern Alberta Development Corporation, Newfoundland, the Department of Rural Agricultural and Northern Development and Quebec the Secretariat des Activites Gouvernmentales en Milieu Amerindien et Inuit (SAGMAI). The first two agencies are primarily concerned with economic development while SAGMAI, as its name implies, is largely concerned with the indigenous population. Economic development in northern Quebec is largely the responsibility of the James Bay and Northern Quebec Corporation.

Three provinces, Saskatchewan, Manitoba and Ontario, established departments of Northern Affairs but the titles are a bit misleading and they vary greatly in the range of their responsibilities. Initially, Saskatchewan established, in 1972, a full service Ministry, the Department of Northern Saskatchewan (DNS), which delivered nearly all of the services in the northern part of Saskatchewan. The Manitoba Department of Northern Affairs, established in 1974, is a limited Ministry in that its mandate is restricted to matters related to local government development (and then only in the more remote parts of the north) and the coordination of federal-provincial agreements affecting the north. The Ontario Ministry of Northern Affairs was established in 1977 and is really a coordinating Ministry because although it has major delivery capacity in some areas its primary role is that of coordinating the northern related activities of the other provincial ministries and of coordinating federal-provincial agreements that deal with northern Ontario.

By the late seventies these new agencies began to exchange ideas via the forum of the Interprovincial Conference of Ministers Responsible for Northern Development. This group first met in Fort McMurray in 1978 and has held meetings almost every year since then. The meetings are a useful means of sharing information and exchanging ideas. The simple fact of the creation of the group signifies the growing awareness of the importance of the provincial north.

The basic differences between these northern
agencies and the typical line ministries is that
they are based upon the criterion of region as
opposed to service, clientele, function or some other
category. They, in fact, represent a good cross
section of the spectrum of ways in which the regional
factor could be handled. At the one extreme there is
the British Columbia position that no concession should
be made to that criterion. At the other end of the
spectrum there was the Department of Northern
Saskatchewan under the New Democratic Party where
most line functions were subordinated to the regional
criterion. A new Progressive Conservative government
thinks the regional criterion less important and is
phasing out the department. In between there is the
Ontario attempt to try and promote a regional
perspective on the part of the line ministries. The
Manitoba Ministry and the other agencies are examples
of attempts to deal with one or a few line matters
by region but not a very wide range of them.

iv) The Policy Making Framework

The policy making framework affecting the provincial north is extremely complex. This is partly
because there are two levels of government involved
and because there are a great variety of relevant
agencies within each level of government that have
different perspectives. It is also partly because
there is an extremely wide range of interests in the
provincial north based upon all kinds of societal
divisions and having widely differing perspectives.

At the federal level the most relevant agencies
are the Departments of Indian Affairs and Northern
Development (DIAND) and the Department of Regional
Industrial Expansion (DRIE). This latter department
was created in 1983 by combining the regional programmes of the former Department of Regional Economic
Expansion and the industry, small business and
tourism programmes of the old Department of Trade and
Commerce.25 DIAND's major responsibility in the
provincial north is for status Indians and, thereby,
the many Indian reserves that exist in the provincial
north. These responsibilities are broad and include
such things as local government and housing on reserves. DRIE's major responsibility is, of course,
the promotion of economic development. Many other

federal departments also have major roles in the
provincial north including the Department of National
Defence and the Department of National Health and
Welfare. The Medical Services Branch of the Department of National Health and Welfare, for instance,
supplies health services to the status Indians on
reserves in the provinces. There are in essence,
therefore, two health delivery systems in the
provincial north.26

     At the provincial level there are the specialised
northern agencies and ministries previously mentioned
as well as a wide range and varying mix of specialised
agencies. To take Ontario as an example, there are
two Ministries with a very major concern for the
north, the Ministry of Northern Affairs and the
Ministry of Natural Resources. In addition, a wide
range of line ministries conduct operations which
have a serious impact on the northern part of the
province including a branch of the Ministry of Culture
and Recreation with responsibility for Indian Affairs.
In addition, there are specialised agencies such as
the Northern Ontario Development Corporation (NODC)
and Royal Commissions of Inquiry, such as the Fahlgren
Commission.

     There are, therefore, bound to be all kinds of
inter-governmental and intra-governmental conflicts
concerning matters related to the development of the
provincial norths. The rivalry between the federal
and provincial authorities over the provincial norths
has already been noted and this problem is compounded
by the fact that the two levels of government have
overlapping responsibilities in some areas as, for
example, in the case of some Indian-related matters
and general economic development. At the federal
level there is a division between those agencies which
push for economic development and those which wish to
protect the environment and it is argued that there
is even a contradiction within one department -DIAND -
between the objective of promoting Indian advancement
and the objective of promoting northern development.
In part, because of this perceived contradiction some
critics have advocated the abolition of the depart-
ment.28 At the provincial level there is the same
division between those advocating development and
those wishing to protect the environment and there is
also frequently conflict between the new specialised
northern agencies and the older line ministries. The
latter tended to resist the formation of the new

agencies and frequently still resent them because they either reduced their empires or 'interfere' in their operations or were seen as hotbeds of radicalism - as one or two of them arguably were.

The range of interests in the provincial norths with which the plethora of governmental agencies must deal is extremely broad. These are perhaps best indicated by placing them on a continuum of those which are for development at all costs to those which are for no further development and even a return to a pristine wilderness. For the purposes of the present analysis, the groups that comprise this continuum are roughly placed into two categories, those for further economic development and those against. An attempt will be made to assess the relative resources for political influence available to each of these sets of interests.

The groups supporting further development of the provincial norths range from those who argue development should take place at all costs to those who argue it should come about only if the environment is protected. Basically, however, the major line of division is between those who support more of the same kinds of development that already exist, and hence see no need to change the hinterland status of the provincial norths, and those who, while not necessarily opposing more of the same kinds of development, also want development that will change the hinterland status of the provincial norths by diversifying the employment base. The groups that support essentially more of the same kind of development are, predictably, the forest industry, the mining industry and many municipalities. The forest and mining industries are especially strong advocates of further development in the provincial north and they are supported by many municipalities either because (as they are frequently one industry towns) they do not wish to become ghost towns or because development brings more jobs, a broader tax base and the possibility of more and better municipal services. The groups wishing for the kind of development that will change the hinterland. status of the region are the chambers of commerce of the larger towns and cities, some labour spokesmen and representatives of separatist organisations. Their basic desire is to expand the employment base to avoid the boom and bust cycle by stabilizing the local economies with the introduction of secondary manufacturing in parts of the provincial north.

141

Although all these groups might not always see
eye-to-eye on the precise nature of the development
that should take place in the provincial north, they
do constitute very powerful political forces. The
forest and mining industries have considerable
resources for influencing policy. They have very
large financial reserves at their disposal and they
are able to promote their views in ways not generally
possible for those groups that oppose development.
In addition, they employ large numbers of people
throughout the north, and most towns and cities are
heavily dependent for their economic well-being on
the employment created by these industries. Moreover, the resources generate considerable export
earnings. The major municipalities and chambers of
commerce have easy access to government. There is,
therefore, an extremely powerful nexus of interests
supporting the development of the provincial north.

The groups opposing further development in the
Canadian provincial north range from those who are
not opposed to development per se but which are
doubtful of the current adequacy of environmental
safeguards to others that really would prefer the
north to be an essentially wilderness area. The
many tourist organisations and some professional
groups, such as foresters, would be in the first
category whereas the more extreme environmental and
Indian organisations would be in the second category.
Usually native organisations do not oppose development
as such but they argue it should have to meet two
absolutely fundamental requirements. First, there
would have to be rigorous environmental safeguards,
largely to protect the traditional economy of hunting,
fishing and trapping. Second, Indians would have to
be allowed to participate fully in development and
benefit from it. This latter condition is sensible
because it is already evident that development without
significant native participation destroys the traditional bases of their life without replacing them with
anything which, in turn, leads to societal breakdowns,
terrible social problems and poor Indian-white
relations.

The groups opposing development do not have
anything like the same resources for influencing
policy as those supporting development. They are
organisationally fragmented and financially weaker
and have no tradition of easy access to a receptive
government. The Indian groups are notoriously
fragmented and the environmental groups, also badly

142

fragmented, saw their issue lose political saliency
as the economic recession deepened.

v)   Policy Outputs I: economic development

The policy outputs in relation to economic
development in the provincial north reflect a desire
on the part of all concerned to produce a climate for
more investment in natural resource development
while at the same time mitigating the various unfortunate side effects of early unplanned private
natural resource development by, first, improving
servicing and conditions of life and, second, by
broadening the base of the economy of the region.
The governments still accept their traditional role
of producing a climate which is conducive to investment and natural resources development but now they
interpret this role rather more broadly and with a
greater concern for northern residents, both white
and native, than used to be the case.

In most of the provincial norths, governments
have placed a great deal of emphasis upon infrastructure development as a means of promoting economic
development. This has taken the form of building
access roads for the forest industry, townsite
development for the mining industry, and transportation and communications improvements generally. Many
of the expenditures on these types of things have been
made under the auspices of federal-provincial agreements dealing with the provincial norths. In the
early 1970's the Department of Regional Economic
Expansion adopted what was called the General
Development Agreement (GDA) approach in which the
Department established broad development objectives
in cooperation with officials from each government
which would prepare proposals for subsidiary agreements. Most of the provinces signed subsidiary
agreements that related specifically to development
in their northern regions. Nearly all these northern
subsidiary agreements reflected a strong infrastructure development approach.30

Another thrust has been upon the delivery of
incentive grants to the major industries already
established in the region. The governments have
argued that such support is needed in the resource
sector to stimulate expansion and modernisation,
especially in the case of the forest industry. Both
the provincial and federal governments fear that if

modernisation of the forest industry does not take place a good part of the industry, one of the biggest in Canada, will vanish with disastrous consequences for the economies of the provincial norths. This is why this one industry alone will have received nearly a billion dollars in government incentive grants over the decade prior to 1985.31

In recent years governments have begun to switch from the 'more of the same' approach implicit in the two policy outputs just mentioned to what could be called a 'job creation' or 'employment-diversification' emphasis. While this shift of emphasis is to be applauded the amounts of money being spent in this area are very small compared with the resource sector. Moreover, much of the money is given to low wage industry such as tourism or to industries closely related to the forest industry. This approach to economic development has also been accused of being relatively ineffective in that it tends to be capital-biased and often results in windfall gains to firms that would have gone ahead with expenditures anyway or were already planning to move into the provincial north.32

In recent years governments have also begun to broaden programmes intended to increase the efficiency of the traditional economy in the provincial norths. This has been done by financing aerial surveys and furbearer population inventories and the extension of loans to inland fisheries operations. There have also been efforts to expand tourism related to the traditional economy and, indeed, tourism in general. While it is usually realised that even an enhanced traditional economy will not provide for a great increase in jobs, it will help to diversify the economies of the provincial norths to some degree. The promotion of tourism, though receiving greater attention, which is usually welcome, is recognised by most residents of the provincial north to be low wage and seasonal and a relatively poor substitute for diversification into secondary manufacturing.

These policies do not amount to a comprehensive set of regional development policies or anything that might be called an overall strategy. They tend to be piecemeal, as one might expect given the number of policy actors involved, and the emphasis tends to vary greatly from province to province. Moreover,

144

they reveal that the governments are concerned largely
to expand resource based industries and certainly
not to changing the very nature of the provincial
northern economies and eliminate the region's hinterland status. The more recent increase in emphasis on
employment diversification and enhancing the efficiency of the traditional economy should be interpreted
as an attempt to mitigate the worst effects of hinterland status which, while welcome, is not intended to
effect a fundamental change of status for the provincial north.

The federal and provincial governments have tried
to retain the political support of the pro-environment
groups in the provincial north by using a judicious
mixture of regulatory and distributive policies.
Regulatory policies have been used to protect the
environment in the provincial north, essentially in
the form of provincial standards for air and water
pollution and, in some cases, mandatory environmental
assessments of major projects. Regulations are largely enforced by fines. Although there have been regulatory measures, neither level of government has consistently given the impression that it takes the need
for environmental protection as seriously as the need
for economic development. Many industries have been
exempted from mandatory environmental assessments and
where they exist compliance orders relating to air
and water standards on individual firms have often
been relaxed and fines are small. Clearly, distributive rather than regulatory policies are preferred
by government and they certainly are by the major
industries of the provincial north. Distributive
legislation provides benefits from general taxation
via such things as incentives and subsidies to
specific industries and groups. Prime examples in
the provincial north are grants to the pulp and paper
industry to upgrade pollution control equipment and
major subsidies by many governments in the form of
help in reforestation.33

vi) Policy Outputs II: social development

The social problems in the Canadian north are
incredibly deep and pervasive especially in the
native north of the smaller remote communities based
upon the traditional economy. It is by no means far
fetched to think of Canada as possessing a third
world area within its own boundaries. Because, however, the region is isolated and is part of a nation

that on the average is wealthy the similarities with
the underdeveloped world go unrecognised by most
Canadians. It is ironic that the kind of measures
Canada often advocates for third world nations are
frequently not adopted here. An example is Canada's
advocacy and promotion abroad of primary health care
and the training of indigenous peoples as health
professionals when only lip-service is really paid to
this in Canada even thought such an emphasis would be
equally useful in the provincial north. This is not
to say that nothing is being done to rectify the
situation in Canada just that there has been a tendency to apply southern solutions to problems and
that this is not the appropriate approach.

     The social problems experienced in the Canadian
provincial north are, of course, the result of some
of the other problems already discussed. Perhaps
the worst problem is that two societies exist side by
side in the provincial north - the white and the
native.34 They exist in the same region but they
are largely separate and grossly unequal. At root
this is a problem of race relations but it does, of
course, have economic and social implications.
Essentially these racial problems will not be solved
until the native population is provided with the
opportunity to participate reasonably equally in all
aspects of the economy and the society of the provincial north. As long as health services, for instance,
are provided by non-natives to the native population,
racial tensions and medical system difficulties will
continue.35 The social problems are also caused by
the remoteness of many of the communities, their small
size and their inadequate economic base. These factors result in a very high cost of living combined
with grinding poverty in many areas and truncated or
non-existent 'hard' services (such as water and
sewer systems, roads and fire protection) and 'soft'
services (such as health, education welfare and
recreational services).

     Most of these problems are reflected in the
nature of the health problems experienced by the
residents of the provincial north for health status
is conditioned by the standard and quality of life.
A clear division can be made between the health status
of the white and native residents of the provincial
north. While there is not conclusive evidence, it
would appear that the health status of the white
population in the northern resource communities is

generally not as good as for southern Canadians.
Even in the larger cities of the provincial north,
such as Thunder Bay, studies have indicated that in
nearly every age category and in nearly every listed
cause of death northern residents die earlier and
in greater proportionate numbers than in the southern
regions of the province.36 The relationship holds
good for morbidity as well as mortality statistics.
Certainly the services available to northern residents
are fewer than for residents of the south. There are
much lower doctor to patient ratios and lower hospital
bed to patient ratios.

The differences between the health status of
northern whites and southern whites pales into in-
significance, however, when looked at in relation
to the differences in health status either between
northern whites and the northern native population or,
especially, between southern whites and the northern
native population. The northern native population
suffers from what has been termed the disease pattern
of an underprivileged society. It has a much higher
infant mortality rate than the southern population
and the Indians and Inuit "suffer from diseases which
for the most part are preventable by relatively un-
sophisticated means".37 These include such things
as respiratory infections, gastroentinitis, middle
ear infections, rampant dental caries and a variety
of nutritionally-based disorders. The health situation of the northern native population has been
characterised by one writer as "A Nation's Disgrace".38

The curative health services supplied to the
population of the provincial north, while not strictly
comparable to that supplied to the population of
southern Canada, are in most respects reasonable.
Certainly enormous progress has been made in this
regard in the past few decades. The Medical Services
Branch of the federal Department of National Health
and Welfare has established an elaborate network of
nursing stations and zone hospitals in the north and
a good system of connectors (air links and satellite
telephones) to primarily serve the northern native
population and many provincial governments have made
notable attempts to improve curative health services
in their northern regions. There are, however,
serious problems remaining. Staff turnover is high,
services are often delivered and managed by people of
a race different from the majority of the recipients
(which produces paternalism and cultural and

147

linguistic problems), there is relatively little emphasis on health education and health prevention and promotion, and there is little coordination of health services with other community and social services. There is a great need to correct these problems especially by shifting the emphasis from curative to a preventative approach and reducing paternalism by rapidly enhancing the role of native northerners in the health care system. Fundamentally, however, nothing will be achieved until it is fully recognised that the health care system, however good, can do little to improve matters if a condition of great economic and social deprivation continues. Poor health statistics are merely symptoms of more funda- mental problems and a health system deals with these symptoms not their underlying causes.39

The problems in the north are also reflected in what can only be termed, in some extreme instances, symptoms of societal breakdown. Here again these symptoms are most evident in the northern native population. With unemployment, poverty, poor housing, poor education, lack of opportunity and recreational facilities, and isolation frequently being the order of the day it is hardly surprising that family prob- lems, alcoholism, violence, mental disorders, poisonings and suicide are rapidly increasing. The statistics are sometimes frighteningly high, so much so that the threat of death from suicide, violence, accidents or poisonings is in some places greater than from infectious diseases.40

While valiant efforts are made by some groups and individuals to combat these problems and improve- ments can be noted, the fact remains that the situa- tion is far from satisfactory. Because of the isolated nature of the communities (and thereby, the travelling time involved for social service agency workers) and their usually small size and fragmented populations, service is normally sporadic and un- coordinated. Moreover, most workers are not trained specifically for service in the north and the service delivery systems are usually based on southern models which are by no means always appropriate. Because of geographic isolation, lack of colleague support, and the range and depth of problems faced it is difficult to recruit and retain staff. While new modes of service delivery, such as the 'cluster' concept, are being experimented with and new, more appropriate methods of training are being developed

(such as the proposed specialised Masters of Social
Work programme at Lakehead University) much remains
to be done. However, as with health services, it
must be remembered that social service delivery
agencies deal only with the symptoms of far more
fundamental problems; they do not and cannot solve
the problems themselves.41

Educational opportunities are also truncated in
the provincial north both for the white population
and the native population, but as with most other
things, especially so far the latter. Educational
opportunities are restricted both in range, quality
and the physical environment in which they occur
and this applies to all levels from kindergarten to
universities. Again all the statistics such as the
participation rates and levels of achievement all too
clearly reflect the problem. As with health and
social services educational services have greatly
improved in recent decades, new approaches are beginning to be tried and efforts are, for instance, being
made to train native instructors. The distance that
remains to be traversed is great especially in
relation to the smaller more remote native communities.
Educational services, like health and social services,
can do little in a positive way to remedy the underlying problems and, in fact, they too treat symptoms
because it could be argued a major role is to educate
northern residents so that they will be able to
migrate out of the region and thereby reduce what
might otherwise become a thoroughly intolerable
unemployment rate. This is perhaps especially the
role of the few universities that exist in the
provincial north. Lakehead and Laurentian Universities
in Ontario (the only other university in the provincial north being the Universite du Quebec a
Chicoutimi) certainly were set up (in the 1960's) as
small general universities on the southern model and
not deliberately as engines of northern economic and
social development. Moreover, their efforts to
develop in this direction have been frustrated at
almost every turn.42

While it can be said that in the field of social
development great improvements have been made it
must also be said that they remain inadequate,
uncoordinated and directed only at dealing with the
symptoms of the problems that plague the provincial
north. All the while that there is no concentrated
large scale effort to provide a larger and more

149

diversified employment base in the provincial north
social development efforts will bear the burden of
trying to cope with an appalling and depressing range
of problems.

vii) Policy Outputs III: local government development

Because the northern portions of most of the
provinces were originally developed almost as if they
were colonial appendages of the southern portions43
the normal structures of local government (city, town,
county, village) common to the south were not established in the north. In some provinces the whole
north has been left more or less unorganised while
in others rudimentary forms of local government have
been undertaken. Even in those provinces that have
experimented with local government structures a
common factor is the far greater degree of governmental control or paternalism in the provincial
norths than in the southern portions of the prov-
ince.44

There are essentially three different types of
communities in the provincial north: organised
communities, unorganised communities and Indian
reserves. They face some problems that are common
and some that are peculiar to each of them. The
problems they face in common are those of long
distances and the resulting poor communications between them. In addition, long distances lead to high
transportation costs which many claim are exacerbated
by discriminatory freight rates. The high transportation costs and captive markets lead to high costs
for almost all goods and services. Moreover, distance,
a relatively small and scattered population creating
a small market, and a lack of skilled force, all
combine to perpetuate economies that are in most
communities heavily dependent upon single industries.
This, in turn, often leads to population outflows,
especially among the young, and slow growth rates
which result in, at best, a limited tax base for
most communities.

The problems encountered by the larger cities
and towns in the provincial north are much like those
of their southern counterparts but with some interesting variations. These variations are fourfold.
First, because the hinterlands of the larger cities
and towns are unorganised in the north they face
severe problems of unplanned fringe growth. The

neighbouring areas have no, or relatively few, controls over land use or environmental abuses, they are dependent upon the larger community for employment, social services and the like and they have lower tax rates which only spurs on further uncontrolled fringe growth. Second, the larger cities and towns, being one-industry towns in the main, lack employment diversification which can create subsidiary problems such as out-migration of the educated young and economic hardship in times of strikes or severe economic downturn. Third, some of the larger towns face problems stemming from very rapid expansion associated with resource booms. Fourthly, they can also face the severe problems associated with a resource bust.

The smaller and more isolated unorganised communities and the Indian reserves face problems in common and these are normally far more serious than those faced by the organised communities. First, they have very low or non-existent tax assessment bases. Governments are the major source of revenue for such communities. Second, physical services are usually very poor. There are often, for instance, no communal water or sewer systems. Other community services such as fire protection and recreation are inadequate if they exist at all. Third, distance from major population centres means high costs for such things as hydro, food and gas which only enhances the poverty suffered by most residents. Fourth, there is confusion or ignorance on the part of many residents concerning the complexity of governmental regulations and procedures and, therefore, a lack of people trained or skilled enough to take on local government responsibilities. It should be noted here that in the provincial north the Metis are frequently squatters on unorganised territory. Thus the problem of land is a major one for them, especially so because lack of ownership frequently means they are ineligible for some economic support or housing schemes organised by the federal and provincial governments.45

The demands placed upon government by the organised and the unorganised communities in the provincial north differs in emphasis. The organised municipalities tend to emphasise the need for economic development and diversification over the furtherance of local self-government for they tend to enjoy a fair measure of the latter. Economic development and

151

diversification is emphasised largely because it brings more jobs, a broader and more stable tax base, and, thereby, the possibility of more and better municipal services. The unorganised communities in the provincial north, although recognising the importance of economic development, place a greater emphasis on the need for the development of structures which allow for a measure of self-government. As with the unorganised communities the Indian reserves also place a great deal of emphasis on local self-government although for rather different reasons. The Metis have long been searching for recognition as a unique cultural group and pressuring for some form of self-government ranging from control of local government to, in the past, the creation of a separate nation.

Governmental outputs intended to promote the main desire of the organised communities, namely economic development and diversification, have already been analysed so governmental outputs in relations to the other problems will be dealt with here. Some of the provincial governments have utilised a number of measures to try and overcome the problems of the organised communities in the provincial north. To overcome the problem of sprawl into unorganised areas, amalgamations have been promoted, annexations have been approved and even one regional government has been established - for the Sudbury area in Ontario. To overcome the problem of relatively weak tax bases, special northern grants, resource equalisation grants and other special grants have been made to strengthen the fiscal capacity of the organised communities. To avert or cushion the problems caused by rapid growth in a resource boom period, special arrangements and structures such as Alberta's New Towns and Ontario's Improvement Districts have been set up. They usually involve a great deal of direct provincial government involvement. Some efforts have also been made to counter the problems associated with resource bust, as in the case of Atikokan in Ontario, but usually very little can be done in this area that does not fly in the face of economic logic.

In response to the demand for increased local self-government on the part of the unorganised communities the provinces have experimented with a rich variety of rudimentary forms of local self-government. There are a wide variety of such forms with differing powers and responsibilities in the various provincial norths. There are the Local Community Authorities and Local Advisory Councils in northern Saskatchewan, the Community Committees and Community Councils in northern Manitoba and the Local Service Boards in northern Ontario. Of particular note is the James Bay and Northern Quebec Agreement46 which brought local self-government to northern Quebec in the form of 8 Cree corporations and a Cree Regional Authority along with 13 Inuit Communities created by the Katavik Act. The very recent concern on the part of the provinces for local self-government in the north has recently been mirrored by the federal government in relation to local government on reserves. In late 1979 the Minister of Indian Affairs and Northern Development announced that his department would shift away from a closely supervised and controlled system to one of setting up elected councils under written constitutions with a wide range of programme, regulatory and financial powers. He said he would "change the role of the department from an administrative role to an advisory and facilitating, resource providing agency".47 The only group for which the future seems to hold little promise at all is the Metis for, although the experiments in the unorganised communities directly affect them, they seem unlikely to receive the specific and separate treatment they desire. The only province in which they have received separate and specific treatment in the area of local government does not provide a model they wish to have elsewhere. In 1940 Alberta passed the Metis Population Betterment Act which set areas aside called 'colonies' specifically for the Metis. Colony residents were called 'settlers' to distinguish them from the rest of the population. Although these 'settlers' can elect their own councils, they are closely supervised by the provincial government. In short, the relationship is rather like that between Indian reserves and the federal government.48

viii) Development and Political Discontent

The political patterns manifest in the Canadian provincial north are partly moulded by the economic base of the region. This encompasses not only the economic base as has existed and does exit now but the economic base that people in the region have felt, and still feel, should exist. I have elsewhere defined these political patterns in the context of one part of the provincial north, namely Northwestern Ontario, but they apply almost universally to the other parts.

I labelled these patterns the Politics of Extraction, Frustration and Parochialism.49   I shall briefly discuss each of them.

The Politics of Extraction is moulded by the economics of extraction that prevails throughout the provincial north. This economics of extraction develops an atmosphere in which much of the local population feels exploited, underprivileged, alienated and unable to control its own destiny or that of the region. Local elites only play a minor role in the decision-making affecting the provincial north. All they can hope to do is somehow influence those who do not make the decisions. Thus the economics of extraction leads to the politics of extraction which, I argue, consists of two processes. The first is attempts by the hinterland to extract fundamental economic or social change or, failing that, as many concessions as possible from the metropolis. I label this the sub-politics of futility because such change goes against the vested interests of the metropolis, the region has no real resources (either economic, social or political) with which to significantly pressure the metropolis and, anyway, there is an ambivalence in the local population about the desirability of such fundamental change. The second process is one of 'keeping the locals happy' on the part of the provincial and federal authorities. I label this the sub-politics of handouts because it consists largely of delivering what many local residents see as merely 'showy' attempts to buy-off discontent by delivery of a few major highly visible developments such as ski jumps and the recreation of old forts as tourist attractions, the delivery of essential services (roads, electrification, airfields etc.) as if they were gifts when residents of the north feel the other regions get such servicing as of right, and the appointment of local residents to cabinet posts of relatively little importance. The overall Politics of Extraction is, therefore, a two-way game with the hinterland region trying to extract what it can from the metropolis and vice-versa. It is, of course, a very uneven fight for nearly all the cards are held by the metropolis. This is a situation bound to lead to frustration and alienation in the hinterland.

The continuing hinterland status of the region and the manifest lack of success of what I labelled the sub-politics of futility has led to what can be called the Politics of Frustration. This takes two

154

forms: a strong undercurrent of radicalism and the
spawning of a number of fringe movements. Both of
these phenomena are indicative of a perception by
many that it is useless to attempt to change the
metropolitan-hinterland relationship through normal
political channels and that either different methods
have to be found or 'anomic' actions are necessary
to alleviate its more malign effects. The strong
undercurrent of radicalism is revealed in the relatively strong support for the New Democratic Party
(NDP), a social democratic party which is Canada's
third party at the federal level and which has
occasionally formed the government in several provinces. The NDP either electorally dominates most
sections of the provincial north or is the second
most influential party in the region. The strong
undercurrent of radicalism is also revealed in the
relatively strong support historically in the region
for radical unions (such as the International Workers
of the World and the One Big Union) and the Communist
Party. This radicalism has had relatively little
impact, partly because of rampant factionalism of the
left and because the politics of handouts has staved
off anything more radical than the occasional NDP
victory. Discontent in the provincial north has
frequently produced fringe political movements that
have no connection with the mainstream political
parties. There have, for instance, been periodic
calls in a number of the provincial norths for se-
cession and the creation of separate provinces. This
has occurred in Labrador, northern Manitoba, northern
Saskatchewan and most notably in northern Ontario.
There have been two episodes of calls for separation
in northern Ontario since the Second World War. In
1950 a man called Hubert Limbrick called for the
formation of a new province called Aurora and when
that came to nothing he began to promote the idea of
a union of northern Ontario with Manitoba. In 1973,
a Mr. Ed Diebel formed a separatist party which
actually succeeded in becoming legally recognised for
purposes of election financing but thereafter went
nowhere. It is interesting to note that the separatist
tendencies in northern Ontario are much like those in
the neighbouring Upper Peninsula of Michigan in the
United States which is a region with similar
problems.50

Many of the residents of the provincial north
have reacted to the politics of extraction by re-
sorting to the politics of frustration. Many others,

however, have given up on an activist kind of response and resigned themselves to passive ones. These I call the Politics of Parochialism which consists of two processes called the sub-politics of sublimation and of dependency. The sub-politics of sublimation usually reveals itself in an almost pathological interest in local politics which sometimes reaches extremes, as in the case of the debilitating rivalry between the two neighbouring towns of Port Arthur and Fort William (later combined to become Thunder Bay). The sub-politics of dependency usually reveals itself in many communities being either company towns or being very closely supervised by agencies of the provincial governments.

It seems most unlikely but these political patterns will change very much in the foreseeable future. The economic base of the provincial north is unlikely to change very much in the near future so the political patterns are also unlikely to change. A new element has, however, been injected into politics in the provincial north and this is the growing political activism and political sophistication of the northern native population. This is, at the moment, aimed largely at achieving local self-government on reserves but may in the future project itself onto a broader arena.

ix) Conclusion

The future of the Canadian provincial north is not bright. The metropolis-hinterland relationship will almost undoubtedly persist. The white north will continue to be dependent upon large-scale resource extraction and will consist of scattered cities and towns subject to boom and bust cycles because they will lack a diversified economic base. In addition, the danger of environmental damage will persist because of the very nature of resource industries. The native north might undergo significant changes because of a new tendency on the part of governments to move away from policies embodying paternalism and assimilation in the face of growing native political activism and assertiveness. The problems of this segment of the northern population are so deep, however, that even if employment opportunities are found along with a greater cultural and political self-confidence really significant progress will certainly take decades and probably generations. Governmental activity in the provincial north is becoming more

156

enlightened and unified but tends to be aimed at
ameliorating the symptoms of regional underdevelopment not eliminating the fundamental problems.

Notes

1. The most detailed effort to define the non-political boundaries of the Canadian north has been made by Louis Edmond Hamelin, Canadian Nordicity: Its Your North Too (Montreal: Harvest House, 1978).

2. See Northern Alberta Development Council, Five Year Review of Activities April 1, 1973 - March 31, 1978 (Edmonton: Department of Business Development and Tourism, 1978) especially the map on page 13.

3. See Saskatchewan The Department of Northern Saskatchewan Act, 1972.

4. See Manitoba, The Northern Affairs Act, 1974 SM. 1974, c56 - cap. N 100.

5. See Ontario, The Ministry of Northern Affairs Act 1977 1st Session, 31st Legislature, Ontario, 26 Elizabeth II, 1977.

6. Quebec, The James Bay and Northern Quebec Agreement (Quebec City: Editeur Officiel du Quebec, 1976).

7. See Government of Newfoundland and Labrador Northern Development Branch (St. Johns: Department of Rural Agricultural and Northern Development, no date).

8. For a description of the two economies as they exist in northern Manitoba see Hickling Johnston Manitoba Northlands Transportation Study, General Appendix (Toronto: Hickling-Johnston, 1975) chapters 1 and 2.

9. Acres Research and Planning Ltd. Mid-Canada Development Corridor: A Concept (Toronto: Acres Research and Planning Ltd., 1969).

10. See Geoffrey R. Weller, "Provincial Ministries of Northern Affairs: A Comparative Analysis" in R.W. Wein, R.R. Riewe and I.R. Methven (eds) Resources and Dynamics of the Boreal Zone (Ottawa: Association of Canadian Universities for Northern Studies, 1983) pp. 480-497.

11. Harold Innis The Fur Trade in Canada: An Introduction to Canadian Economic History (Toronto: University of Toronto Press, 1930).

12. M. Watkins, "The Staple Theory Revisited" Journal of Canadian Studies Vol. 12, pp. 83-95.

13. See, for example, Roy E. George A Leader and a Laggard: Manufacturing Industry in Nova Scotia, Quebec, and Ontario (Toronto: University of Toronto Press, 1970).

14. See, for example, Thomas J. Courchene, "Alternative Regional Development Strategies in a Federal State" in Canadian Council on Rural Development Regional Poverty and Change (Ottawa: Canadian Council on Regional Development, 1976) pp. 91-206.

15. Wallace Clement, "A Political Economy of Regionalism" in D. Glenday et al (eds) Modernization and the Canadian State (Toronto: MacMillan, 1978) pp. 89-110.

16. Carl Cunei, "A Class Perspective on Regionalism" in D. Glenday et al (eds) Modernization and the Canadian State (Toronto: MacMillan, 1978) pp. 132-156.

17. Henry Veltmeyer, "The Underdevelopment of Atlantic Canada" Review of Radical Political Economics, Vol. 10 1978, pp. 95-105.

18. See, for example, Economic Council of Canada Living Together: A Study of Regional Disparities (Ottawa: Supply and Services Canada, 1977).

19. See Hamelin op.cit. chapter 4.

20. See, for example, the Treaty 3 brief to the Ontario Royal Commission on the Northern Environment in North of 50°, No. 2, 21st December 1977, page 16.

21. An impression of the problems can be obtained from works such as Warner Troyer No Safe Place (Toronto: Clarke Irwin, 1977); K. Lie, "The Plight of Ontario's Northern Forests" Alternatives Vol. 7 Autumn 1978, pp. 17-25 and Jamie Swift Cut and Run: The Assault on Canada's Forests (Toronto: Between the Lines, 1983).

22. See, for example, Sudbury and District Chamber of Commerce A Profile in Failure (Sudbury: Sudbury and District Chamber of Commerce, 1976).

23. See Gordon Brock The Province of Northern Ontario (Cobalt: Highway Bookshop, 1978) and J. Aitken "The Scary Things I hear About Canada" Weekend Magazine 6th May 1981.

24. These different ways are described in Geoffrey R. Weller, "Provincial Ministries of Northern Affairs: A Comparative Analysis" op.cit.

25. The restructuring is detailed in Peter Aucoin and Herman Bakvis, Organisational Differentiation and Integration: The Case of Regional Economic Development Policy in Canada, a paper presented to the annual meetings of the Canadian Political Science Association, Vancouver, British Columbia, June 1983.

26. See Geoffrey R. Weller, "The Delivery of Health Services in the Canadian North" Journal of Canadian Studies Vol. 16 No. 2 Summer 1981, pp. 69-80.

27. See Ontario, Royal Commission on the Northern Environment Interim Report and Recommendations (Toronto: Royal Commission on the Northern Environment, 1978).

28. See Richard Paton New Policies for Old Organisation: Can Indian Affairs Change? (Ottawa: Carleton University School of Public Administration, 1982).

29. The line-up of interests is described in Geoffrey R. Weller, "Resource Development in Northern Ontario: A Case Study in Hinterland Politics" in O.P. Dwivedi (ed) Resources and the Environment Policy Perspectives for Canada (Toronto: McClelland and Stewart, 1980) pp. 243-268.

30. See, for example, Canada Canada-Manitoba Subsidiary Agreement: Manitoba Northlands (Ottawa: Department of Regional Economic Expansion 15th September 1976) and Canada Canada-Ontario Subsidiary Agreement: Northwestern Ontario (Ottawa: Department of Regional Economic Expansion, 23rd May 1976).

31. See, for example, Ontario Statement by the
    Ontario Treasurer, Frank S. Miller on Ontario's
    Program to Assist the Provinces Pulp and Paper
    Industry (Toronto: Ministry of the Treasury,
    31st January 1979) and Canada Principal Elements
    of National Development Policy in Support of
    Canadian Forest Industries: Background Notes
    (Ottawa: Department of Regional Economic
    Expansion, February 1979).

32. These criticisms can be seen in Ontario Economic
    Council Northern Ontario Development (Toronto:
    Ontario Economic Council, 1976) and Ontario New
    Democratic Party Briefing to the NDP Caucus on
    the Performance of the Ministry of Northern
    Affairs and N.O.P.C. (Sault Ste. Marie: Ontario
    New Democratic Party, 29th November 1978).

33. Examples of the balancing act performed by gov-
    ernments in this area can be found in Douglas C.
    Nord and Geoffrey R. Weller, "Environmental
    Policy and Political Support" in Allan Kornberg
    and Harold D. Clarke (eds) Political Support in
    Canada: The Crisis Years (Durham, North
    Carolina: Duke University Press, 1983) pp. 252-
    269, and in Geoffrey R. Weller, "Resources
    Development in Northern Ontario: A Case Study
    of Hinterland Politics" op.cit.

34. This estimation is made by C.E.S. Franks,
    "Fractures in the Mosaic: Canada's Provincial
    Norths", a paper presented at the annual meetings
    of the Western Social Science Association,
    Denver, Colorado, April 1982.

35. This problem is referred to in Peter Ruderman
    and Geoffrey R. Weller, "Health Services for
    the Keewatin Inuit in a Period of Transition.
    The View from 1980 Inuit Studies, Vol. 5, No. 2
    1981 pp. 49-62.

36. See Thunder Bay District Health Council Panorama
    of Mortality (Thunder Bay: Thunder Bay District
    Health Council, 1978).

37. Canada Indian Health Discussion Paper (Ottawa:
    Medical Services Branch, Department of National
    Health and Welfare, December 19th, 1979).

38. Paul Grescoe, "A Nation's Disgrace" Edmonton

161

Journal (*The Canadian* supplement, April 23rd, 1977).

39. See Geoffrey R. Weller, "The Delivery of Health Services in the Canadian North" op.cit.

40. This is discussed in mocrocosm in P. Driben and R. Trudeau *When Freedom is Lost - The Dark Side of the Relationship Between Government and the Fort Hope Band* (Toronto: University of Toronto Press, 1983).

41. Many of these problems are discussed in Connie Nelson *The Northern Model for Service Delivery to Children* (Thunder Bay: Thunder Bay Children's Services Steering Committee, April 1981).

42. See Geoffrey R. Weller, "Universities, Politics and Development: The Case of Northern Ontario", a paper presented at the International Symposium on the Role of Universities in Developing Areas, Ben Gurion University of the Negev, Beer Sheva, Israel, December 27-29th, 1983.

43. See M. Zaslow *The Opening of the Canadian North 1870-1914* (Toronto: McClelland and Stewart, 1971).

44. For a general account of local government in the provincial north see Geoffrey R. Weller, "Local Government in the Canadian Provincial North" *Canadian Public Administration* Vol. 24, No. 1, Spring 1981 pp. 44-72.

45. See D. Bruce Sealey and Antoine S. Lussier *The Metis: Canada's Forgotten People* (Winnipeg: Manitoba Metis Federation Press, 1975) and J. Sawchuk *The Metis of Manitoba: Reformulation of an Ethnic Identity* (Toronto: Peter Martin Associates, 1978).

46. Quebec, The James Bay and Northern Quebec Agreement, op.cit.

47. The Honourable Jake Epp, Minister of Indian Affairs and Northern Development *Speech to the Executive Planning Committee* (Quebec City: 20th November 1979).

48. See Paul Driben *Cultural Isolation and Self-*

Image Among the Metis (unpublished manuscript, no date) p.3.

49. See G.R. Weller, "Hinterland Politics: The Case of Northwestern Ontario" Canadian Journal of Political Science, Vol. 10, No. 4, December 1977, pp. 727-754.

50. See Geoffrey R. Weller, "Algoma and Superior: Prospects for Political Separation in Northern Ontario and Northern Michigan" a paper presented at the annual meetings of the Western Social Science Association, Denver, Colorado, April 22-24, 1982.

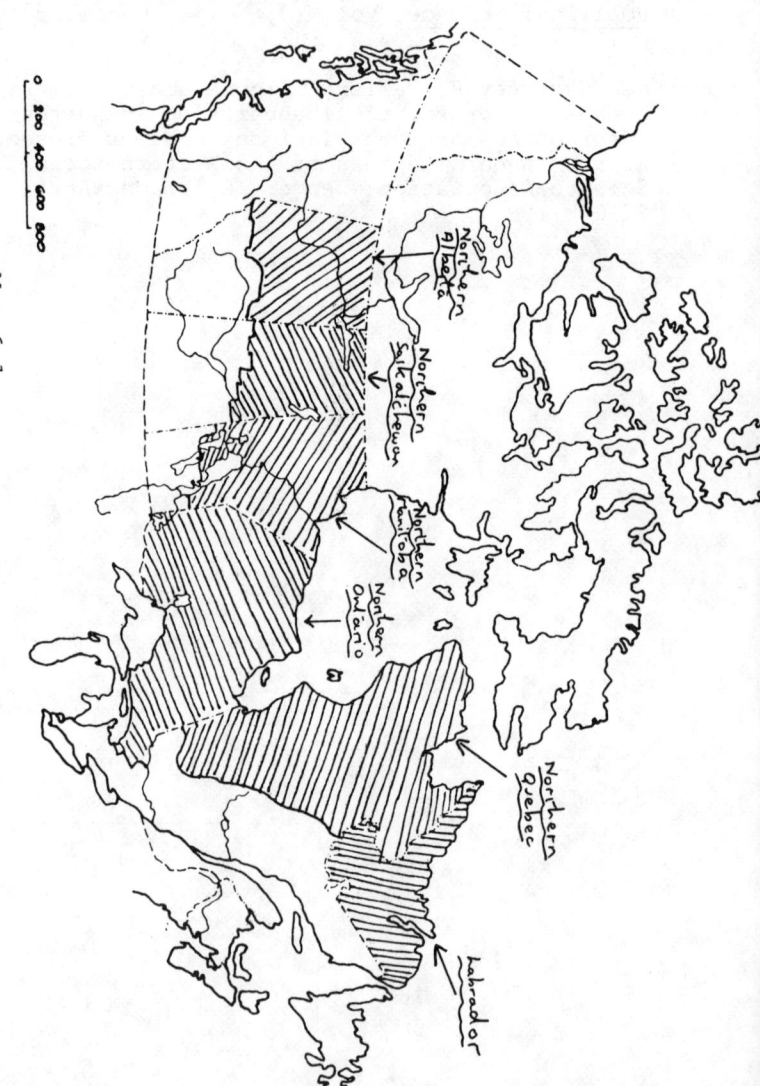

Map 6.1
Canada: the provincial north

Northern Alberta
Northern Saskatchewan
Northern Manitoba
Northern Ontario
Northern Quebec
Labrador

0 200 400 600 800

164

Part Two

REGIONAL POLICIES

Chapter Seven

Government Organization for Regional Development Policy:

lessons from the Canadian experience

Peter Aucoin

i)   Introduction

The Canadian experience in the area of regional
development policy is an important one from the perspective of comparative public policy for two reasons.
First, successive federal governments have had to pay
serious attantion to the question of regional development simply because regionalism is a central political
concern in Canada. The Canadian experience, accordingly, is one in which regional development policy has
been an item continually on the political agenda.
Second, various different approaches have been applied
not only in terms of policies and programs, but also in
terms of government organization for policy-making and
administration.

This chapter focusses on one aspect of this Canadian experience, namely the evolution of government
organization for regional development policy. This
evolution is described briefly and analyzed in light of
the ideas, interests and institutional factors which
account for the several instances of organizational
change which have occurred over the past twenty-five
years. In the second major part of the chapter an
attempt is made to assess whether organizational "learning" characterized the successive alterations to organization for this field. On the basis of this assessment
an attempt is also made to determine whether there are
important lessons or generalizations which emanate from
this Canadian experience and which may be of interest
beyond the Canadian case.

ii)   The Evolution of Government Organization for
      Regional Development Policy

The Canadian experience in the field of regional
development policy is a complex one for a number of
reasons. Three reasons deserve particular attention.
First, and most obvious perhaps, is the fact that
Canada has a federal system of government which in large

part reflects real differences in regional identities, cultures and traditions. This system of government, in turn, tends to reinforce and enhance these regional differences by virtue of the considerable powers exercised by the ten provincial governments which, it is argued, make ample use of the powers to engage in "province-building."[1] Given that the federal government also has considerable powers, the general consequence is what can be referred to as "intergovernmental governing": in virtually any jurisdiction each level of government has some role, whether it be education, fisheries or economic management. Although federal and provincial governments may be politically autonomous, and constitutionally have exclusive jurisdiction over most specific areas of responsibility, their functions and activities are by and large interdependent. A regional development policy that ignores the reality does so at great risk of being torn to shreds in the intergovernmental arena of federal-provincial relations.

The second reason why the field of regional development policy is complex is the crucial spatial dimension of Canada's national economy.[2] On the one hand there are significant regional disparities across this continental country in resources, size of and access to markets, and per capita income--structural differences between regions which have existed for well over a century. On the other hand, the regional effects of national policies are such that economic costs and opportunities, levels of employment, consumer prices and interest rates differ widely in different parts of the country. All of these differences are widely recognized: equally important, however, is that these differences have at various times been attributed to federal government policy, lending fuel to the argument that the federal government has a major responsibility for reducing these regional disparities.

The third reason for complexity stems from the interaction of two fundamental features of our national institutions of government.[3] On the one hand, the federal government is organized according to the British tradition of Parliamentary government which in its Canadian version is characterized by what many consider an excessive concentration of powers in the hands of the executive branch, namely the Prime Minister and Cabinet. In large part, this fact is also responsible for a highly centralized system of policy formulation and decision-making notwithstanding the highly regionalized character of Canadian political life, a character that extends to the leading political parties including the only two--Liberal and Conservative--which have held power in the federal arena. On the other hand, this same executive branch has had to be the principal institutional mechanism for the accommodation of regional interests, given that our Senate is an upper or second chamber of Parliament with little if any political clout, notwithstanding the fact that its composition is more heavily weighted in favor of regional considerations rather than representation by population. This accommodation of regional interests in Cabinet is achieved partly by attempts to secure regional representation in the Cabinet and partly by a tradition of recognizing the right of certain ministers to involve themselves in all matters of government that affect their regions. With few exceptions, nonetheless, the actual organization of Cabinet portfolios and thus administrative departments and ministries (as well as boards and corporations) is along functional, and not regional, lines.

The combined effect of these several factors has served to make the regional dimension of Canadian politics a dominant one. At the same time, this has not meant that regional development policy has been of the highest priority; nor has it meant, as already indicated, that government organization for such policy has been well established. Over the past twenty-five years there has been an evolution of policy and organization, however, which has seen regional development become increasingly central to and integrated with national economic development policy in its broadest sense. In terms of organization, the latest stage in this evolution has just recently been affected, but not to everyone's positive evaluation as will be noted

For the purposes of this chapter, four distinct organizational approaches or stages can be identified.4 The first stage involved the establishment, beginning in the late 1950s, of a number of separate and distinct boards and agencies focussed on specific regions in particular and rural areas in general. These organizations, each of which was attached to the portfolios of individual Ministers with larger departmental responsibilities, constituted the initial and not unexpectedly ad hoc and uncoordinated efforts of two governments to respond to demands that all regions be able to benefit from national development. Needless to say these demands were most strongly pressed by those regions which had not shared equally in such development.

167

In this post-war period a number of factors has contributed to the development of these demands. First, there was a general demand that all Canadians should be treated equally with respect to public services and levels of taxation, regardless of their province or region of residence. These demands resulted in the extension or establishment of several different federal-provincial financial arrangements which, while too complicated to be outlined here, served to provide for a greater equalization of provincial government revenues and a number of federal-provincial shared-cost programs.5 Second, and partly related to the first factor, there were increased demands for federal government intervention to promote economic development and equity. In many of these demands, of course, a regional dimension was present. Third, and especially in response to federal government initiatives as a result of this second factor, there were the inevitable calls for the coordination of governmental interventions.

In light of these demands and responses, and the coming to power of a Prime Minister commited to national unity and rationality in governing, the first stage in regional development policy and organization gave way in 1969 to a second stage in which a comprehensive and coordinated effect was to be made to overcome the regional disparities which had plagued the nation since its inception. The organization to achieve this goal was the new Department of Regional Economic Expansion (DREE) headed by a senior Cabinet Minister for the new portfolio.6

The creation of this portfolio and department was not only in recognition of the new priority to be given to regional development, it also constituted an organizational response to what were perceived to be organizational deficiences in the previous regime of several uncoordinated boards and agencies. The organizational arrangements for regional development policy in the first stage lacked coordination for at least three reasons. Perhaps the most important reason was that "regional development policy" was not conceived of in any coherent manner, theoretical or practical. In part it meant rural as opposed to urban development; in part it meant industrial development in the hinterlands as opposed to the heartland; and in part it meant infrastructure development for the poorer as opposed to the wealthier regions of the country. Each part was dealt with by a separate agency although with obvious overlaps in mandate.

The boards and agencies involved in this first
stage, moreover, were precisely that--boards and
agencies. There was no single minister or department
whose sole or primary function was to promote and implement regional development policy. Although these
boards and agencies formally reported to or operated
within the portfolio/department organizations of
ministers, lines of accountability were often not clear;
indeed, the placement of some boards and agencies was
often determined on the grounds of the political
interests of ministers and not, therefore, in accordance
with any cogent set of organizational principles.

In addition, certain boards and agencies were frequently regarded as poor cousins in their various
departmental "homes" and hence few if any departments
became regionally sensitive by virtue of having some
responsibility for these boards or agencies. The major
line departments were organized, as noted, along
functional or sectoral lines and little inclined to
incorporate regional development considerations into
their policies and programs. As a result, they were
also not inclined either to promote or to accept the
coordination of their policies and programs with those
of other sectoral departments in the name of regional
development.

The second stage in regional development policy,
ushered in with the creation of DREE, was meant to
provide a more coherent and comprehensive policy focus
and to overcome the above noted organizational
deficiencies. It not only assumed responsibility for
the several existing boards and agencies and their
programs, it had as its responsibility the design and
implementation of new regional development policies and
programs. Along with its comprehensive mandate, it had
its own new funds to spend. It was also expected to
cooperate with and, when so authorized by Cabinet, to
coordinate the activities of sectoral line departments
in order to achieve the stated goals of regional
development. In short, DREE was meant to be a major
organization within the federal government, particualar-
ly given its coordinating mandate.

Although DREE was established as a department for
the design and implementation of regional development
policy, it was structured initially as a highly centralized organization. Its minister was a powerful member
of the Cabinet; its deputy minister was an influential
public servant; and its style or mode of operation

conformed to that which concentrated power in Ottawa,
the nation's capital. It reined in authority from
officials in the boards and agencies it had inherited;
it abolished previously established federal-provincial
intergovernmental consultative mechanisms which had
operated at the regional level; and in many instances
it by-passed or ignored provincial governments when new
departmental programs were introduced. It also located
the majority (approximately 70%) of its officials at
its headquarters in Ottawa. Finally, it changed the
policy orientation of regional development policy to
one that focussed almost exclusively on "growth poles,"
that is the development of large urban centers with the
provision of infrastructure projects and industrial
incentives. The assumption in this approach was that
once these centers were developed they in turn would
provide for the development of surrounding regions.7

Within three years of its establishment DREE found
itself under attack from several quarters. Although
its strong backing from the Prime Minister and the
political and bureaucratic clout of its minister and
deputy minister had made the department a powerful one,
provincial governments became increasingly dissatisfied
with its unilateral and aggressive approach both to
federal initiatives for regional development and to
intergovernmental relations; and other federal departments became upset both with its preferred access to
new budgetary allocations and with its interventions
into their areas of responsibility. In one sense,
DREE's very accomplishments in the political and bureaucratic arenas were the principal cause of this groundswell of criticism.

The federal government's response was to replace
the minister and deputy minister; and, with new political and bureaucratic leadership, DREE initiated a policy
and organizational review of itself. The outcome of
this was a reorientation of policy, including a new
mechanism for intergovernmental relations, and a major
reorganization of the department. This introduced the
third stage in the government's organization for
regional development policy.

The reorganization of DREE entailed a massive turn-
around from a highly centralized department with its
staff concentrated in Ottawa to a highly decentralized
department with its staff concentrated in regional and
provincial offices. This organizational structure was
made necessary by the new policy approach and its

170

intergovernmental requirements. In turn, the latter
reinforced the truly decentralized structure of the
department.

In brief, the new policy orientation involved a
shift from the previous stress on the "growth pole"
approach in a limited number of poorer provinces and
regions to a multi-dimensional approach wherein all ten
provinces were to be involved. The instrument for this
new policy was what were called "General Development
Agreements" (GDAs).8 These GDAs, to be entered into by
the federal government and each provincial government,
were agreements on general goals to be pursued over a
ten year period within each province; that is they were
specific for each province. Under the umbrella of these
GDAs, "subsidiary agreements" were to be negotiated on
a bilateral basis to determine the projects that would
be the means to achieve the goals of the GDAs. Unlike
previous DREE initiatives, the GDAs, subsidiary agreements and the specific projects which the latter entailed were to be joint endeavours by the federal and provincial governments, although the federal government
was to pay the lion's share of the cost of these endeavours. Although Cabinet approval at both levels of
government was to be required for general and specific agreements,the design and implementation of them
was to be responsibility of joint committees of public
servants with equal representation from both governments.

In many respects, the GDA era of approximately the
past decade was unique, especially in light of the
heightened level of competition and conflict between
the federal and provincial governments during this same
period of time. The GDA approach was considered
successful from certain perspective for a number of
reasons. The provinces liked this approach not only
because the federal government contributed the major
share of expenditures but because its approach was
sufficiently flexible to allow a very large range of
projects to be considered eligible for subsidiary agreements, some of which had a very tenuous connection to
regional development. At the bureaucratic level those
DREE and provincial officials involved in the design
and implementation of subsidiary agreements enjoyed considerable discretion and thus were able to develop projects in line with their professional views on what was
required for regional development.

171

At the same time, however, there were also concerns about and criticisms of DREE, its GDA policy approach and the federal government's general organization for regional development policy. As was the case with DREE in its first form, both its successes and its failures were counted against it, paradoxically by its supporters and opponents alike.

Inherent in the organization and approach of DREE, as well as its position within the federal government's policy and administrative structures, were a number of features which, in the long run, helped to bring about its demise. Chief among these features were its own decision-making system, its relationships with provincial governments, its source of funding and its relationships with other federal line departments.

The decentralized organization of DREE was well designed perhaps from this point of view of DREE officials in the field, that is in their regional and provincial offices, and their counterparts in provincial government departments in that the major project design and negotiation activities were undertaken at this level. Professional administrators from one level of government worked closely with professional administrators from another level of government. However, this very intergovernmental administration led to a widespread perception that these officials enjoyed a great deal of autonomy from their political masters in their respective Cabinets, not to mention in their respective legislatures, and, particularly as far as DREE officials were concerned, from their federal DREE headquarters and other central agencies and departments of the federal government. This perception of autonomy from political intervention was a concern given the crucial constitutional principles of responsible government and thus ministerial accountability to Parliament and legislatures as well as to the public. This autonomy was viewed as tantamount to the operaton of a third level of government and a bureaucratic one at that.

In some large part this perception was a function of the actual design of a decentralized DREE. It was also a function of the intergovernmental approach contained in the GDA policy; that is, the approach was meant to give officials the responsibility for jointly designing and thus, in effect, negotiating federal-provincial agreements and projects. Once this responsibility was exercised by both sets of officials,

172

political executives at each level were anxious not to delay or endanger the agreements so reached. At the federal level, moreover, DREE had its own budgetary allocation from which to fund these jointly designed projects and this facilitated acceptance at the federal level of such projects even when there were Cabinet ministers and other departments not entirely happy with what was being proposed.

At the same time, however, there was an increased concern on the part of the federal government, especially the Cabinet, that DREE's programs, dominated as they were by federal government expenditures on subsidiary agreement projects, were not securing the desired degree of political credit and visibility for the federal government and, of course, the federal governing party. Provincial governments and provincial ministers, it was argued, were both taking and being given public credit for projects within the provinces and administered through provincial departments but which were in largest part being financed by the federal government. This concern became particulary acute during the late 1970s and early 1980s with respect not only to DREE programs but other areas where the federal government had provided massive outlays from the federal treasury such as in health care and higher education.

Added to this public political concern was an intragovernmental political concern at both ministerial and bureaucratic levels of the federal government. DREE's programs, as noted, were financed by the federal government through federal-provincial agreements. As such DREE was able to obtain approval for its expenditures from Treasury Board, the Cabinet Committee then responsible for these expenditure decisions, in a way that made secure its funds for these intergovernmental programs; indeed, up to a certain level expenditure approval could be given by regional officials. Needless to say this treatment of DREE and its expenditure proposals was perceived by other ministers and their departmental officials as preferred treatment, especially once expenditure restraint became the order of the day in the late 1970s. This perception was in good part animated by envy on the part of other ministers and their officials, given that they had to operate with restricted budgets, but it was also provoked by the fact that many of DREE's projects so funded were in areas of their jurisdiction and were projects which from their national sectoral perspectives should not always have outranked their own proposals.

For many ministers and officials, DREE's budgetary allot-
ment was uncontrolled by the criteria of expenditure
decision-making to which they were subjected.

Although many of DREE's initiatives brought it into
the policy fields of other line departments, DREE's
capacities to bend the regular programs of other line
departments was limited. In some areas, some departments
were willing to join with DREE on particular projects
but never to the extent that the original designers of
DREE had hoped. DREE did have some financial incentives
to offer other departments but its capacity to "coordinate" either the design of the programs of other departments or their implementation in the field was clearly
limited. Few line departments became more "regionally
sensitive" in their programs or structured their departmental organizations to fit the decentralized and
therefore regionalized pattern of DREE. A common view,
and a concern to those interested in regional development, was that line departments felt relatively little
need to pay much attention to regional development since
this was DREE's responsibility.

The above noted conditions might well have persisted had it not been for larger political and organizational concerns at the center of the federal government. In the late 1970s there emerged an increased
concern for greater coordination of the wide range of
departments and agencies whose programs, expenditures
and regulations related to economic development. A
number of shortcomings were identified and among them
four are related to our purpose here. First, no single
portfolio or department was able to exercise sufficient
leverage to define, let alone to integrate, the field
of economic development policy. Second, the Cabinet
committee system was not structured in such a way as to
focus or integrate decision-making at this level on
this broad area of policy. Third, the increased dispersal of federal line departments to the regions had
occurred without sufficient attention to the need for
coordination in the "field." And fourth, the decision-
making system throughout the federal government did not
provide for a sufficient integration of policy and
expenditure decisions.9

In late 1978, the Prime Minister decided to effect
major budget cuts in federal spending while, at the
same time, giving highest priority to new initiatives

in the field of economic development programs which
during a time of restraint meant of course that intense
interdepartmental competition was inevitable. The
shortcomings in federal organization and processes,
noted above, were thus brought to center stage. The
conclusion was that the existing machinery of government
was incapable of providing the required degree of
coordination and integration in governmental decision-
making. The result was the creation of a new Cabinet
Committee, named the Board of Economic Development
Ministers, chaired by a senior Minister who became
President of this Board, a new portfolio served by a new
central agency secretariat called the Ministry of State
for Economic Development.

The roles of this new portfolio, Cabinet Committee
and central agency secretariat constituted an organization innovation in a number of respects.10 Most
important, in general terms, was the fact that this new
structure integrated at the ministerial level functions
which under the Cabinet committee system to that point
had been separated, namely policy and expenditure
decision-making. This new committee had powers to
allocate budgetary resources for the programs of the
departments and agencies within its sector; indeed it
was now required to do so when approving program proposals. In this respect, and for the area of economic
development policy only of course, it assumed powers
which heretofore were vested in a separate Cabinet
Committee for budgetary decision-making, namely the
Treasury Board. Ministers from all departments included
within the mandate of this new committee, including the
Minister of DREE, now had to decide on the priorities
of their and their colleagues' proposals in terms of
both their policy merits and expenditure priorities.
At the bureaucratic level, the secretariat which served
the Cabinet committee--the Ministry of State for
Economic Development--assumed functions previously performed by the Privy Council (Cabinet) Office and the
Treasury Board Secretariat for sectoral policy Cabinet
committees and the Treasury Board, respectively.11

In 1979, a change in government took place and the
above organizational system was extended to integrate
all major fields of government policy; that is social
development policy and external and defense policy in
addition to economic development policy. Although this
new government did not survive a year in office, when
it left the organizational concepts of sectoral Cabinet
committees, with policy and expenditure decision-making

175

responsibilities, headed by Ministers of State with
their own central agency secretariats were firmly established as the organizing principles of the Cabinet
decision-making system.

This new system had been imposed upon the old
order from top-down, however; that is upon the existing
structure of portfolios and departments. It was not
surprising then that the strengths and weaknesses of the
federal government's approach and organization for
regional development policy, now part of this new
structure for economic development policy, would
quickly surface. In 1982, accordingly, another major
reorganization occurred which resulted in the demise of
DREE. A fourth stage of government organization for
regional development policy was thus introduced.

The 1982 reorganization contained four elements of
interest insofar as the evolution of organization for
regional development policy is concerned.12 First, it
integrated responsibility for the regional programs of
DREE (that is other than those funded through the GDA
regime) and the industry, small business and tourism
programs of the Department of Industry, Trade and
Commerce (with this department's trade branch transferred to a reorganized Department of External Affairs)
through the creation of a new Department of Regional
Industrial Expansion (DRIE).

Second, the Cabinet Committee on Economic Development and the Minister/Ministry of State for Economic
Development were renamed to signify the intention of
the government that "the regional perspective be brought
to bear on the work of all economic development departments and in all economic decision-making by the
Cabinet": hence the Cabinet Committee on Economic and
Regional Development (CCERD) and the Minister/Ministry
of State for Economic and Regional Development (MSERD).
In light of this intention of the government, all
departments in this field were directed "to improve
their regional capabilities and to build the regional
dimension into their internal policy development and
decision-making processes," now that "responsibility
for economic development in the regions...(would) not
be the distinct mandate of a single department." These
departments were expected to take advantage of "the
availability of specialized personnel (individuals
already in regions and now part of DREE)" to assist
them in carrying out this directive of the Prime
Minister.13

The third major element in this reorganization was the establishment of a system of provincial offices as part of the MSERD organization. These offices, headed by a Federal Economic Development Coordinator of "senior rank" were given four main functions, namely:

> to provide an improved regional information base for decision-making by the Cabinet Committee on Economic and Regional Development, for use particularly in the development of regionally sensitive economic development strategies;

> to give regional officials of sectoral departments a better understanding of the decisions and objectives of the Cabinet;

> to better coordinate the implementation of government decision affecting economic development in the regions; and,

> to develop regional economic development policies for consideration by Cabinet.14

The establishment of these new offices was of critical importance because it was the decentralized organization of the Ministry that, in large part, was meant to ensure that the advantages which obtained with the decentralized DREE were maintained while the disadvantages which obtained with the limited capacities of DREE to coordinate sectoral departments were overcome.

Fourth, and finally, the federal government announced that the GDA approach would be discontinued when the agreements expired. They were to be replaced by a new set of agreements which were to require federal sectoral departments to become involved in ways they seldom if ever did in the DREE-GDA approach. Some projects were to involve these departments in the actual administration and delivery of programs, as opposed to implementation by provincial government departments, thus increasing federal visibility in the provinces. In this way, federal policies and programs were to be "tailored" to regional development and not just to the development of various departmental sectors. Without DREE to assume responsibility for negotiations with the

177

provincial governments, sectoral departments were to be required to play a lead role in the design and management of these new federal-provincial economic and regional development agreements. The role of MSERD was to coordinate the planning and implementation but not the actual design or implementation of these agreements.

As might be expected, the introduction of this fourth stage of government organization for regional development policy was not greeted in all quarters with great enthusiasm.15 Almost without exception, however, the critics of the reorganization compared the experience of the DREE organizational approach to the potential of the new organizational approach and found the latter wanting. Since experience with the latter was too brief to assess it in other than a speculative way, I shall consider its potential in the following section where its perceived strengths and weaknesses can be better contrasted to the previous three stages in government organization for regional development policy.

iii)   Lesson from the Canadian Experience

Generalizations about the comparative effectiveness of organizational approaches for any area of public policy are difficult to make for at least two fundamental reasons. First, there is clearly no right or best way to organize a government for any major set of undertakings such as are involved in the broad field of regional development policy. There is no one right or best way if for no other reason that there are many ways that can be effective given the particular priorities and mix of objectives which a government may wish to pursue at any given point in time. Second, the significance of organizational structures and processes is limited as a determinant of public policy precisely because organizational factors are but one set of determinants of public policy among many. Policy ideas and political interests, in addition to various environmental conditions and resources, always loom large as determinants of public policy.16

To the extent that organization does count, however, there are a number of considerations that emanate from the Canadian experience which may be of relevance to political systems in which regional development policy is an important item on the political and policy agenda and is there for the same basic reasons as are found in Canada; namely regional disparities which are the result both of disparities in

natural endowments and of disparities in the effects of
national policies. As a further condition on the
relevance of the Canadian experience to other political
systems, regional development policy must be pursued as
an effort to overcome specific regional disparities as
well as to adjust national development in the light of
regional considerations. Regional development policy
per se involves more than a regional aid or welfare
policy. If the former is a government's choice then
all that is required is an aid dispensing agency; if the
latter is the approach then the organizational issues
involve no more than a central coordinating mechanism
for sectoral departments. If, on the other hand,
regional development policy is to be pursued simultaneously with national development policies for specific
sectors of the economy, then a more complex set of
organizational issues must be addressed. It is with
the challenges of this approach that the Canadian
experience offers the following lessons.

First, whatever organizational systems are developed for regional development policy an essential feature
of the same must be a significant degree of decentralization to the regions in question. Decentralization is
not merely a matter of the dispersal of operating staff
to the regions but rather of developing in the regions
the policy research and development capacities of the
government and of ensuring that some delegation of
administrative authority takes place in order to provide
the necessary coordination of program design and implementation. The need for a decentralization of government organization to serve these two functions is two-
fold.

On the one hand, the very nature of the problems
to which a regional development policy is addressed is
one that is characterized by regional differences and
usually differences of a complex variety. To design
solutions to the disparities which exist requires a
thorough and on-going understanding of the particular
problems of development in a given region. This demands
that staff who are responsible for developing policy be
given the necessary opportunities to come to the
required understanding of a region's problems. In
almost every circumstance this means full-time residence
in the region in question. Policy development requires
on-going research "in the field," in short, and the
organizational method to achieve this is a decentralized
staff.

On the other hand, knowledge derived from field research is but one condition for effective regional development policy. Another is that the government possess the capacity to coordinate program design and implementation in the field. Without this capacity the classic divorce of staff and line functions will lead to regional development policies that are ignored, mis-understood or misused by the officials of line depart-ments in the design and implementation of their programs.

The DREE experience in the third stage which was outlined in the previous section serves to demonstrate the critical significance of a decentralized approach to government organization.17 That this approach was not abandoned with the demise of DREE but was to be extended to other line departments, as well as to the Ministry of State for Economic and Regional Development, testified to the organizational learning which occurred in Canada over the past twenty five years. In part, of course, federal officials are required in the field because Canada is a federal system and there is need for interaction between federal and provincial officials. More important, however, is the fact, a fact only gradually accepted, that centralized program planning simply does not work where the subject in question involves widely different regional conditions which demand different responses each with a different mix of policy instruments. This is not to suggest that there cannot be central policy objectives; rather, it is to say that the means to realize these objectives need to vary with local circumstances. How a government decen-tralizes to achieve these ends is another matter and is related to two separate but related organizational issues; namely those of organizational differentiation and integration.

Organizational differentiation had been the norm in the Canadian experience up to the recent 1982 reorganization and elements of this remain. The central issue in regard to organizational differentiation is to ensure that a particular policy or policy objective is best served by the organizational design of a govern-ment. In the Canadian experience and within the Canadian tradition regional development policy has presented a challenge to organizational designers pre-cisely because it is one of those fields of public policy which cut across and encompass a number of other, if not all, major fields of public policy. The actual organizations used in Canada have gone from the most specific, e.g. the early boards and agencies for agricultural and rural aspects of regional development policy, to the most general, e.g. the umbrella portfolio/ministry of state secretariat put in place in 1982. In between a centralized and decentralized quasiline portfolio/department, i.e. DREE, was used.

For the purposes of organizational differention, the single most important lesson from the Canadian experience lies in the need to have a political and bureaucratic presence in the decision-making processes of government. This two-fold presence is necessary because of the very nature of regional development policy as a policy field which, as noted, cuts across and encompasses other policy fields. If the entire political executive and bureaucracy are responsible for regional development policy but no single minister and agency has a particular responsibility, then in all likelihood the normal course of decision-making will push regional development policy off the political-bureaucratic agenda when its objectives and priorities compete with those special and specific responsibilities (and interests) of ministers and bureaucrats.

This, in essence, is what critics or at least skeptics suggest would happen under the 1982 reorganization. However, even in this reorganization the federal government did not entirely shed all aspects of the previously highly differentiated organizational system. Most important, it retained a separate budgetary fund for regional development programs and activities and it established with MSERD a bureaucratic presence in the form of the ten provincial Federal Economic Development Coordinators whose principal responsibility was the regional dimensions of Canadian economic development policy.

Although neither of these features may be sufficient to provide the required political and bureaucratic presence for regional development policy, they at least indicate that in the organizational differentiation-integration trade-off the government was unwilling to go the whole route to integration in complete contradiction to its past experiences. But, in eliminating a specific portfolio for regional development policy it may have taken an unnecessary step in that direction, unnecessary that is because a separate Minister of State for Regional Development (that is a minister without a line department or program implementation responsibilities) could have been appointed with

responsibility for the operations of the Federal
Economic Development Coordinators who, in effect, could
collectively constitute a secretariat for this portfolio.

The third lesson from the Canadian experience, and
perhaps the one which accounts best for the 1982
reorganization, is the requirement that government
organization for regional development policy exhibit a
high degree of organizational integration. Since
regional development policy cuts across and encompasses
other departments it is essential that the policies,
programs and expenditures of these departments serve,
in some major part, the objectives of regional development. Proponents of a concerted approach to regional
development are fond of pointing out that for all the
millions spent annually by DREE, including its GDA
schemes, these amount to only roughly 1% of the annual
federal budget. The effects of these expenditures on
regional development are dwarfed by the effects of
expenditures of other federal sectoral programs many of
which either are not at all sensitive to regional considerations or, worse, actually serve to exacerbate the
regional disparities which regional development policy
is meant to reduce. Indeed, it is argued that even
minor changes in the activities of several sectoral
departments, that is in their programs, expenditures or
regulations, would result in major alterations to inter-
regional disparities. The same argument can be extended
to other areas of federal government policy, in taxation
or procurement policies, for example.19

The significance of these arguments was not lost
on federal officials and as much if not more than any
considerations they accounted for the decision to move
from the differentiated organizational regime that was
represented by DREE to the integrated organizational
regime represented by MSERD. Under the former regime
DREE simply did not possess and was not given the
leverage to tailor or bend the activities of sectoral
and other departments to serve a comprehensive regional
development policy. In neither the political nor
bureaucratic arenas was it able to fulfil its original
expectations.

The prospects for a more effective regional
development policy as a consequence of the establishment of MSERD were dependent upon a number of factors,
in addition to the actual political priority given to
this objective. Chief among these factors were the
analytical capabilities of MSERD to provide the

required regional development dimension to policies for economic development; second, the decentralization of sectoral and some service departments (e.g. the Department of Supply and Services) in order to ensure that the necessary regional sensitivities was introduced in the design and implementation of their programs; and, third, the coordinating leverage which MSERD was to bring to both political decision-making, especially with respect to the expenditure budget process, and administration in the field. Not only is each of these conditions critical to the effectiveness of an integrated organizational system, the very nature of an integrated system requires that all three conditions be met.

iv) Conclusion

The evolution of the Canadian federal government's organization for regional development policy and the lessons which can be derived from this experience, it must be acknowledged and emphasized, constitute but a single case in the context of comparative government organization for this field of public policy. As a single case, however, the case does encompass a wide range of organizational options for the empirical reason that the Canadian government has, in effect, experimented over time with different major alternatives. Moreover, as the account and analysis serve to demonstrate, the four stages in this evolution represented organizational learning on the part of the federal government.

In 1984, however, further organizational changes were effected, partly for reasons that had little to do with the question of government organization for regional development policy per se. At this point in time it is not at all clear that the federal government has learned from its own experience as outlined in this chapter!

Notes

Research for this chapter was supported by a grant from the Dalhousie University Research Development Committee, using funds supplied by the Social Sciences and Humanities Research Council of Canada. The author gratefully acknowledges this support.

The author also wishes to acknowledge the assistant of his colleague, Dr. Herman Bakvis of Dalhousie University, with whom he is associated in this research project. Professor Bakvis need not accept any responsibilities for this present chapter, however! The first published result of our joint research, on which this chapter draws, can be found in Peter Aucoin and Herman Bakvis, "Organizational Differentiation and Integration: the case of regional economic development policy in Canada", Canadian Public Administration, 27 (3), Fall 1984, 348-371.

1. See, for example, Alan C. Cairns, "The Governments and Societies of Canadian Federalism", Canadian Journal of Political Science, 10(4), December 1977, 695-725.

2. There is an extensive literature on this subject. Two useful works are N. H. Lithwick (ed.), Regional Economic Policy: the Canadian experience (Toronto: McGraw-Hill Ryerson, 1978) and Economic Council of Canada, Living Together: a study of regional disparities (Ottawa: Supply and Services Canada, 1977).

3. For a general introduction to these matters, see R. J. Van Loon and M. S. Whittington, The Canadian Political System (Toronto: McGraw-Hill Ryerson, 1976).

4. On the first two stages see, A. Careless, Initiative and Response: the adaptation of Canadian federalism to regional economic development (Montreal: McGill-Queen's, 1977).

5. For a description of these arrangements, see D. V. Smiley, Canada in Question (Toronto: McGraw-Hill Ryerson, 1980).

6. See Richard Phidd and G. Bruce Doern, <u>The Politics and Management of Canadian Economic Policy</u> (Toronto: Macmillan, 1978), especially on the transition from the initial organization of DREE to its decentralized form.

7. See N. H. Lithwick, "Regional Policy: the embodiment of contradictions", in G. Bruce Doern (ed.), <u>How Ottawa Spends Your Tax Dollars</u> (Toronto: James Lorimer, 1982), 131-146.

8. For a superb case-study of this approach, see Donald J. Savoie, <u>Federal-Provincial Collaboration: the Canada-New Brunswick General Development Agreement</u> (Montreal: McGill-Queen's, 1981). The analysis which follows on this third stage draws extensively on this account as well as on interviews with officials across Canada conducted by the author and Herman Bakvis.

9. See R. Van Loon, "Stop the Music: the current policy and expenditure management system in Ottawa", <u>Canadian Public Administration</u>, 24 (2), Summer 1981, 175-199.

10. See Richard French, <u>How Ottawa Decides</u> (Toronto: Canadian Institute of Economic Policy, 1980).

11. On the system prior to these changes see, G. Bruce Doern and Peter Aucoin (eds.), <u>Public Policy in Canada: organization, process and management</u> (Toronto: Macmillan, 1979).

12. Office of the Prime Minister of Canada, <u>Release</u>, "Reorganization for Economic Development", 12 January 1982.

13. The above quotations are taken from <u>ibid</u>.

14. <u>Ibid</u>.

15. See, for example, Standing Senate Committee on National Finance, <u>Government Policy and Regional Development</u> (Ottawa: Supply and Services Canada, 1982) and Atlantic Provinces Economic Council, "Analysis of the Reorganization for Economic Development: background and policy direction", Halifax, October 1982.

16. See Peter Aucoin, "Public Policy Theory and Analysis", in Doern and Aucoin (eds.), _Public Policy in Canada_, 1-26.

17. See again Savoie, _Federal-Provincial Collaboration_.

18. On the development and early experience with the organization system of "ministers/ministries of state" see Peter Aucoin and Richard French, _Knowledge, Power and Public Policy_ (Ottawa: Science Council of Canada, 1974).

19. See I. McAllister, "How to Re-make DREE", _Policy Options_, March 1980, 39-43.

Chapter Eight

DREE and SDRW: Canadian and Belgian Experience in Regional Economic Development

Maureen Covell

The concept of region is a multi-dimensional one, encompassing, along with the notion of definable geographical area, implications of economic and often cultural or ethnic specificity. Although all dimensions of regionalism have elicited governmental activity in the post-war period, it is the economic aspect of regional differences that has been the object of the largest amount of governmental output. Regional differences in prosperity and economic growth have given rise to an outpouring of scholarly material analysing conditions, reasons, and remedies; to an abundant polemical literature (often overlapping with the first category) demanding measures to redress the imbalances, and to a wide variety of governmental policies designed to address or at least give the appearance of addressing the situations described and decried. I will be looking at policies designed to alleviate regional economic inequalities in Canada and Belgium. The chapter will focus on two institutions created to carry out these policies, Canada's Department of Regional Economic Expansion (DREE), and Belgium's Society for Walloon Regional Development (Societe de Developpement Regional Wallon - SDRW). The two institutions have been chosen both because each was designed to play a major role in its country's attack on regional disparities and because, by a coincidence that is not really a coincidence, they have almost the same life span. DREE was created in 1969, SDRW in 1970. DREE was condemned to death in January 1982 and executed in 1983, while sentence was passed on SDRW in July 1983 and carried out in 1983. Because this time period saw the rise and demise of similar attempts to deal with regional economic differences in several other countries, a comparison of the two institutions may not only illuminate the Belgian and Canadian experiences but also tell us something about the usefulness of trying to deal with regional differences via the type of strategy they represent.

Neither DREE nor SDRW can be considered a success, even in the minimal sense of self-preservation. This

chapter will argue that, beyond the specific contex-
tual reasons for this failure there are more general
reasons, rooted in conceptions of the nature of regions
and the causes of regional economic disparities that
were shared by Belgian and Canadian policy makers.
Briefly put, analyses and policies tended to concentrate on the economic aspects of regional disparities
and on economic causes. At the extreme, there was an
assumption that regions are objective, 'given' entities and that regional differences are the natural
result of the free interplay of economic forces.
Since this chapter is a study of two institutions
shaped by these assumptions, it will deal with Canadian
and Belgian regions as defined by the creators of
those institutions and discuss their analysis in some
detail. However, it will argue that, as stated in the
first paragraph, a 'region' is a construct based on
many dimensions. The causes of regional differences
are also multi-dimensional, and it is in the neglect
of non-economic dimensions, particularly the political,
that many of the causes of the failures of regional
policy can be found.

i)   Regionalism

        Regional differences in prosperity and economic
growth have been a constant feature of the economic
history of most countries. However, the type of
attempt to deal with these differences represented by
DREE and SDRW is of more recent origin. As a 1970
OECD study of regional policies stated:

>   The rise and decline of particular
>   territorial areas of national
>   economies is not a new historical
>   phenomenon, but the concept of
>   region as a means of furthering
>   economic growth and ensuring the
>   sharing out of the fruits of ma-
>   terial and social progress among
>   people living in all parts of a
>   country is becoming increasingly
>   relevant in modern society.1

        Why did this emphasis on regional development
occur when it did? The answers must remain speculative, but several political and economic changes
that took place at the same time as the development
of regional policies seem to have contributed to the
growing consciousness of regional disparities and to

the development of government action as a response.
First, in both Belgium and Canada the 1950's and 60's
saw an increasing politicization of regional differences. In Canada this politicization took many forms,
including the 1956 election of a Conservative government that based part of its appeal on a mobilization
of votes in disadvantaged peripheral regions such as
the Prairie provinces and the Maritimes. Not only was
this government the source of some early regional
programs, but the defeated Liberal party was not slow
to draw the conclusions its loss of power suggested.
The 1960's also saw the development of the 'Quiet
Revolution' in Quebec, a complex phenomenon that both
ended the province's traditional isolation from the
Canadian political system and raised the question
whether its future relationship with that system would
be one of integration or separation. This development
was also likely to make the Liberals 'region conscious'
since their status as a semi-permanent governing party
depended on their domination of Quebec representation
in the national parliament. In the case of Quebec,
the multi-dimensional nature of regional discontent
was given a degree of recognition and a combined strategy of increasing recognition of Francophone culture,
increases in Francophone access to positions of influence at the centre, and improvement of economic
conditions in Quebec was formulated. The discontents
of Anglophone regions, however, were treated as almost
entirely economic in nature and source.

Politicization of regional differences in Belgium
has a long history, but until the 1960's this politicization had been expressed in debates over language-use
in the regions and in national politics. It was not
until the post-war reorganization of the economy that
Belgian politicians, particularly those from the
Walloon region, began to stress the economic aspect of
regional differences. This new emphasis led to the
creation of a political party demanding increased
autonomy for the region, the Rassemblement Wallon.
This party joined with parties from the Flemish region
to demand a constitutional revision decentralizing the
unitary Belgian state. Their electoral successes had
sufficient impact on the traditional governing parties
to lead to a considerable amount of decentralization
and finally to the constitutional revisions of 1970
and 1980. However, for most of the period under discussion, the regional policies of successive Belgian
governments represented an attempt to avoid this
political solution by treating the problem as if it

were purely one of economic distress.

Other economic and political changes also pushed governments in the direction of establishing regional policies. First, the post-war diffusion of Keynesian economics led to a widely-held belief that governments not only could, but also should intervene to prevent economic hardship. The same period that saw the creation of DREE and SDRW also saw the creation of other programmes designed to contribute to economic growth and equity. The prosperity of the 'golden sixties' made its own contribution. Prosperity arrived, but not for everyone. This highlighted the structural problems of disadvantaged regions in a way that the shared hardships of depression and war had not. Moreover, even without raising taxes, governments had a lot more money to spend. Again, DREE and SDRW were only two among many programmes designed to distribute government funds in a visible way to target groups of people.

ii) The Philosophy

Orientation would almost certainly be a more accurate word than philosophy to describe the ideas behind regional policy in Belgium and Canada. Certainly neither DREE nor SDRW was the result of a coherent ideology of the sources of economic growth at the national or regional level. It has been suggested that the various economic rationalizations that accompanied the development of regional policy were simply camouflage for a pragmatic political decision to grease squeaky wheels.2 However, discussions of the programmes contain several recurring themes suggesting some specific economic beliefs, however dimly held. These beliefs did not always create a congenial environment for the operation of DREE and SDRW.

First, both Belgium and Canada operate under liberal market economies, with political cultures in which faith in both the causative powers and sanctity of economic forces have been only slightly modified by the Keynesian overlay. According to these beliefs, market forces determine the prevailing distribution of prosperity and misery in a country, and, over time, their operation leads to the most efficient and beneficial use of the resources available to the country. In the case of regional disparities, this credo leads to the assumption that there is a necessary trade off between aid to disadvantaged regions and overall economic growth. Moreover, in both Canada and Belgium there are powerful interest groups ready to enforce compliance with the ideology. Business groups in both countries were quick to denounce the 'strings' attached to various industrial incentive programs, while the richer regions in each country predicted that dire economic consequences would result from policies diverting resources from the 'productive' prosperous regions to the 'unproductive' depressed regions.

This fixation on economic forces also colored the identification of the regions to be assisted and the analyses of the causes of and cure for their condition. Belgian regional policy identified distressed regions according to 35 criteria, most of which were never published. Among those made public were structural unemployment, an actual or imminent decline in important economic activities, an abnormally low standard of living, and slow economic growth.3 DREE's criteria focussed on structural unemployment, lower than average per capita income, and stagnating economic growth.4

Analysis of the causes of regional disparities also stressed economic factors. Lack of resources, lack of infrastructure, isolation, and a population with few or inappropriate skills are the most frequently mentioned causes of a failure to prosper.5 The outlines of a cure were less evident. Politically costly solutions such as allowing large scale emigration to reduce the pressure on employment opportunities were rejected in both Canada and Belgium.6 The most popular available theory of economic development, growth pole theory, required too much government intervention and ran too much against the political goal of distributing funds to as many grateful voters as possible to be attractive to policy makers in either country. In the end, regional policy in both countries involved a variety of general industrial incentives and infrastructural investment, backed by a vague belief in the efficacy of pump priming.7

A final element that entered into the creation of DREE and SDRW was what might be called the bureaucratic dream of fully synoptic decision-making, based on the belief that knowledge is power.8 A major part of the mandate of both organizations was the gathering of information and the setting of regional priorities in a process designed to incorporate both technical and political actors. However, the questions asked

in this process concentrated on economic causes: the
discovery of the other aspects of regional problems
had to depend on serendipity.

iii) <u>Belgium</u>

The Walloon region of Belgium was one of the first
major industrial regions of 19th century Europe. The
industrialization was based on coal and steel with
the later addition of glass and textile industries,
and financed largely by capital from Brussels. In
conjunction with colonial trade, Walloon industry
formed the economic basis for a Francophone political
elite located in Brussels and for a Walloon working
class with wages above the national average, firmly
institutionalized in a network of Socialist (and to a
lesser degree Catholic) trade unions, parties, and
social insurance societies. Some depressed rural
areas, 'isolated' from the main industrial areas,
remained, but until the Second World War, industrial
Wallonia was both source and symbol of Belgian prosperity.

The crisis that came after the war was political
and psychological as well as economic.9 The post-war
period saw the coming to power in the other Belgian
region, Flanders, of a new entrepreneurial and political elite. The roots of this elite lay in the nine-
teenth century Flemish nationalist movement. To
put the matter very simply, the leaders of the Flemish
movements argued that the backward status of their
region had three causes: the lack of status of the
Dutch language, the lack of political power correspon-
dent to Flemish numbers in the Belgian population,
and the lack of control over soruces of wealth. Their
goal was not only to raise standards of education,
political participation and economic welfare for the
general population of Flanders, but also to create a
Flemish intellectual, political and economic elite.
By the post war period, this elite began to claim the
power in the central government reflecting the Flemish
majority in the Belgian population, thereby threatening
the position of the old Francophone elite. Less involved in colonial trade then the old elite, the new
Flemish elite was more open to the new international
sources of capital that were beginning to appear in
Europe. The combination of internally generated financial resources, international capital, and state
power led to a reversal of traditional Belgian economic and political relationships. The old elite fought
a political rear-guard action, but did not rejuvenate

192

itself economically through new investments in Wallonia.10

The Walloon region was therefore faced with an aging industrial plant and with the structural decline of its most important industries, beginning with the collapse of coal in the 1950's. As important, it was faced with crises of consciousness and of political as well as economic leadership. Political activity in Wallonia had been based on class and religious consciousness in the context of a unitary, Francophone-dominated Belgium. The interests of the region were largely perceived as class interests to be defended against the sources of economic power located in Brussels. Moreover, the main political force in the region, the Socialist party, was committed to a national strategy of unity with the weaker Socialist movement in Flanders. Under these circumstances, regional consciousness developed only slowly in response to the shift of economic and political power to Flanders.

The combined loss of economic prosperity and political power did eventually lead to a regional crisis of confidence in the Belgian state. The first large scale manifestation, and a major stage in the development of this crisis was the 1960-61 general strike against austerity measures introduced by the government as part of the adjustment to decolonization. The strike, planned as a nation-wide demonstration of class solidarity, took place as planned in Wallonia, but not in Flanders. This division of the 'Belgian' working class was as traumatic to Walloon opinion as the eventual failure of the strike itself. It turned a class confrontation into a regional one, and undermined the arguements of those who favored cross-regional solidarity with the Flemish 'little brother'.11 A political party demanding Walloon regional autonomy was created, and regionalist movements appeared in the other political parties, including the socialists. The continuing decline of the region, and its political consequences, were the main forces behind the creation of institutions such as SDRW.

EARLY POLICIES

It would, of course, have been politically impossible to design a regional policy for Wallonia alone. The Flemish claimed, with justice, that they

193

too had their depressed areas, and one of the unpublished criteria for the designation of assisted
region was no doubt the requirement of some balance
in expenditures between Flanders and Wallonia.

The first large scale regionalization plan was
passed in 1959. It consolidated earlier legislation
and identified two types of region to be assisted:
depressed rural areas and declining industrial areas.
The designated regions were not to include more than
15% of the country's population.12 The program aimed
at the modernization of existing plants and the creation of new industrial activity in the depressed
areas through incentives in the form of low interest
loans, loan guarantees and tax exemptions.13 In
addition, provinces and communes were enabled to form
organizations to study development needs and to undertake small scale infrastructural projects such as
industrial parks. The program was never considered
satisfactory: by 1964 investment undertaken under
its provisions was only 6% of all investment in the
country from 1959-64.14 If anything, the provincial
and communal associations had proved too successful:
an OECD assessment stated that they "have proliferated
to such an extent as to make coordination of their
action very difficult".15 Finally, the program did
not have the expected political pay-off: demands
for regional autonomy continued to grow.

As a result, a new regional assistance law was
passed in 1966. The number of regions qualifying for
assistance was increased to take in areas that included
35% of the Belgian population. The incentives were
made more alluring, so much so that they drew criticism from the Commission of the European Community as
falsifying competition. Evaluation of the legislation was mixed: its proponents argued that it was
responsibile for the creation of 135,000 new jobs,
while other studies questioned whether it had actually
influenced decisions to invest.16 From the Walloon
point of view, the most important characteristic of
the program was that investments under it went mainly
to Flanders, and that the decline of the Walloon
region was continuing.17

At the same time, the Belgian government was
altering other aspects of its economic organization
and spending policies to take account of regional
demands. Two posts of Secretary of State for Regional
Economic Affairs were created in 1966. At first part

of the Prime Minister's Office, they were moved to a more strategic position in the Ministry for Economic Affairs in 1968. An interdepartmental commission for regional policy, grouping civil servants and members of ministerial cabinets was also created. On the spending side, a Fund for Economic Expansion and Regional Reconversion was created. As its title indicates, it spent on both national and regional levels: by 1970 about one-third of its overall expenditures had been directed at regional assistance projects.18 Central departments, such as the Ministry for Public Works, added a regional component to their budgets.

SDRW

These regionalization programs and internal changes all represented attempts to meet the economic grievances of Walloon regionalists without giving them the political autonomy they demanded. In the overall context of Belgian politics of the period, they represented, along with the language laws of 1961-3, the last stand of the unitarist political elite, threatened simultaneously by Walloon demands for economic federalism and Flemish demands for cultural federalism. The 1970 Terwagne law, which set up the SDRW as part of a collection of regional economic institutions was one of the last of these last stands. It was passed five months before the revision of the Belgian constitution that laid the basis for political regionalization, and represents both an affort by the old elite to give concessions that would avoid the revision, and an attempt by regionalists to get some type of regional economic institution in case the proposed (and at the time still vague) constitutional revision did not occur.19

The law set up three types of institution. First, it set up a National Planning Bureau which had, in addition to its functional divisions, three regional sections. National and regional level planning were to go on simultaneously with coordination at a relatively late stage in the process. This absence of early interaction was mitigated by the fact that the regional sections lacked personnel and so were dependent on the assistance of the national level functional divisions for much of their work.20

The law also set up regional economic councils, (Conseil Economique Regional Wallon (CERW) for

195

Wallonia). These were advisory councils composed of
members of the national parliament and provincial
councils, and of representatives of trade unions,
business, and agricultural interest groups. They
co-opted a number of 'technicians' and were joined in
their deliberations by the provincial governors. The
councils were to study the economic problems of their
regions and to give advice on a whole series of topics including the use of funds from various sources
designated for regional economic development, the
regional component of the plan, and the use of the
credits granted to Wallonia in compensation for the
money spent on the Flemish port of Zeebrugge. In
addition, they could be consulted by any government
ministry for information relevant to its activities
in the region, and could, on their own initiative,
emit an opinion on 'any problem of regional economic
interest'.21

The SDR's were created both to assist the CER's
in gathering this information and to carry out policies of their own. They were given the form of a
parastatal, with a governing board composed of interest group representatives and delegates from the provincial level of government. They were mandated to:
study, plan for and promote development in their
region; establish a list of regional sections of the
Planning Bureau; cooperate with national ministries
in the planning and execution of policy in the region;
and undertake their own investment projects in the
absence of private initiative.22

This mandate could, depending on the resources
available, and the degree of organizational initiative
applied, either remain largely theoretical or become
almost infinitely expandable. Unfortunately for
SDRW, the full mandate was never carried out: with
the exception of a few small projects its contribution
remained largely at the level of study, proposition
and publicity. Even in this role its existence was
tenuous. Although the law establishing it was
passed in 1970, it was not in fact set up until 1973
and did not become fully operational until 1975. By
1978, rumors of its abolition were already beginning
to appear in print.23 There are several reasons for
its sad history. I will discuss the ones peculiar
to Belgium here, and the more general reasons in the
conclusion.

First, the resources allocated to SDRW were not

large enough to allow it to play a major role in the
regional economy. Its annual functioning budget was
only about 64 million Belgian francs (about 2.5 million Canadian dollars) and even these sums often arrived
late. The sum of 394 million francs (about 15.5
million Canadian dollars) allocated for investment
projects also arrived years after it had been promised. Its arrival did permit SDRW to undertake some
economic activities but created a conflict over strategy. Should this money be used in attempts to rescue
the failing traditional industries of the region or to
start new enterprises? The evident human (and political) costs of allowing already existing industries to
go under pushed SDRW to concentrate on rescue
attempts.24

The personnel of the society also expanded slowly.
Put at 84 in 1978, its growth was hindered not only
by budget problems, but also by a policy of hiring
outside regular civil service procedures. This strategy was designed to attract more flexible, entrepreneurial employees to the agency, but laid it open
to protests from the civil servants unions and
accusations that political connections rather than
entrepreneurial talent were the main criteria for
engagement. In fact, disputes among the region's
political parties over the political balance of those
to be hired did cause delays in recruitment.

There were several reasons for this lack of
resources, reasons arising from the difficult environment in which SDRW had to operate. First, the organization was caught in the battle between regionalists
and unitarists that dominated Belgian politics in
the 1970's. The law that created SDRW reflected the
unitarist suspicion of creeping federalism and one of
its provisions was a major cause of the delay in
bringing the agency into existence. As part of their
defense against regionalism, the unitarists had
secured the provision that the SDR's be created by
the provinces rather than established directly at the
regional level. The Walloon Socialists, with the
assistance of their associated trade union, were able
to use their domination of the provincial level of
government in the region to get SDRW established with
a regional jurisdiction.25 However, this took time,
and in the eyes of the unitarists the resulting
organization did not have a status much superior to
that of the earlier intercommunal and provincial
development societies. Moreover, it was dependent for

much of its investigative activity on commissions from government ministries. Unitarist ministers were not likely to give it such commissions, and even favorably disposed ministers often turned to sources more directly under their control such as their ministerial cabinets.

The SDRW was born into a crowded and rapidly changing institutional environment. There were many other institutions that performed similar functions of investigation, consultation, and investment. For a country whose government has the reputation of avoiding interference in the economy, Belgium has a large number of input and output economic policy institutions. Some are non-governmental: political parties, unions, employers' associations all have 'study bureaus' that periodically address regional issues. At the consultative level, there are several institutions that regularly associate interest group representatives with the formation of policy. In the area of investment, there is not only the Economic Expansion Fund mentioned earlier, but also a National Investment Society, and, by 1979, Regional Investment Societies, all with considerably greater resources.

In the area of policy-making, national control remained strong: when it was surrendered it went to new regional political institutions who jealously guarded every area of jurisdiction they were able to wring out of the central government. In 1974 regional ministerial committees were set up; in 1979 regional 'executives' were established in the national government, and in 1980 a further constitutional revision set up an autonomous level of government with authority over a range of economic activities.27 SDRW was caught in this political evolution: too much for the dominant unitarists of 1970, it was too little for the federalists of 1980, and it was they who abolished it in 1982.

In this crowded and changing environment SDRW was not able to play the role of catalytic investor its proponents had aspired to on its behalf. Its main accomplishment were undertaking of the first serious interdisciplinary studies of a range of problems such as urban energy policy and waste disposal that were important if not exactly central to Walloon economic revival. These studies were useful to the new regional political executive, which spent the first year and a half of its autonomous existence without a functioning bureaucracy. In addition, in collaboration with CERW, SDRW participated in a war of statistics, communiques and conferences designed to increase the Walloon share of the national budget. The effects of these activities are difficult to measure: in any event, they were not enough to save the institution.

The end of SDRW was of a piece with its history. When the new Walloon Regional Council voted to abolish it, it was also decided that the personnel would be transferred to the new regional civil service with their (much higher) salaries and fringe benefits intact. The law was passed in July 1982, but the necessary executive orders to carry it out were not immediately passed. Instead, in early 1983 the Walloon executive announced that the condemned institution was going to hire 125 new functionaries who would, of course, benefit from the same rights of transfer as those already in place. The deadline for application was so close to the date of the announcement that only those with prior knowledge of the hirings - for example, superfluous members of the ministerial cabinets of the Walloon executive - were likely to be able to assemble the necessary documentation in time. The civil servants' unions launched an official complaint, but to no avail. The new employees were hired and SDRW then duly abolished.

iv) Canada

Although the history and scale of the two countries are quite different, Canada, like Belgium, is characterized by important regional differences in prosperity and growth rate. As in Belgium, some of the disparities are long-standing, while others are relatively new: formerly prosperous regions now suffering the effects of deindustrialization. Again, the nature of the regions is also similar: depressed agricultural areas and industrial areas dependent on a small number of industries in structural decline. Problems of geographical isolation are greater in Canada, and more Canadian regions, isolated or not, are dependent on a single seasonal primary industry. Problem areas include the whole Atlantic region, Eastern Quebec, northern Ontario, and portions of every other province. Cultural differences make these regional disparities easily politicizable. Like Flanders and Wallonia, Canada's regions have been created by a combination of factors including the existence or importance of various resources, and the location of control over political and economic power at both the national and international level.28 In addition, like Belgium, Canada faced a major challenge to its national unity during the period, in the form of a growing assertion of Quebec's regional identity.

The first regional programs of any scope were created by the Diefenbaker Conservative government, a government which drew much of its appeal from its articulation of the resentments of the peripheral regions against 'Central Canada'. Their programs included the Agricultural and Rural Development Act, specifically aimed at the Prairies and the Maritimes, and the Atlantic Development Board, which had a mandate to examine the overall problem of Atlantic Region underdevelopment. Liberal governments of the 1960's amplified these programs, and, reflecting their own political base, began a series of industrial incentive programs, including the Area Development Agency (1963).29 Much of the agency's money went to relatively prosperous areas with high cyclical unemployment located in Ontario strongholds of the Liberal party.30 In 1969 the government created the Regional Development Incentive program (RDIA). Under the program, areas were designated for assistance under the criteria of high unemployment, low income levels, and the probably region-wide impact of assistance. However, as the OECD evaluation of member states' regional policies remarks: "no rigid statistical criteria (were) used for this purpose".31 In fact the number of designated areas tended to increase over time as much in response to political pressures as in answer to changing economic conditions.32

One of the major roles assigned to DREE when it was created in 1969 was the coordination of these various programs. The overall mandate of the department was even broader than that assigned SDRW: to "facilitate economic expansion and social adjustment" in the designated regions.33

The new organization had more resources to back up this mandate than SDRW.34 DREE was a government department, with major political figures as both minister and deputy minister. Moreover, it had several concrete functions assigned to it: the coordination of federal government regional assistance programs, the coordination of the regional impact of

the policies of other federal ministries, the assertion of a visible federal spending presence at the
local level, and, not incidentally, the generation of
support for the Liberal party.35 In its regional
assistance programs, it was to apply a combination
of industrial incentives, infrastructure development,
and social and resource development. In its early
years the program had a strong tinge of the growth
pole conception of development, a philosophy that also
provided a useful justification for concentrating
expenditures in populated areas.

The extent of DREE's mandate aroused the territorial instincts both of other federal ministries
and of the provincial level of government, suspicions
that were increased by its early behavior. Protests
against DREE's mode of operation led to a reassessment in 1972-3 and to a reorientation of its
approach.36 Coordination with the provincial level
of government was emphasized and the department
itself decentralized. An attempt was made, via the
mechanism of General Development Agreements with the
provinces, to substitute some degree of coherent
planning for the earlier free-wheeling approach to
assistance. These changes bought the department six
more years of existence, but were not enough to save
it in the end. In 1983 it was dissolved and its
activities transferred to two other departments as
part of a wholesale reorganization of government
economic policy.37

Several of the reasons for DREE's demise are
similar to those responsible for SDRW's failure. Like
SDRW, DREE was born into a crowded and changing
institutional environment. It had to cope with the
hostility of other federal departments who resented
its attempts to coordinate and its tendency simply
to ignore their policies in the field, and was
vulnerable to the accusations of other economic departments that its activities threatened overall
national economic growth. As Quebec moved from a
quiet revolution to a separatist one, the Canadian
government, like the Belgian one, moved towards political solutions to the problems of regionalism.

In addition, the prevailing economic ideology
worked against DREE. Manufacturers' groups objected
to the controls implied by the direct grant form of
industrial incentive.38 A Senate committee on regional policy objected to the use of regional policy
for 'industrial structuring' and doubted the

ability of politicians and bureaucrats to 'pick winners' among the industries competing for assistance.39 Richer provinces argued that regional disparities were the result of the natural flow of investment to more productive areas and that artificially distorting the flow would lead to disaster for everyone.

Finally, DREE had become at best politically useless and at worst embarrassing for the government. Although its supporters argued that it had probably kept regional disparities from increasing, they could not demonstrate that DREE had made major progress towards eliminating them. It had certainly not stemmed the development of Quebec separatism. Ironically, given the criticisms mentioned above, the agency was also criticized because its actual pattern of expenditures was often unplanned and incoherent. Critics accused the agency of using partisan political criteria in the allocation of funds. In the end, DREE was considered to have failed even in the task of attracting political support. For the Senate committee on regional policy, the "reason above all others" for the dissolution of the department was that "the Federal government was getting no political credit for its money".40

v)   Conclusion

What do the histories of DREE and SDRW tell us about the possibility of redressing regional disparities via the type of institutional creation and industrial incentive strategy they represent? It could be argued that this is hardly a fair question. The establishment and life span of the two agencies were so riddled with partisan political considerations that their operation can hardly be considered a test of the economic assumptions behind the policies. However, an examination, not only of their histories, but also of those of similar institutions in other countries suggests that this type of approach to regional problems is so prone to 'political' distortion that this characteristic must be considered in any evaluation. DREE and SDRW were set up in response to the political as well as to the economic manifestations of regional disparities. This origin, as well as their control of money and the supposed visibility of their expenditures made political use of them inevitable. A recommendation that such institutions be better shielded from 'politics' in the future runs against political rationality for those establishing them.

A more directly economic criticism of the two institutions questions what an OECD report describes as the assumption that regional disparities are fringe problems.41 The argument that regional problems are the result of the whole of government policy and can only be addressed by a revision of that policy rather than by adding new policies is a common one. Writers in Wallonia and the peripheral regions of Canada go further and argue that the depressed status of their regions is the result of deliberate government policy. They argue that their regions are depressed, not only because of a lack of economic resources or capital, but because of a lack of political power, because they are excluded from the coalition of regions represented by the government, and over the long run the political regime of their countries. If this is so, it could be argued that the failure of DREE and SDRW to revive economic growth in depressed regions is not important since this was not their real function. Rather, they were to mitigate the political effects of over-all government policy. However, even given this conception of their purpose neither institution could be considered a success: each seems to have created rather than dissipated political embarrassment for its creators. In a sense DREE and SDRW treated the political as well as the economic aspects of regional disparities as fringe problems. If it is true that regional disparities are not solely economic in nature, it is also true that they are the result of the totality of political as well as economic relationships in a country. Regional disparities raise questions of relative political power as much as they do questions of relative economic resources.

If this is so, then some suggestions can be made for a revised perspective on regional disparities. First, if political as well as economic factors are at the root of regional differences in prosperity, then the prevailing use of a country's resources might well not be the most economically rational use, and the assumption that there is a necessary trade off between overall national growth and regional re- development can be questioned. However, there are probably political as well as economic limits to a government's ability to redistribute resources to less prosperous regions, since redistribution perceived as excessive by the dominant regions will threaten that government's political base. Under these circumstances, redistributive policies are likely to remain fringe policies.

These limitations suggest that regions should not rely on largesse from the centre for their redevelopment. This point is reinforced by the example of the reversal of Flanders' status, which suggests that some type of internal regional consciousness and political organization must be part of any attempt to mitigate regional underdevelopment. It cannot, however, be said that the example of Flanders 'proves' that disadvantaged regions can solve their problems by a total strategy of self-reliance. The Flemish had the advantage of constituting a majority of the Belgian population, a potential political resource that is not available to the inhabitants of most underdeveloped regions. Also, much of the post-war prosperity in Flanders was the result of changes in the sources of capital and the importance of resources that were not under the control of Flemish elites. Nor should the example be taken to show that the creation of a regional capitalist class is the only route to regional redevelopment. Walloon political elites, particularly from the Socialist party, have argued that Walloon economic redressment should not involve the recreation of relationships they fought at the national level. The Flemish example does suggest that some of the conditions for regional redevelopment can be created internally and that the conditions for taking advantage of external changes can also come from within the region itself. It can be argued that regional political consciousness is a necessary part of regional economic redressment, and that centrally designed policies should include major elements of real decentralization and regional autonomy.

The need for regional political consciousness is further underlined by the differences in success between DREE and SDRW. Although neither changed the overall pattern of government policy, the fact that DREE was able to command resources on a much greater scale than SDRW reflects the greater degree of regional consciousness and political organization that exists in Canada. If regimes are coalitions of dominant regions, depressed regions must find a way of making their voices heard at the centre and controlling their own sources of prosperity.

Notes

1. Organization for Economic Cooperation and
    Development (OECD) The Regional Factor in
    Economic Development (Paris: OECD, 1970) 9.

2. Ibid., 18.

3. OECD, Regional Problems and Policies in OECD
    Countries Vol. 2 (Paris: OECD, 1976) 53.

4. Department of Regional Economic Expansion
    The New Approach (Ottawa, 1976) 9.

5. For a summary and critique see Ian McAllister
    Regional Development in the European Community:
    a Canadian Perspective (Montreal: Institute
    for Research on Public Policy, 1982) 25-27.

6. Justifications for this differed. Canadians
    argued that emigration was as much a cause of
    economic depression as a consequence, while
    Belgians argued that their country was so
    crowded that there was nowhere to go.

7. For convenient comparative summaries of the
    policies, see the OECD publications listed above.

8. For a full discussion of this ideology, see
    Sutherland and Lazar, "Knowledge for Development",
    chapter ten.

9. There is a voluminous literature on 'the decline
    of Wallonia'. This analysis follows that of
    writers such as Michel Quevit "Economic
    Competition, Regional Development and Power in
    Belgium" in Antoni Kuklinski (ed) Polarized
    Development and Regional Policies (New York:
    Mouton, 1981) 357-77, and Michel Molitor "La
    face cachee des problemes institutionels belges:
    Leurs racines economiques" La Revue Nouvelle
    (Brussels) 1979, 9, 149-62.

10. For a discussion of the consequences of this loss
    of economic leadership, and a discussion of
    possible sources of replacement, see
    Quevit, "Economic Competition", 152.

11. Figures of participation by sector and region
    are given in Valmy Feaux Cinq semaines de lutte

sociale: La greve de l'hiver 1960-1961 (Brussels: Institut de Sociologie de l'Universite Libre de Bruxelles, 1963) 169-81.

12. Raymond Riley Studies in Industrial Geography: Belgium (London: Unwin, 1976) 57-62.

13. See ibid, 47.

14. For an outline, see G. Richard Thorman Foreign Investment and Regional Development: The Theory and Practice of Investment Incentives with a Case Study of Belgium (New York: Praeger, 1979).

15. OECD The Regional Factor 48.

16. Thorman, Regional Development.

17. For summaries of the argument, see the articles by Quevit and Molitor already cited.

18. OECD The Regional Factor 85.

19. See "Regionalisme et decentralisation economique: Debat en marge du projet de loi 152" Socialisme (Brussels) 1970 350-365 (Terwagne was a Socialist minister); Jean Beaufays "Politique economique regionale" in Centre Interuniversitaire de Droit Publique Etudes sur le regionalisme en Belgique et a l'etranger (Brussels: Bruyland, 1973) 229-351, esp. 305-10.

20. Annick Messiaen "La planification regionale en Belgique" Critique Regionale No. 4 (1981) 5-34.

21. "Les Conseils Economiques Regionaux" Centre de Recherche et d'Information Socio-Politiques (CRISP) Courrier Hebdomadaire No. 584 (1972).

22. Bernard Anselme "Les organes regionaux de decentralisation economique d'aujourd'hui et demain" Socialisme (1978) 259-66.

23. For example, "Soldes avant liquidation", L'Evenement July 1978

24. SDRW Rapport Annuel 1978 et seq.

25. "Debat en marge du projet de loi 152".

26. L. Roeylants "Les principes de l'action budge-
taire des gouvernements, 1961-79" CRISP
Courrier Hebdomadaire No. 878 (1980).

27. Jacques Brassinne "Les institutions de la Flandre,
de la Communaute francaise, de la Region wallonne"
CRISP Dossier No. 14 (1981).

28. For a discussion, see H.M. Stevenson "Political
Identification" Chapter 1 in this collection.

29. OECD Regional Problems and Policies gives a
summary of these programs, as does DREE The New
Approach.

30. Anthony G.S. Careless, Initiative and Response:
The Adaptation of Canadian Federalism to Regional
Economic Development (Montreal: McGill-Queen's
University Press, 1977) 100.

31. OECD, The Regional Factor 112.

32. Careless Initiative and Response 133. The Report
of the Standing Senate Committee on National
Finance, Government Policy and Regional Development (Ottawa: Supply and Services, 1982) makes
the same point several times.

33. DREE, The New Approach, 9.

34. For a more detailed analysis of DREE, see Peter
Aucoin "Decision-making in Canada" Chapter 7
of this collection.

35. Careless, Initiative and Response, 165.

36. Careless gives an excellent account of DREE's
early years.

37. See Aucoin, "Decision-making in Canada" for an
account of this process.

38. Senate Committee Report 31-2.

39. Senate Committee Report 8.

40. Senate Committee Report 80.

41. OECD Regional Problems and Policies 35.

Chapter Nine

Regional Development: experiences from the EEC

Ian McAllister

i)   Regional Development: issues, goals and policies

Few countries have had an easy time specifying
appropriate regional development goals or managing
regional development programmes.   Certainly Canada has
not; certainly none of the European Community member
countries has.   It is hard on other continents also to
find exceptions.   Brazil has its intractable Northeast,
Pakistan severed in two.   African countries have had
their complications: Nigerian regional conflicts have
not been patched up by oil wealth; the Sudanese south
is vastly less developed than the north; Ghana's
northern region has far less development than the
south.   Now in her fourth year of independence,
Zimbabwe has already weathered complex regional
difficulties, aggravated by the legacy of history, her
southern neighbour and a ravaging drought.

Each nation has to determine which are her
development priorities and which are the regional
issues that must be tackled most strenuously. Outsiders
can present comparative experiences and perhaps some
insights; they cannot presume to identify appropriate
goals, nor should they place themselves in roles where
they seek to recommend solutions.   That, properly, is
the stuff of politics - the preserve of the domestic
politicians.   Even the analysis of problems is usually
more properly done by the country's own nationals.
Problem definition requires a sensitivity - one that is
best developed at home: it requires an appreciation of
cultural and historical niceties.   Imported theories,
such as dependency or staple theories, while useful in
some settings, can also place blinkers on local
analysis.

Even in the same country one man's dream of
development is often another's nightmare.   Steel plants
and major highways can bring affluence, exciting new
technology and open up new territories...They can also
generate pollution, dual economies and social discord.
Development used often to be defined rather narrowly as

rapid economic growth, driven largely by capital, and measured by soaring gross national product 1; nowadays economists warn that such views were tritely simplistic. They emphasise the income inequalities that aggregate indicators can mask; they note the corrosive inflation and structural distortions that can come from unbalanced growth (especially when concentrated in a very few towns).2 Development now is more and more defined to embrace a sense of 'balance', a capacity to adjust to changing external circumstances as well as to altered internal priorities, a mix of social as well as economic changes. The 'appropriate' form of development is now no longer seen as 'obvious', nor are traditional 'economic principles' so clearly the 'right basis' for development plans. For example, that familiar anchor - the concept of 'comparative advantage' - only really helps one understand a static world, it does not provide a prescription for future specialisation; nor should past configurations dictate future investment patterns, albeit they may temper them.

Development for whom? Development at what social costs? Development at what risks? Development over what time period? Development under whose auspices - surely not the multinationals? But where does foreign investment fit? How, if sought, can it be controlled to relate to national and regional goals? Such questions have to be asked and answered. They are important when national policies and strategies are designed. They are just as salient at the regional level. As circumstances change, so also might the appropriate answers.

Regions themselves have to be agreed upon - and again that very process can have many shapes. Administrative regions, problem regions, geographical regions, political regions, 'solution' regions (such as poles of growth), ethnic regions, homogeneous regions, international regions...the list goes on and on. It warns of pitfalls unless treated seriously. Regions that may be convenient for administrative reasons, may well prove economically unviable, and so on.

The appropriate list and weighting of development goals for a region, given all these caveats, is obviously not easy to draw together, let alone to get consensus on. Ideas such as 'self-sufficiency' are tempered by 'at what costs to the region and to the nation?'. Yardsticks of regional 'equity', such as average per capita income, regional measures of output or services, can mask substantial inequalities; they can also be prescriptions, if all regions are to get similar treatment, for balkanisation and uncompetitive industry. 'Equality of opportunity' has a breath of the brave new world - but how far is even that to be taken? Should a family living in the middle of a desert or on top of a mountain be provided with schools comparable to those in populated areas? Where do cut-offs lie? To what degree should jobs be moved to people? To what extent should policies emphasise mobility of people to jobs? So many jobs, moreover, in today's societies are heavily subsidised even when located in the wealthier, industrial regions.

It is, of course, easy to ridicule extremes. Regional development issues, however, are rarely extremes - they are normally blurred. Regional development goals and policies are generally the product of compromise - of compromise between ill-defined concepts of efficiency and ill-defined concepts of equity. They are the product of compromise between embarking on challenging but uncertain futures and holding back, propping up the sleepy industries, the familiar villages, the social patterns of a past that is often romanticised as some 'golden age' by those who have never lived through it. It is little wonder that governments have problems tackling regional development in an assured manner: they have normally been guided by very mixed signals. Canada3 and the European Community4 are no exceptions. It is unlikely that any African nations will find regional development policy making any easier.

While the balance of this chapter focuses on aspects of the EEC regional development experience from a Canadian vantage point, from the perspective of the African continent, three aspects may be of note:-

a)   In evolving agreements, such as the Lome Conventions, and in interpreting them, the European Community (for all the good-will that may sometimes exist) will inevitably be conscious of its own domestic regional problems. To those in developing countries, with sometimes rather tougher difficulties to resolve, these might sometimes appear not large problems. To the Community, however, they certainly are serious and they constrain the readiness of the Community to be outward-going in external relationships, particularly with developing countries that are often competing in many of the same product markets as the poorer regions of the EEC.

b)   The EEC framework as a whole, for all the internal wrangling among the ten member nations, has weathered innumerable problems and survived. The longer-term benefits to be gained from broad regional associations appear significant (for example, in energy efficiencies and in economies to be gleaned from greater industrial specialisation); yet the EEC experience suggests shorter-term conflicts may be inevitable and sometimes they will require more drastic restructuring of agreements than international bureaucracies can seemingly cope with fast (for example the recurrent difficulties over the Community Agricultural Policy and the Community budget). Were the Community a full-fledged federal entity, such as Canada, Australia or West Germany, it is inconceivable that such distortions in expenditure patterns would have been able to continue so long.

c)   A large number of instruments to facilitate more balanced regional development have been established within the EEC at large. While some of these instruments are at the Community level, others have been designed by the separate member governments. Such instruments have many lessons of the 'nuts and bolts' kind - and a study of them can be productive. However, to be reasonably effective such regional instruments require substantial political direction, as well as coherent links with the broader national development goals and policies in such sectors as industrial policy, transport policy, social policy, fiscal and monetary policy. Regional instruments are of little benefit unless they are both integrated with, and reinforced by, broader national policy and planning frameworks.

ii)   Regional Development Problems and the EEC: severe problems as distinct from short-run adjustment issues

     The main regional problems in the European Community can be viewed in two groupings. Some are essentially short-run adjustment problems, the product of changing economic structures or social preferences and customs. In some cases some workers may have to move short distances to new jobs as a consequence of plant closures, or new industries will be brought in -

212

but the problems are essentially of short duration. They are not discussed in this chapter. The other group of regional problems, however, is deep-rooted. The problems have persisted over many years - and, in many cases, have weathered all kinds of government programing efforts. It is this latter structural cetegory that caused the European Community to join with member governments to reinforce their efforts in regional development policy.

Where are most of these kinds of severe problems to be found? The more peripheral regions of the Community have tended to be less economically vibrant, according not merely to the more traditional clutch of economic indicators - such as per capita output and regional unemployment rates, but also when the criteria are broadened to include various social data and productivity yardsticks.5 Even though a large proportion of the populations of these peripheral areas are linked to a rural way of life, agricultural productivity measures are generally low in comparison to central EEC standards. The gap between the richer, more industrialized regions - places such as Hamburg being extreme examples - and the poorer less developed areas, such as regions in Ireland and (yet more impoverished) Southern Italy and Greece, is substantial. In some of the more extreme examples, the ratios (for yardsticks as average per capita output) come out as high as 6:1 in favor of the wealthier regions.

The main kinds of regional problems that have proven persistently difficult fall into relatively few categories.6 They are not all, by any means, solely rural in nature. Some indeed, such as urban congestion and pollution, are the product of rapid economic growth; others, such as obsolete industrial towns, are its aftermath. Seven main problem categories will illustrate the range:

a)   Old industrial areas that are facing problems in adjusting to sweeping structural and technological change. In addition to high unemployment levels and the run-down character of much of their industrial plant, these areas usually suffer from severe environmental degradation and poor quality social infrastructure. Productivity measures are low. Such areas include Genoa and its weak shipbuilding industry; much of the northern U.K., with its historic reliance on steel, shipbuilding and textiles; coal and steel

213

areas such as Charleroi in Belgium, and so forth. It
is a relatively long list and one that raises difficult
social and political problems as well as complex
economic ones. For example, when is a major steel
plant and its dependent community 'obsolete'? At what
stage should radical and not 'piecemeal' surgery be
applied? How far should governments go in propping up
towns based on old industrial plants? Should they so
routinely seek to enable such towns to diversify into
other fields through subsidised industrial estates,
labour and capital or does this risk a second round of
distortion, namely the poor location for the new
activities that have been 'bribed' to locate there? In
Canada, with its huge distances between many towns,
this is of major concern. In densely-populated Europe,
however, it has far from been resolved.

b)   Urban growth problems, where the cities are
dominating very broad areas yet have failed to digest
effectively the influx of people - often daily
commuters - from outlying communities. Many such
communities have been swollen not only by people from
the rural areas of their own country, but also
(especially in the 1960s) by migrant workers from other
parts of the Community and from outside. In turn, many
of the suburbs have themselves become enmeshed in the
urban sprawl. London, Paris, Milano, Lyon,
Amsterdam...the list can go on and on - indicative of
the sweeping move from agriculture and rural-based
activities over the past decades and the rapid growth
of the urban concentrated service industries in Europe,
a sponge-like growth that now threatens to have reached
a 'plateau'. Among the issues are appropriate
immigration policies for the Community, the degree to
which urban controls are both practical and politically
acceptable, and the extent to which rural development
can become more labour-intensive, given income
elasticities of demand for agricultural production.

c)   Rural stagnation problems, where adjustments to
the changing face of agriculture have either been slow
or, at best, not fast enough to enable farmers to earn
decent livings even when protected through C.A.P.
Inadequate infrastructure and lack of alternative
employment opportunities within the region has been a
characteristic of many such rural areas - as already
noted they are particularly serious in the more
peripheral regions of the Community. Prior to 1973
there was a widespread haemorrhaging from these
regions, of the younger and more versatile workers, to

214

more prosperous parts of the same country (for example from Southern Italy to the Milano-Torino triangle) or outside the country to industrial growth points of the Community, particularly in West Germany. Since the economic slowdown of the past few years, there appears to have been a damming-up process taking place in these poorer regions with disturbingly high unemployment levels as one outcome. Were the more industrialised parts of the Community now booming, a fairly radical approach to revitalising these depressed areas might be conceivable - even at the expense of the richer farmers in the more Northern areas of the Community. At this juncture, however, such a stance would appear politically impossible. The entry of Greece has further aggravated the situation, since its agricultural produce is in direct competition with areas such as Southern Italy.

d) <u>Frontier regions abutting the East European bloc</u>. This problem, peculiar to West Germany, is nevertheless deep-rooted and a daily reminder of the European war history. West Germany has developed incentives to encourage greater developments along these extreme and artificial borders, with some assistance from the European Community.

e) <u>Mountain village areas</u> where inadequate infrastructure compounds the problems of isolation and terrain. This applies particularly to parts of Italy, France and Greece. The degree to which such areas can be provided with adequate rural services, especially in the face of poor long-term economic prospects, is a complex social and political issue.

f) <u>Environmental destruction problems</u>. These clearly present problems of major proportions that are being treated very differently by member countries. West Germany, France and the Netherlands appear to be quite successful in their integration of environmental guidelines into regional development planning. Italy, in particular, appears to be far from on top of the problems.

g) <u>Ethnic divisions</u> are also frequently linked to regional economic difficulties. Affected groups periodically perceive themselves to be ignored by their national governments and believe they are eligible for additional regional development aid and improved representation. The extreme case is perhaps that of Belgium - where equal treatment of Flanders and

Wallonia is now so emphasised that incentives are given, regardless of the industrial problems that have particularly hit Wallonia while Northern Belgium has been booming (until the past year or so).

All but one of these problem categories can find their Canadian counterparts. For example, industrial Cape Breton - with its aged steel plant - is a prime example of an old industrial area that has had seemingly unlimited subsidies poured in without signs of real success on any appreciable scale. The area limps along largely on the proceeds of patronage. The urban growth problems are similarly to be found - perhaps Montreal being the extreme 'problem' case. Rural stagnation and its challenges are faced in areas as far apart as Newfoundland, the Gaspe of Quebec and the Interlake of Manitoba. The isolated mountain areas are perhaps best matched by Canada's more Northerly communities, such as Nain or Makovik in Labrador. The environmental destruction problems are perhaps less severe in Canada - with only one tenth of the EEC population and a land area of some ten times the size. But a Northern ecology gives for fragility and the proximity to the U.S. is far from unproblematic - in such cases as the pouring of industrial waste into the Great Lakes and acid rain. Ethnic issues, particularly focussing on Quebec, have played a major role in Canada's regional policy frameworks. Only, thus, the border with the East European bloc is a radically different category. Canada is hardly seeking to populate its Northern defence lines.

iii)   Frameworks for Regional Policy Responses

The discussion has so far focussed on problems. What are the general EEC policy responses? Essentially the broad (as distinct from localised) policy responses have been at two main levels - that of the national government level and that of the European Community level.

a)   National Government Regional Policies7

The national government level of response to regional problems has been far from homogeneous or sustained. It has varied, as one might expect, very greatly from country to country and, within a country, from government to government. Some systems, such as the French and British, have been relatively centralised in their approaches: yet they have sought to balance the capitals with other poles of growth.

216

Others, particularly West Germany with a federal system, have sought to bring a degree of harmony to different approaches. Belgium, with its Flemish-Walloon situation, has been dominated by tensions to match favours equally, regardless of economic circumstances. Italy has sought to tackle extreme Southern disparities, yet also has many Northern and Central problems. The Netherlands have excelled in detailed land use planning, because of the very congested nature of their remarkable country. They have even encroached upon the sea.

The range of regional policy instruments, used by the member governments, has been vast (for examples, see Table 9.1). It has included tax concessions and a galaxy of direct subsidies to industry, all kinds of infrastructure support, training and research and development assistance, investments by state corporations, advance factories, mobility aids and so on.[8] In the case particularly of Paris and London, controls on industrial expansion within the cities have also been imposed. In Italy, a minimal proportion of public sector expenditures has had to be funnelled into the South.

Several strands of theoretical logic have played a role in defending such programmes (even though sometimes only after the event). They include the broad concept of growth centres, both as a balance to major cities and also as "poles" of attraction for more rapid growth of depressed regions; and the concept of inter-industry economies, bolstering the case for state involvement through mechanisms as industrial estates and state corporations.

In general terms the 1960s saw the national governments being relatively innovative and energetic in much of their regional development programming.[9] However, since 1973 there seems to have been a more conservative approach followed; in large part this was brought on by the radical change in the economic climate, but in part - no doubt - it was a reflection of the rather patchy nature of the results of some of the regional policies in the 1960s. Despite some massive investments, the record had frequently not lived up to the aspirations and promises: Southern Italy was not the only region that could claim its 'cathedrals in the desert', nor were all the industrial estates bursting with clients, even before the oil crisis.[10] Le désert français was served by some

grand, but rather uncompromisingly unlinked, super-
highways that fed out from Paris - but the 'desert' had
not gone away!11

Yet, there seems some consensus that the 1960's
saw a modest reduction of regional disparities in most
countries as well as many obvious improvements in local
infrastructure facilities.

The post-1973 era, in contrast, appears to have
witnessed a widening of many of the gaps once again.12
The national governments have increasingly been faced
by the spectre not merely of relatively high levels of
unemployment in the less prosperous regions, but of
mounting unemployment levels - particularly among the
young, older workers, women and disadvantaged groups -
on a national scale. In such circumstances
considerations of regional balance appear to have been
diluted as national governments have focused on key
sectoral developments such as energy, transport and the
recurrent nightmare of the steel industry.

b)   European Community Level Regional Policies

The European Community level of regional policy
has sought to be complementary to, and not in
competition with, national regional policies.13 It has
always been viewed in terms of 'additionality'. Commi-
ission programmes have been designed not to displace
national regional efforts, but to reinforce them. A
second principle has also been important - namely the
goal of bringing greater harmony to the overall
regional efforts of the Community at large, as distinct
from more balkanisation of effort and unproductive
competition, for example in the form of competing
grants for the same industrial plant, between regions.
Prior to 1973, the European Community level approach to
regional development appears to have been somewhat less
aggressive than post 1973.

1958 - 1973 Policies

In the earlier phase of the European Community's
life, before the six founding members were joined by
the U.K., Ireland and Denmark, much of the concern was
to ameliorate such damaging impacts the abolition of
trade barriers between member nations would have on the
poorer regions. The European Investment Bank was then
the only major regional development instrument at the
Community level, although even it was not exclusively

an instrument for regional development. While other
Commission programmes and activities had substantial
regional effects, initially they had few regional
guidelines. Just as it still is, the EIB was
fundamentally a development bank. It raised its funds
on the European and international capital markets, as
it does today; and - just as now - it loaned these
funds to a variety of projects - industrial,
agricultural, transport and energy projects, as well as
other infrastructure activities such as irrigation,
water supply and sewerage works. Many loans went
directly to the industry concerned; some others were
through the mechanism of a global loan system - whereby
lines of credit were opened to regional or national
financial institutions and they, in turn, made
sub-loans to small and medium size industrial ventures,
chosen according to criteria agreed upon with the EIB
(see Table 9.2 for an overview of EIB lending patterns).

The EIB, when it was established in 1958, adopted
two principles of importance to this discussion and it
has faithfully pursued them. The first was to loan the
bulk of its funds in the less developed regions of the
Community. Over 2/3 of EIB loans have met that
guideline between 1958 and today. As of January 1984,
the Bank had made loans in excess of 24,000 million
European Currency Units, and some 40% had gone to
investments in Italy. The second principle was to
foster projects of common interest to more than one
state, as a mechanism for strengthening the fabric of
the EEC. Some 40% of the EIB loans have been for
projects that fulfill that principle. Some loans, of
course, were able to meet both criteria.

The European Investment Bank was, I think it fair
to say, a product of a viewpoint that was widespread in
the late 1950s, that capital was essentially the engine
of growth - and that its selective infusion into
developing regions and countries was at the hub of the
development process. Inadequate attention was paid to
cultural differences and infrastructure depth as
between the industrial heartlands of Europe and their
poorer regions, many of which resembled Third World
countries in many regards. Nor has the pull of the
metropolis nor the dragging effect of dependency been
adequately appreciated. This was the era of the
Harrod-Domar growth model, of post-Marshall Aid
euphoria, and the like. Probably more was expected of
the EIB's involvement in regional development than

would today appear to have been reasonable. It was also a time when regional disparities appear to have been viewed more as aberrations from the expected economic norm (whereby capital should quickly be attracted to labour surplus/low wage areas and surplus labour to labour scarce/higher wage areas). Being a time of national boom - there was optimism that regional problems could quickly be resolved. Exactly the same kind of thinking was apparent in Canada. Cultural differences tended to be downplayed. Hence, other potential European Community regional instruments, such as the Social Fund, played a most passive role up to 1973. Even agricultural policy, forever the big spender, was not particularly sensitive to regional imbalances in the earlier period. The European Coal and Steel Community played very much a sector specific role; most of its endeavours were focussed on the old industrial area category of the problem.

It is also important to note that, prior to the 1973 period, regional development was viewed as something of a secondary consideration to the European Community as a whole. The central rationale for the EEC was trade rationalisation and the strengthening of the economic muscle of the Community at large. There is little, in the Treaty of Rome, about regional development. Moreover, the years leading to 1973 saw substantial overall economic prosperity and growth. There was a widespread mood of optimism about the adjustment process. It should be emphasised that every one of the six member countries then had some rapid growth regions within its borders - an important factor politically for such an economic philosophy to have held credibility.

Post - 1973 Policies

1973 was a watershed year. The oil embargo and its aftermath shattered much of the self-confidence on the European economic scene. The entry of three new members (the U.K., Denmark and Ireland) added new dimensions to the regional problems the Community already was experiencing - particularly in Italy. The shipbuilding problems of Scotland and Northern England were now placed beside those of places like Genoa; U.K. textiles were floundering against external competition - subsidies and cross-subsidies were so rampant that any untangling was inevitably going to be a political nightmare and contain enormous social implications, unless alternative employment was forthcoming. Ireland, similarly, brought a low-productivity rural sector that contrasted sharply with that of the South of England or the Netherlands; it added to the French agricultural dilemma. Yet even without the events of 1973, it had been becoming clear that the European Commission, itself still lacking a real European Parliament, was going to be challenged to play a greater role in fostering a regional development framework within the Community at large.

But how far was the Commission to go? The traditional view was that West Germany had been the major beneficiary from the EEC trade policies, France had 'cleaned up' from the agricultural policy, Italy had been helped, particularly, by the regional development work of the EIB. Moreover, the entire Commission budget still accounted for less than 1% of EEC GNP and there were strong pressures to ensure its containment.14

Over 70% of that total budget was fuelling the agricultural policy - and much of the funds were going to wealthier farmers in richer regions via dairy and cereal subsidies.

What have been the main changes in European Community level approaches to regional development - post 1973?

First, there has been a steady trickle of studies - many of considerable merit as informative and analytical documents. These are certainly useful for those interested in comparative ideas and approaches. But studies, for all their merits, do not generate development.

Second, there has been a steady stream of exhortation from the Commission and from committees, such as the Economic and Social Committee. The tenor of these pronouncements has been consistent. A recent (fifteenth) General Report (1981)15 will give the flavour:

> In view of the widening regional
> disparities in the Community and
> the deterioration in the causes of
> imbalance brought about by the
> economic crisis, the Commission
> considers that Community regional
> policy must be more sharply focussed
> on the most important regional

problems and its instruments made
more effective...

Third, in 1975 the European Regional Development
Fund was established. Its annual disbursements (less
than commitments because of time lags) are still only
some 5% of the total Commission budget (see Table 9.3).
Or if comparison is made to the nearest Canadian
equivalent to that fund, the recently absorbed
Department of Regional Economic Expansion, DREE, had a
budget about half of the size of the ERDF. Yet the EEC
population is more than ten times that of Canada's.

Fourth, the European Social Fund and the European
Investment Bank have both expanded their activities -
with the larger proportion of their funds going into
the poorer regions. There has been a continuous flow
of directives to these instruments - as to all of those
managed by the Commission - to be more regionally
sensitive in their priorities and programmes, as well
as to target more narrowly on those perceived in
greatest need, such as the young, women, the aged.

Fifth, the Community Agricultural Policy has
continued to grow absolutely though not relatively to
the overall Community budget. Nevertheless more than
70% of the 1983 budget still went to agricultural
policy; some 7 times as much as has been routinely
disbursed by the European Regional Development Fund
will have been spent under the Agricultural Policy on
dairy subsidies alone. The greater proportion of the
agricultural budget still finds its way to the
wealthier regions, despite efforts - especially under
the guidance section - to impact increasingly on the
poorer regions.

Sixth, the European Parliament has emerged,
slightly faltering and still defining its role. Thus
far it does not seem to have cut much ice regarding
regional policy, nor can it be expected to in the near
future.

Finally, the attitude of the member governments to
the entire Community budget process has tended to
remain one of striving for their 'fair share', rather
than the development of a framework that would take
serious account of the extreme regional imbalances in
the Community. For example, there is no regional
adjustment programme - such as the Canadian federal
fiscal equalization programme16 - to serve as a

transfer conduit from richer to poorer regions. Nor is any such a framework apparently on the horizon, despite periodic reports on the subject. Indeed the very approval process on the budget has become more and more divisive in recent years.

Postscript on the European Regional Development Fund

Some further remarks on the European Regional Development Fund are warranted. This is becoming something of the centrepiece symbol of European level regional policy - just as DREE once did in Canada - with all the same risks, as other agencies are tempted to shirk their own regional development responsibilities.

The European Regional Development Fund was established as a grant allocating agency to enable the European Commission to play a more supportive role in regional development. Two principles have underpinned its aid:

a) The grants have been viewed as supplemental to the regional development assistance given by member governments, hence are tied to their own regional development programmes; effectively the national governments are reimbursed some of the costs

b) ERDF aid is limited to designated areas; the criteria for area designation are normally determined by the respective, national governments.

All but some 5% of ERDF grants have been allocated within the framework of a national quota system.17 Over time the ERDF has fostered a programming approach by the member governments - of between 3-5 years duration, so there is a clearer framework for fund assistance. Not all governments have responded to this approach with enthusiasm, but over time improved documentation has been emerging from the process - and, through such a mechanism, the ERDF has started to play something of a catalytic role. Some of the regional development programmes (for example for the Netherlands) are good models for regional planning documentation, at least for industrial countries.

Much of the ERDF infrastructure assistance has

223

tended to favour industrial estate complexes with energy projects also gaining increased attention. About 30% of total ERDF aid has gone to projects in the industrial and service sectors (as distinct from infrastructure) and a large proportion of all ERDF grants has gone to relatively big projects (i.e. 10 million e.c.u.'s and over).

In the overall scheme of things, and even in comparison with the European Investment Bank, however, the ERDF is relatively small. Over the first nine year's of the Fund's life (1975-83), actual payments totalled some 5,046 million e.c.u.'s (or 55% of commitments), while in 1983 alone the E.I.B. advanced loans of 4,247 e.c.u.'s. One issue is whether the Fund should be radically scaled upwards. An ERDF official, in making a case for more resources, remarked (to the author) that, given the dimension of the Community's regional problems, ERDF annual disbursements represented the allocation of but one packet of cigarettes to each man, woman and child living in the less wealthy regions. Even in the context of Community budget priorities, the ERDF expenditures pale beside those poured into subsidies for dairy or cereal production in the more affluent regions.

Yet, while the Regional Fund is small, it still is one extra brick in the fabric of the Community. By its very existence, it serves to confront members with the challenge and the dimensions of the regional problems that, to a large degree, will have to be tackled by their own member governments. From a regional policy vantage point, it is definitely a useful addition. It may be small - but on the bright side it is in the 'right direction'.

iv) Conclusion

In absolute terms, such as miles of roads built, new schools opened, improved medical services and the number of industrial estates, the European Community (just as Canada) can demonstrate much progress in the less prosperous regions. Some fraction of that progress can be directly associated with both the regional policies and programmes of the national governments and also with Community level development agencies.

In relative terms, most regions that were substantially behind the richer regions in 1950 are

still so in 1984. The same is the case in Canada:
Alberta, because of its oil and natural gas reserves -
is a rare exception. Relative disparities that
promised to narrow during the decade before 1973, now
seem to have broadened again in the post-OPEC oil
embargo era as unemployment and plant closures and
slow-downs became Community-and Canada-wide.

A widespread reassessment and some disillusionment
with regional policies has been one result. A number
of questions are being asked with increasing frequency.18
To what extent should policy focus be narrowed to urban
redevelopment from broader regional development? To
what degree should emphasis be placed on basic needs or
on manpower training, rather than on strategies for
industrial development in peripheral regions? To what
extent should the state play an interventionist role or
simply 'patch up' emergency problems - leaving market
forces to determine the appropriate directions and
priorities? Are regional development programmes really
cost-effective investments, in contrast to programmes
(in more prosperous regions) with shorter 'pay-back'
periods? To what extent should policies seek to stop
disparities widening, as distinct from narrowing them?

In the European Community and Canada many of the
problems and approaches have had a certain similarity,
including the difficulty of clarifying goals and
gaining consensus on quite broad regional development
directions. One final note should, however, be made of
a sharp difference.

Regional policy in Canada, over the past fifteen
years at least, has largely been set against the
backcloth of Quebec. The federal government has been
concerned that Quebec could separate if, among other
things, the Quebec electorate felt their economy was
falling too far behind that of Ontario, in particular.
That concern has coloured the shaping and
administration of all recent federal regional
programmes in this country.

In the case of the European Community - regional
development policies have been set against a very
different kind of scenario. The Community has been
expanding geographically. 1973 saw three additional
members with new adjustment complications; 1981 has
seen Greece join; Spain and Portugal are lined up. Such
new members from the Mediterranean region will

generate more competition problems with many of the
poorer regions of the present Community - for example
the Mezzogiorno and its wines, citrus fruits and
cottage industries. They will also compete for the
scarce regional aid funds and this will increasingly
confront the Community with tough questions about how
far goals of improved standards of social services,
basic infrastructure and more equalised regional
employment opportunities and incomes should be
advocated. Or is it to be a Community of very unequal
partners? How far can richer members, such as Germany,
be squeezed to transfer funds to the less prosperous
parts, particularly when Germany herself is
experiencing severe economic difficulties? The debate
is far from ended.

Notes

1. For a useful discussion, see A.K. Caincross, "The Place of Capital in Economic Progress", in L.H. Dupriez (ed), Economic Progress, Papers and Proceedings of a Round Table held by the International Economic Association, Louvain, 1955. This is reproduced by Gerald M. Meier, Leading Issues in Economic Development (Oxford: Oxford University Press, 1970 (second edition)) pp. 180-185.

2. For a current assessment, see Malcolm Gillis, Dwight H. Perkins, Michael Roemer and Donald R. Snodgrass, Economics of Development (New York: Norton, 1983) pp. 261-285.

3. For a controversial review of Canadian regional development approaches, see Ralph Matthews, The Creation of Regional Dependency (Toronto: University of Toronto Press, 1983). For a more orthodox account, see N.H. Lithwick, Regional Economic Policy: The Canadian Experience (Toronto: McGraw-Hill Ryerson, 1978).

4. For a useful overview, see Paul Romus, L'Europe et les regions (Paris: Fernand Nathan, 1979).

5. For a painstaking comparison of regional disparities, see William Molle, with Bas van Holst and Hans Smit, Regional Disparity and Economic Development in the European Community (Farnborough: Saxon House, 1980).

6. For further discussion, see Ian McAllister, Regional Development and the European Community (Montreal: The Institute for Research on Public Policy, 1982) pp. 1-27.

7. Among useful reviews on national policies for regional development in the EEC are: Miles M. Hansen, Public Policy and Regional Economic Development (Cambridge, Mass., Ballinger, 1974); Organisation for Economic Cooperation and Development, Regional Problems and Policies in OECD Countries (Paris: OECD, 1976); R. Petrella (ed), Le developpement regional en Europe (The Hague: Mouton, 1971); R.H. Williams (ed), Planning in Europe (London: George, Allen and Unwin, 1984).

227

8. See, for example, Douglas Yuill, Kevin Allen and Chris Hull (eds) Regional Policy in the European Community (London: Croom Helm, 1980).

9. McAllister, Regional Development and the European Community pp. 44-48.

10. K. Allen and M.C. MacLennan, Regional Problems and Policies in Italy and France (London: Allen and Unwin, 1970).

11. J.F. Gravier, Paris et le désert français en 1972 (Paris: Flammarion, 1972).

12. See, for example, Commission of the European Communities, The Regions of Europe (Second Periodic Report on the Social and Economic Situation and Development of the regions of the Community) (Brussels: Com (84)40 final/2, 4 April 1984).

13. Among the more useful documents on Community level regional policies are the annual reports of four main Community instruments that focus (to varying degrees) on regional development. These are: the European Investment Bank, the European Regional Development Fund, the European Social Fund and, because of its scale rather than because it has yet any clear regional focus, the Common Agricultural Policy. A detailed review of Community level regional policies is to be found in McAllister, Regional Development and the European Community.

14. For a good discussion, see the Report of the Study Group on the Role of Public Finance on European Integration, Chairperson D. MacDougall (Brussels: Commission of the European Communities, 1977).

15. Commission of the European Communities, Fifteenth General Report on the Activities of the European Communities in 1981 (Brussels: Office for Official Publications of the European Communities, 1982).

16. For a useful review, see Economic Council of Canada, Financing Confederation (Ottawa: Canadian Government Publishing Centre, 1982) pp. 11-36.

17. In 1984 this approach was marginally changed to give the Commission somewhat greater flexibility in the allocation of ERDF grants. Minima and maxima ranges have now been identified for each member country, effectively increasing the non-quota element to some 12%. The world 'quota' is no longer used. It is premature to speculate whether the Commission will actually gain much greater influence in its relationships with the member governments as a result of this adjustment.

18. See, for example, David Pinder, Regional Economic Development and Policy :Theory and Practice in the European Community (London: George Allen and Unwin, 1983) pp. 105-106.

Map 9.1

Synthetic Index of Inequality in the EEC
(Based on GDP and Unemployment, Average 1977-1979-1981)

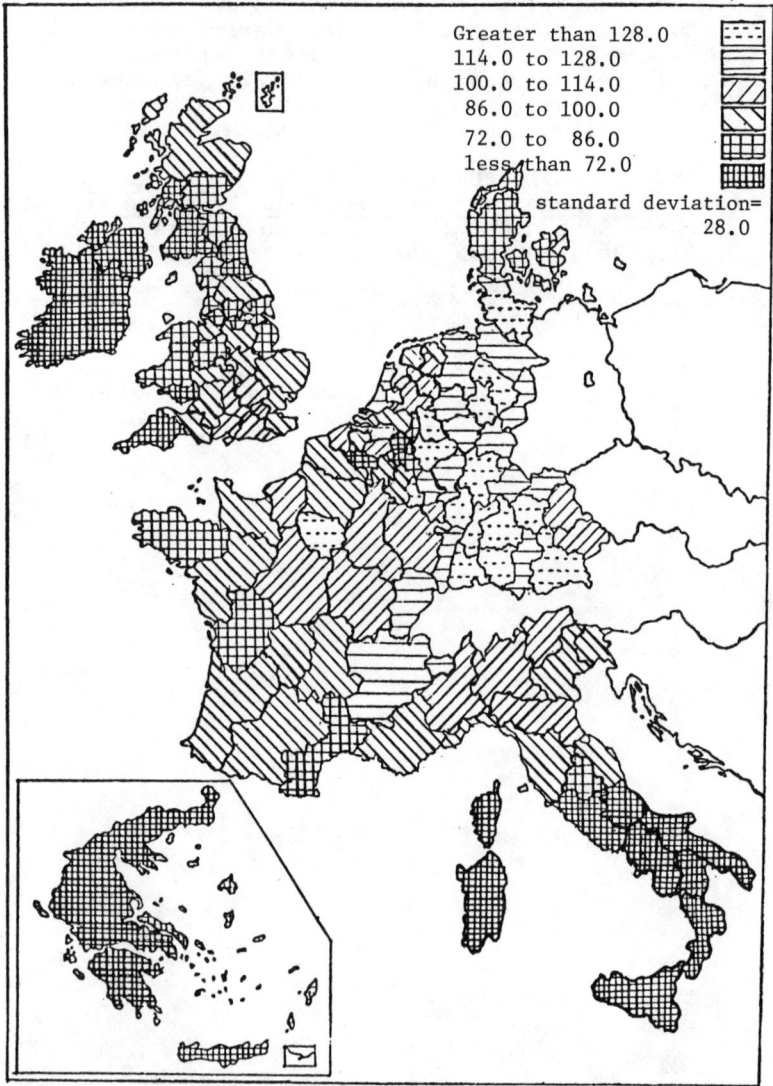

Greater than 128.0
114.0 to 128.0
100.0 to 114.0
 86.0 to 100.0
 72.0 to 86.0
less than 72.0

standard deviation=
28.0

The Greek Regions have been added to this map even though they were not included in calculating the synthetic index.

Source: Commission of the European Communities The Regions of Europe Brussels: Com(84)40 final/2, 4 April 1984, 7.1-1.

Table 9.1.1

FINANCIAL INCENTIVES APPLIED IN THE FRAMEWORK OF REGIONAL ECONOMIC POLICY IN THE COUNTRIES OF THE EEC

Category	B	DK	G	F	IRL	I	NL	UK
1. Capital grants (investment grants & investment allowances)								
--buildings	A	A	A	A	A	A	A	A
--equipment	A	A	A	A	A	A	A	A
--working capital	-	B	-	-	B	-	-	-
--rationalization & reorganization	-	-	B	-	B	B	-	-
2. Ready built factories	-	B	-	-	B	-	-	B
3. Ready built factories & industrial sites at reduced prices (including factory rent concessions)	B	A	-	A	B	B	B	B
4. Soft loan schemes (interest rebates and/or concessionary loans)	A	A	A	B	B	A	B	A
5. Credit facilities								
--medium and long-term credit banks	-	-	-	-	-	B	-	-
--loans with state guarantee	B	B	B	-	B	-	B	-
6. Labour grants (employment premium)	B	-	-	B	B	-	-	A*
7. Tax exemption								
--accelerated depreciation allowance or special depreciation allowance	B	-	A	A	A	B	A	B
--from profits	-	-	B	B	B	A	-	-
--from income	-	-	B	-	-	-	-	-
--export profit tax relief	-	-	-	-	A	-	-	-
--from consumption of energy (oil, natural gas)	-	-	-	B	-	B	-	-
--other tax exemptions (business tax exemptions, local registration fees, turnover tax, property income)	B	-	-	A	B	B	-	-
8. Training (very often applied nation-wide)	-	B	B	B	B	-	B	B
9. Transfer premiums								
--decentralization idemnity & decentralization allowances	-	B	-	B	-	-	-	B
--decentralization grant for artisanal subcontractors	-	-	-	B	-	-	-	-
10. Incentives to incite labour to leave problem regions	-	-	-	-	-	-	-	B
11. Incentives to incite labour to move to problem regions	-	B	B	B	-	B	B	B
12. Capital removal grants or allowances for the relocation of firms	-	B	B	-	B	-	B	B

231

Table 9.1.2

FINANCIAL INCENTIVES APPLIED IN THE FRAMEWORK OF REGIONAL
ECONOMIC POLICY IN THE COUNTRIES OF THE EEC

Category	B	DK	G	F	IRL	I	NL	UK
13. Equity participation	-	-	-	B	B	B	-	B
14. Reduction of public utility tariffs								
--transport	-	-	-	B	-	B	-	B
--electricity	-	-	-	-	-	-	-	-
15. Preferential regime for public tender	-	-	B	-	-	B	-	B
16. Regional allocation of public orders (government expenditure)	-	-	B	-	-	B	-	B
17. Regional allocation of public investment	-	-	-	-	-	B	-	-
18. Social security concessions	-	-	-	-	-	A	-	-
19. Marketing assistance to firms	-	-	-	-	-	B	-	-
20. Location controls (disincentives included)								
--location tax (levies)	-	-	-	A	-	B	B	-
--building licence	-	-	-	A	-	-	-	A
--notifications in respect of new industrial buildings, installations and offices	-	-	-	-	-	B	B	-
21. Deconcentration of administration, consultancy & data processing activities (research activities grant included)	-	-	-	B	-	-	B	B
22. Redistribution of fiscal receipts	-	-	B	-	-	-	-	-
23. Artisanal schemes	-	-	-	B	-	-	-	-

Legend: A - a major instrument of a country's regional policy.
B - an instrument available for some very specific regional purposes.
* - The regional employment premium was abandoned in January 1977; however a labour premium is applied in Northern Ireland.

Source: N. Vanhove and L.H. Klaassen, Regional Policy - A European Approach (Farnborough: Saxon House, 1980), pp. 310-12 (drawing on a series of OECD and EEC publications).

Table 9.2

Financing provided, by the European Investment Bank, from 1958 to 1980, and 1983.[4]

	1980 Amount (million e.c.u.)	1980 %	1973-80 Amount (million e.c.u.)	1973-80 %	1958-80 Amount (million e.c.u.)	1958-80 %
COMMUNITY						
Belgium	153.2	5.2	318.6	2.6	385.8	2.6
Denmark	99.3	3.4	307.1	2.5	307.1	2.1
Germany	14.2	0.5	547.4	4.4	901.0	6.1
France	279.0	9.5	1739.8	14.0	2310.2	15.5
Ireland	376.0	12.7	1076.9	8.7	1076.9	7.2
Italy	1290.3	43.7	4752.7	38.2	6165.0	41.4
Luxembourg	--	--	--	--	9.0	0.1
Netherlands	--	--	62.3	0.5	105.2	0.7
United Kingdom	688.0	23.3	3421.3	27.5	3421.3	23.0
Non-Member Countries (1)	50.8	1.7	200.8	1.6	200.8	1.3
Sub-Total (2)	2950.8	100.0	12426.9	100.0	14882.3	100.0
OUTSIDE THE COMMUNITY from the Bank's own resources	371.4	67.8	1381.5	69.3	1537.2	64.6
from budgetary resources	176.3	32.2	631.2	30.7	844.1	35.4
Sub-Total	547.7	100.0	1994.7	100.0	2381.3(3)	100.0
TOTAL	3498.5	--	14421.6	--	17263.6	--

Source: European Investment Bank, January 1981.

(1) Loans granted for energy projects in Austria, Norway and Tunisia but of
direct importance to the Community.
(2) Including loans from the resources of the New Community Instrument for
borrowing and lending (1979:277 million e.c.u., of which 105.3 million in the
U.K., 86.7 million in Ireland and 85 million in Italy; 197.6 million e.c.u.,
of which 137.8 million in Italy, 41.7 million in Ireland and 18.2 million in
Denmark).
(3) Of which 351.4 million e.c.u. in Greece prior to its accession to the
Community (341.4 million e.c.u. own resources. 10 million e.c.u. budgetary
resources).
(4) Loans granted by the EIB for 1983 were 4,682.9 million e.c.u. (exclusive of
a further 1,211.8 under the NCI facility, the bulk of which went to Italy
and Greece for earthquake reconstruction). Source: Commission of the
European Communities: Seventeenth General Report, 1983. Brussels, pp.62-63.

Table 9.3

European Regional Development Fund grants (by Member State)[1]

	1983		1975–83		
	Number of invest-ment projects	Assist-ance approved (million ecu)	Number of invest-ment projects	Invest-ment involved (million ecu)	Assistance approved (million ecu)
Belgium	42	8.88	346		77.84
Denmark	102	22.40	659		105.52
FR of Germany	232	43.75	2021		456.09
Greece	209	361.48	694		823.10
France	961	285.42	3647		1369.03
Ireland	103	102.16	795		551.30
Italy	1035	818.96	7993		3493.55
Luxembourg	0	0	9		6.94
Netherlands	14	20.14	65		120.16
United Kingdom	955	458.44	5185		2172.44
Community	3683	2121.61	11745	70141.60	9175.97

[1] Over the first nine years of the Fund's operation, from 1975 to 1983, payments totalled 5046 million e.c.u. (or 55% of assistance approved - a lag occurring between the approval process and actual payments for projects undertaken).

Source: Commission of the European Communities, Seventeenth General Report of the Activities of the European Communities in 1983, Brussels, 1984, p. 154. (It should be noted that this table is not identical to that in the source, due to some errors in the former).

Chapter Ten

Knowledge for Decision-Making: more beating of dead

horses who still won't lie down

Sharon Sutherland and Avrim Lazar

i)   Introduction

Ideologies are seductive because they promise what
is most wanted. They are irresistible when there is any
possibility that they might deliver on their promises.
The modern official, elected and appointed, is necessarily attentive to the system of myths called "rational
government." The promise that the complexities of
governing in the modern world--the competing interests,
the multidirectional and interacting effects of each
decision, and the richness of alternative views of
"reality"--can be reconciled by the application of
demonstrable, scientific certainties is not easily
shrugged away. Simplifying models with their manageable
number of variables and orderly one-way relationships,
equations with their if-then certainties, and the
precise quantities expressed in statistical series are
the charms that promise to control the stream of difficulties that can follow a decision in any part of the
global village.

In its benign form, rationality in decision-making
indicates only the use of reasoned arguments and evidence in choosing one alternative before others. But
more and more frequently since the advent of the information age, the process of gathering and combining evidence is elaborated until its separate keepers begin to
believe that a perfect process should generate perfect
outcomes--and, at the least, that no outcome is fully
satisfactory unless and until its formative stages have
been fully and perfectly processed. In other words, the
process of rational decision-making comes to be valued
for itself. This is what is intended by the term
"rationality ideology."

The promises of the rationality ideology are seldom
stated in a very direct way simply because they are so

235

obvious: real knowledge for decision-making.

To those who subscribe to the rationality ideology, a decision-maker in a rational system is, first, armoured in facts, second, girded by a model that is true to the causality of the immediate situation, and, third, armed by reliable knowledge of the smaller system's place in a larger system that is accurately aligned with world historical forces. Such a decision-maker is by definition productive, in harmonious interplay with other forces, and well-placed to anticipate and deflect shocks from beyond the boundaries of the fully-articulated system. In this view, traditional politics is denigrated--a clumsy struggle of raw interests, bumbled through in ignorance.

It is easy to recognize this rationality ideology at work in the large-scale rationalist planning projects of the 1960's and early 1970's. The social indicators movement, for example, was a potent myth across Europe and North America. It was believed that a wide-spread sophistication in the conduct of both hard and soft scientific research, joined to the new capacity to record, retrieve and report, could be used by all governments to bring about development and to prevent shocks to national systems. It is much less easy to recognize the distortions introduced by wishful thinking about what might be attained by rationality if "reason" were to be applied retrospectively to events that have already occurred: the past can seem like an open book to us simply because it has already happened and we have a memory of it. "Systematic retrospective rationality" is a useful label for the large-scale use of the techniques of applied scientific research to ascertain exactly what government programs have accomplished in the past (and are accomplishing currently)-- this information to be used in forward planning. This earnest backward search for landmarks passed in the dark is currently designated by a variety of names--program evaluation, effectiveness evaluation, program results and impacts studies. The basic assumption is that it is a duty to establish systems to learn precise lessons from the past--not just general strategies--so that no lessons will be lost. It is thought that government officials can and should track costs and benefits from various program modalities in a very conclusive scientific manner, assess these results against the standards pledged in official statements of goals and objectives, and then use the information for accountability and to improve the outcomes of government action in the future.[1]

Thus rationalist technique is intended to generate facts to substitute for the primacy of political choice in future action.

In this chapter we criticize attempts to ambitiously and systematically enlarge the use of pure reason in policy-making for two reasons. First, the attempts never work. Second, they can cause positive harm: they are not a good star to steer by. The harm comes about because the systematic attempt to achieve rationality in all spheres creates a profound and qualitatively new confusion of the traditional, formal political process with the management process. The management process in this confusion acquires unjustified legitimacy--and thus gradually and perhaps irreversibly enlarges its scope for action at the expense of the traditional political process. The "rationality process" takes on the attributes of a separately valuable goal rather than being seen simply as a means to assist in guiding political choice. An example may be useful: in the Canadian federal system there is a growing if implicit norm that a problem is really fair game for a "political" solution via intervention by a Minister only after "normal" intra-bureaucractic policy analysis procedures have been exhausted and have not suggested a feasible technical solution.2 Thus the traditional political process, wherein a Minister imposes an outcome (i.e., a value--his legitimacy stemming from his link with a majority of the electorate) begins to be seen as second best. (But of course the rational-technical bureaucratic process is not politically neutral, even though the agenda is difficult to discern).

One can see this trend to worship process rationality as a different and more serious phenomenon from that identified in case studies of individual decisions where "the facts" are used by bureaucrats to divert individual substantive outcomes from directions first set by the political leadership. Where these occasions are individual, independent campaigns across the shifting politics-administration front, we are talking about a campaign to make these individual forays unnecessary--an alteration to the decision-making culture. With this shift, "political" matters are routinely pushed back on the agenda, or are re-described as predominantly managerial problems. Political actors lose control of the political agenda to administrators.

The following sections of this chapter sketch the main reasons that retrospective-rationalist schemes

cannot succeed in the first of the two basic tasks they
set for themselves: a) the routine creation of conclusive information about program accomplishments for all
significant areas of public expenditure, and b) the
effective use of such conclusive knowledge to guide
future expenditure and improve bureaucratic and political accountability. The model that is in place in
Canada is described as a case study of a retrospective-
rational system. Canada--of all developed Western coun-
tries--almost beyond doubt has the most highly developed
system to encourage routine development of information
through applied research undertaken in administrative
settings. The final part of the chapter is an attempt to
suggest suitable (or at least more suitable) directions
for getting appropriate, cheap, fast, and suitably-
reliable information for use by governments. It is not
intended to enter the debate about whether or not social
science is possible per se. This chapter leaves aside
the prior question, making only the less ambitious claim
that a pure social science, even though feasible in
another setting, could not be performed one day after
another in administrative settings to generate pure
truth on a routine basis.

ii) Generic Problems with the Mission

There have of course been many warnings, from a
variety of scholars of administration, against ambitious
schemes for rational planning. Critics have charted the
failures of dirigist and even of more modest "indicative" planning. As long ago as 1959, Charles Lindblom
in his article "The Science of Muddling Through" made a
forceful case for cautious tiny steps that built from
the status quo--i.e., for no planning as such.
"Muddling through", a term Lindblom used to connote a
guarded optimism, brought small successes and avoided
flashy disasters. (More recently Lindblom has, in
Usable Knowledge, suggested strategies for weighing
specialized research knowledge against ordinary knowledge, and hinted at alternative strategies to what
might be called head-on social scientific attacks on
public problems.)3 Yet while scholars could reject
rationality in the abstract, they could not reject it
as their pratice--it is, after all, the world view of
scholars. And managers, ever vulnerable to the promise
of idealized rationality, embraced it, showered schemes
to improve rationality in decision-making with resources, and put them as close to the centre of governments as they could manage. Hence in the 1960s and
1970s system-makers were in many Western countries given

unprecendented resources to develop bases of knowledge
and information on one particular policy area to pano-
ramic indicators of progress in all policy areas.4   As
the rationalist systems were put into operation, the
earlier "in principle" critiques were importantly sup-
plemented by critiques that were themselves empirical.
That is, "science-oriented" analysts were driven to
look, more or less dispassionately, at the quality,
actual utility to real decision-makers, and potential
usefulness of the information that had been generated.5
They were shocked at the low quality and uselessness of
most of the work they reviewed.

        Through this broad literature that first warned,
and then documented the failures of ambitious attempts
to routinize the collection of facts for decision-
making, a number of problems are mentioned time and
again.   These most significant "generic" difficulties
we summarize below.

a)   Vague Goals or Multiple Implicit Goals: In the
application of the rationality ideology, measurable
goals must exist to serve as standards against which
the accomplishments of public policy efforts can be
assessed.   But many valid and important public programs do not have clearly-defined goals that can be
translated with acceptable accuracy into measurable
indicators of what the program should be doing.   Some
programs are legitimately best thought of as symbols to
remind the population of national dreams--Canadian
"multiculturalism" programs are an example.   Members of
our various national and racial groups are photographed
with arms thrown around one another's shoulders, or
doing their vibrant dances without let or hindrance,
and these images serve as ikons to exhort tolerant
behavio r from the population.   Another dream-reminder,
perhaps less obvious, is the subsidy for postage on
indigenous Canadian magazines.   It is hoped that the
potential subscribers will be led, by price if nothing
else, to prefer our Maclean's to the other place's Time
magazine.

        And even pragmatic programs can elude attempts to
stipulate worth.   There is a wealth of evidence and
viewpoints on the Canadian Defense Program, for example.
The guns and warheads and men can be counted, but
whether they are too few or too many, and for what, we
are unable to agree (presumably until a war concentrates
our minds upon a goal).

Another example of necessary spending is for mental hospitals. Again we do not know what goal we seek. Must hospitals routinely and effectively cure the insane so that they become productive members of society? This seems to be an impractical demand. Should they then merely offer comfort to the insane and protect them from harm? Should they at the same time maintain public order? If the programs are meant each to accomplish several goals, then one must ask whether the goals will necessarily be compatible and if not, which goal should be given priority. To ask for a priority is generally to return the ball to the political level. (The empirical work, if it does anything, will then show the politicians which of the multiple goals is most realizable within current constraints. This creates an interesting if gratuitous pressure to stay with the status quo).

Demands for a clear expression of a single quantifiable goal can also obviously be a form of political debate. The quantities that one chooses to examine can show who wins and who loses, depending on what baseline is chosen. Thus the provision of a single, quantified goal will often mark a fairly arbitrary political trade-off. The policy struggles vis-a-vis the representational characteristics (representational of Canada's founding nations--the French and the English) of senior federal bureaucrats affords an example. Not until 1970 could a simple administrative doctrine be formulated that fairness demanded that the public be served in its own language, and that the Francophone working-level in the federal public service would require management in its own language for reasons of efficiency.6 The tool that would enable the "solution" of the problem at the administrative level--that would result in allocation of more jobs to francophones--was the decision that the characteristic of speaking French, or being willing and able to learn the other language, could form an element of merit in job competitions. Now, however, the situation is quite changed. Hence English-speakers demand to know why certain positions are designated as "bilingual imperative", and by whom. The issue is being repoliticized by demands for the lately-administrative facts from English-speakers who now believe that they are disadvantaged in the quest for high appointed office.

In a different vein, demands for quantification can lead, consciously or unconsciously, to substantial biases toward areas that most readily meet auditing criteria. For example, there is some evidence from agencies that make grants for development projects that

240

resources "migrate" to technocrats. New projects and grass-roots producers are disadvantaged by the reporting standards necessary to receive grants. A desire to reward objective output leads to rewarding a paper process that can be epiphenomenal to attainment of the main goal.

In summary, at best the needs of the model for precise goals will be frustrated by many useful and traditional government activities. At worst, "rational investigation" can readily disguise an attack on an earlier political trade-off, or it can re-enforce the status quo by being blind to seemingly obvious characteristics of a situation. Indeed, it can do both at the same time. Like most human actions, rational processes in context are founded on some arguments and make others.

b) Little Knowledge, "No Results": Related to the "goals" problem is the knowledge problem. The rationality ideology simply assumes we can possess the demonstrable, causal knowledge that can give us the technical capacity to do what we think we want to do. This is a far-fetched assumption. Much of what we need does not now exist, and in some areas is highly unlikely to be created. All governments use resources in ignorance of the exact outcome that should "scientifically" be expected. They do so out of cultural and political values.

Empirical research conducted to explore a contemporary problem, even if conducted painstakingly according to the positivist model of proof, will as often enlarge the area of uncertainty as reduce it--because the results will inevitably suggest other, sharper enquiries. Programs of research are seen to be necessary, because a sole study can seldom provide information that can tip the scales to a decisive use of resources in an innovative way. But whole programs of research are more suitably part of the process of science--not of administration.

Further, even when whole programs of research have been conducted, "rational" administrators and decision-makers are capable of ignoring their imperatives. A compelling scenario can capture the field. For example, it is now accepted that the Canadian National Energy Program initiated in 1980 was founded on premises that contradicted the majority of evidence-based predictions. The NEP was designed to deal with the worst-possible future. Those who implemented it did not assign a heavy value to the difficulties that would be caused by the policy itself if the dreaded future did not come about.

The "no results" problem is of course the cause of the "no knowledge" problem in the policy sciences. But it is fair to say that it is more acute in research conducted by and for administrators than in research conducted in traditional research settings. This is simply because administrative research is much more likely to accept compromises in the model of proof. Typically, studies of administrative success that appeal to scientific standards will find that they cannot establish a positive program effect, or that any effect they can discern is minor. The scientific model of proof involves overturning the null hypothesis. In program language, the null hypothesis states that the manipulation in question (the program) is not demonstrably causally linked to the variables in the problem set (made no difference to the problem or situation). In the science model, the logic works against false positive claims because lack of reliability in measurements "dilutes" the strength of results. Thus the effect is conservative.

But precision of measurement is almost impossible to achieve in field settings. Likewise, programs are not mechanically administered, but involve important areas of discretion. The result is that all kinds of error dilute effect. Thus the programs appear to be ineffective, but as an artefact of the research, quite apart from their merits or demerits. Some researchers recognize this problem, yet claim that it is insignificant because the top decision-maker can weight the probability that the research is in error in an ultimate, Baysean calculus of probabilities of specified outcomes following upon a given decision.7 But this argument is disingenuous, not least because of its assumptions about the characteristics of top decision-makers. Our leaders may not have progressed past pie-charts, as American legislative auditors have lamented.8 More directly, the basic point is that research conducted in administrative settings can be so flawed that the margin of error is indeed unknown and inestimable, and therefore there is only a fiction to weight in the Baysean calculation.

Perhaps the earliest and best-documented example of the strategic use of the "no results" phenomenon to obtain a substantive effect in a policy field is in the corrections field in the United States.9 Study after study found no effect toward rehabilitation from a great variety of programs. Observers and policy makers were moved to despair: if "nothing worked", why try anything to attempt to rehabilitate offenders? A simple "show me" became a useful weapon for those who were a priori against a program: as soon as the onus was on program proponents to prove that their initiative could be successful, they were lost in the swamp of method. It look some years before comprehensive critiques of the "no results" consensus were available to those who wished to work with offenders.

A strategy for the use of research in political ways is thus clear. If one is opposed, one pushes for the statement of measurable objectives against which the success of the effort can be scientifically assessed. The objective research leaves the impression that the program accomplishes little or nothing. If one supports something, the incentives are to deflect direct study. Encourage study of anything but the core of your effort. Depending on the kind of political apparatus that is in place, the strategic, sub-political use of research can be more or less destructive.

Again the application of the rationality ideology is seen to be at best ineffectual and at worst a covert pursuit of political values. The pursuit is outside the normal political forums where the public or their representatives express their values and argue for their own views and interests.

c) No Rule for Choosing Between Methods: In implementing the rationality model, the researcher/program evaluator/analyst/consultant will typically only use one of the compendium of techniques that are appropriate and affordable for investigation of the chosen problem. Major examples of approaches and techniques are cost-benefit analysis, experimental research, censuses or samples through survey methods, and the various designs for statistical analysis of administrative data. Each approach-cum-method has its own characteristics, and each will generate a qualitatively distinctive report. Each is "most appropriate" on certain soft criteria for any given project. Virtually no-one can be equally at home with all methods. There is no objective rule to guide the choice between methods. (In fact, a first task for a critic is to assess the qualitative biases inherent in the choice of method). This is another indication that the problem is not one of technology, but rather one of choosing which values should be maximized in any particular situation. Again we see choices at the administrative level potentially filling the space normally occupied by traditional political action. And because our myths claim that all our action is based on fact rather than on chosen values, we draw closer to the mocked situation wherein, to change political direction, it becomes necessary to re-write "objective" history.

Scholars who are interested in methods as an object of study bear no responsibility toward those who are oriented to subject fields, and want only useful research tools. The same publishing house that kept us at the edge of the state of the art when program evaluation methods were being elucidated now keeps us at the state of the art in the debunking exercise. The November 1983 Sage publisher's catalogue announced a new edition of Struening and Brewer's Handbook of Evaluation Research and on the same page advertised Beyond Method by Gareth Morgan. Where Struening and Brewer deal in "hard data," Morgan deals with softer stuff. His theme is that researchers actively create "knowledge" as a result of the assumptions that guide the research process. He juxtaposes "21 different research perspectives that highlight significant links between assumption and method." Therefore, despite the use of rational techniques, the outcome of any one research project is frankly open to choice based on values.

d) Personnel: Impossible demands for total objectivity, impartiality and precision in task execution will be made of the personnel who are to accomplish the research. If there is no bridge, the person who is supposed to cross the water is required to have some special qualities. Alas, the system still ends up being peopled with people. In the absence of clear procedures and decision-rules, and manageable amounts of work, people see what they have been taught to notice, favour some things over others, and cut corners on one study so they can get on to another. This of course is one of the oldest criticisms of "systems" approaches. Its applicability to the rationality ideology will be obvious from the arguments sketched above.

e) Research 'in vivo': The problems associated with the rationality model are not limited to absurd attempts to implement it wholesale. Even modest, pragmatic attempts to generate conclusive knowledge on a systematic basis will fail to routinely create the kind of

244

information that can in itself justify choice. Certainty in research always declines as one gets closer to real life and further from the elegant simplicity of the laboratory. In studying government programs one is close to the limiting extreme. The possibility of adequate controls and thus certainty all but disappears because the object of study is continually changing and being acted upon by factors which are themselves continually changing.

This series of families of problems is perhaps a re-statement in a more concrete manner of the "little knowledge, no results" problem--but put in real terms to convince "practical" people.

One family of problems stems from rapid changes in the environment. The object of the policy--the problem-- does not remain stable through the administration of the program nor through the cause of the research that studies the program's result. Major variables cannot be controlled or suspended so that the net effect of the program (conceived as a manipulation) on the problem can be determined. Say that a government implements a year-long patrol of highways to decrease traffic fatalities and injuries. What would have happened without the program? Because we had it, we can't know for sure. A number of other factors may have varied significantly during the year, for an unknown impact. Some that suggest themselves are the weather (visibility and traction), driver training and licensing regulations, regulations governing alcohol or stimulant consumption, types of automobiles and other vehicles on the roads, congestion of main arteries perhaps through repaving operations, and factors affecting the installation and use of seatbelts or other safety equipment. We can only deduce what the patrol program's net effect was by conducting a series of soft comparisons with fatalities for that period in other jurisdictions.

Even program boundaries, although ostensibly under the full control of the administrative apparatus, may well be shifted before the research can be completed. The earlier-noted 1975 review of all evaluation activity in the United States (note 5) showed that research projects of less than 18 months duration generally yielded information of doubtful reliability. It was not unusual for a large evaluation study to last five or even ten years. The framework that specifies the boundaries of the planning entities--the programs--normally evolves at a considerably faster rate. That is, what

constitutes a program is a rolling choice. Reformula-
tions of programs make it impossible for the researcher
to gather the base or comparison data against which the
proposed program's accomplishments might be measured.
That is, the cost base shifts so that even this kind of
prosaic certainty will elude us. In Canada, there is
the example of the Guaranteed Annual Income Experiments
of the early 1970s. Data generated in this research
are still being analysed in the Department of National
Health and Welfare. Canadian social policy has evolved
almost without direct reference to the result of the
experiment.

And even when a program has remained stable over
time, it most often does not represent an entity that
has a basis in a testable scientific theory. Instead,
problem sets and research entities arise from the
bureaucratic context. Data are gathered along lines of
contemporary administrative or political expedience.
It is unlikely that their scrutiny will yield up the
laws of nature in the form desired.

Baseline data is also very scarce. It is probably
worth re-stating a truism that seldom occurs to people
when they have been directed to "find out" something:
one observation by itself will generally be meaningless.
Only once the investigation is well underway, or when a
result is being interpreted, does it become clear that
without some "norm" or earlier set of observations the
new information is meaningless. As well, statistical
series that were supposed to serve to norm current
information can be irrelevant or misleading because
definitions have been altered at crucial junctures in
the past. "Banks" of information that were supposed to
shed light on one another prove to be collected on
incompatible assumptions. Or it is found that the
event that is forcing the current round of decision-
making is quite different from any that went before--or
even that the rules that used to relate variables no
longer seem to apply.

f)   Costs and Benefits of the Activity not Identifiable:
The use of resources on large-scale rational systems and
on the scientific model of proof for program accomplishment is a choice like any other. It reveals priorities
for the use of resources, and can be challenged for
evidence of success like any other priority. Further,
the choice to devote resources to systems that promise
to direct, control and hold to account in itself embodies values and makes claims about the nature of

reality. Demands for accountability in the use of public resources that go far beyond what is customary elsewhere in the society are a sign of pathology. They are covert attempts to delegitimize a line of action. So far of course, the benefits of elaborate rational systems have not been tested against their overt goal: to ensure that a fair public benefit--known in advance, chosen by political actors rather than by officials, and net of the cost of the system--has been achieved for the expenditure of resource. A demand to prove the benefits of rational systems is of course as dishonest as the challenge to "prove rationality" of any activity. In general, comprehensive costs--both direct and indirect-- are not calculated. The results are difficult to pin down because changes for the better cannot be attributed definitely to the one factor alone, or allocated in part in an exact way. Hence benefits are more often claims of disasters averted--going to hell in a hand-basket--then of positive triumphs. In short, like other government activities, the pursuit of a rationality model for decision-making is based on values--in this case a belief in elaborate, system-wide research--and not on certain knowledge of actual results.

iii) Case Study: Decision-Making in the Canadian Federal Government

     The central rational system in the Canadian federal government is the Policy and Expenditure Management System (PEMS). It is an elaboration of a planning-programming-budgeting system10 that is too sophisticated to mention planning in the label, but is in fact determined to do long-term planning and to use the plans to control the budget. It significantly involves a linking of the political stratum with the bureaucratic system for rational management. The purpose of the linking is ostensibly to enhance the capacity of the top bureaucratic level to be responsive to direction from the political level while (and, arguably, by) controlling initiatives that emerge from the departmental administrations. Advocates and detractors alike are agreed that PEMS is a thorough-going attempt by the government to organize its operations in order to achieve the full benefits of the rationality model of decision-making.

     In the federal government, therefore, the entire expenditure budget of each department is divided exhaustively into program entities in the planning-programming-budgeting sense. In the program budget, expenditures are grouped and described under the "goals"

247

that government intends to achieve through that application of public resources. Every expenditure is conceived to have a potentially-measurable outcome that is publicly expressed in its own program goal. The whole of the government's activity is described in a manner designed to be represented in an integrated, results-oriented systems diagram.

Each program's anticipated result is to be audited against actual accomplishment by whatever innovative research method suits the problem. The usual entities for audit--the organizations, the sets of accounts and records of transactions, the management information systems, the routine safeguards for use of machine-readable information, the processes for hiring personnel, and so forth--are of course scrutinized by traditional methods. This information is foundational for the government's professional program evaluators who conduct or commission original research to establish whether, and to what extent, official planning objectives have been achieved. The "external" auditor of the government then conducts his own determinations of economy and efficiency and provides critiques of government's work for his own forum--the Public Accounts Committee of the House of Commons.

Both bureaucratic and political decision-makers at the highest levels must, in theory at least, pay close attention to the findings of rational information-gathering by program evaluators and auditors. Each major sector of government is headed by a committee of the political cabinet that has decision-making authority delegated to it from the full cabinet. Each sector is provided with a fixed budget by an inner cabinet that represents what the country can afford for that priority. Each sector/cabinet subject committee has its own secretariat. These sectoral secretariats are made up of the senior officials of the sectoral departments and a dedicated staff to serve them. Any new policy proposal from a department that has spending implications must be screened and assessed by the permanent secretariat on rational grounds before it can be submitted to the political policy committee for approval in principle and later funded in competition with all existing programs (whose habitual-incremental budgets are scrutinized by Treasury Board). These "A-base" budgets for established program entities take the first bite out of the cash allocation for the sector. Funds can be freed from the existing program base if the sectoral politicians can agree. It is part of the annual planning

cycle that existing programs are evaluated for their
success by departmental "evaluation units." Hence
decisions to free funds are ideally taken in the light
of information gathered in the routine program evaluation exercise.11 Ineffective programs are in this
manner to be replaced by programs that are better in
context. The limited total resource for the sector and
the constant pressures to spend more and to take on new
functions is itself the incentive to cut expenditure on
ineffective programs. One can describe the idealized
process as one of continual review of the sectoral
expenditure base, by the medium of the objective evaluation of each and every program (program component/
planning element) in that base.

The significance of using the program budget to
present the estimates of expenditure to Parliament is
considerable. It is an attempt to unite bureaucratic
categories of the budget--the ways that the money really
is spent--with political categories that state goals
and thereby represent the promises made to the electorate. Everyone is supposed to be able to talk about
the same thing, to debate its merits. And not only
spending projections, but in fact the accountability of
both politicians and the highest officials is also for
the program entity--that is, for the goals that were
used to present the plans to spend the money. In 1977,
the Government passed legislation that allowed the
external auditor (officially styled the Office of the
Auditor General of Canada) to conduct his own applied
research--quite free of the accounts of expenditure or
any normal financial control system--and express "audit"
opinions on entities of his own choice. The incumbent
at the time and his successor have chosen to increasingly emphasize the program entities as the shape of the
PEMS system has become more clear. It is important for
some of what follows to understand that while the
Auditor General tables his report with the Public
Accounts Committee of the House of Commons, he takes no
direction from either the government or this committee
as to his choice of audit topics, audit entities or
methods. He is as independent in his sphere as a
provincial government.12 The government-side central
agency, established in 1978, is the Office of the
Comptroller General. From 1977 to the present, it has
guided the establishment of departmental "evaluation
units," and tried to set feasible standards for the
normal conduct of evaluation research.13

In summary, we have in Canada a system that guarantees that all expenditure is classified under a goal-type heading, and that information will be generated in the bureaucracy on each and every such entity.14 The system further guarantees that information will be aggregated upward, by placing sectoral decision-makers in a situation of controlled competition for known, limited resources. Every penny is spent under the heading of one or another promise, and every promise is monitored to see whether it is being kept. Promises that are not kept are, at the least, candidates for a close scrutiny to see if the resources can be devoted to a more fruitful enterprise

a)   Current Problems in the Canadian Implementation

The new apparatus for rational decision-making in the Canadian Federal government is scarcely five years old, but already many incisive critiques exist.15 Observers are agreed that the system centralizes control over resource allocation by the complexly differentiated cluster of central agencies that serve the cabinet. (It seems to be assumed that this means that political control is enhanced). It is further argued that the principles underlying choices and negotiations at the highest levels of decision-making are more often explicitly stated. Even purely political "end runs" on the rationalist-administrative system have become, if not more rare, at least much more visible. Because the system has become so formal, agendas tend to be both formal and known in advance because the participation of key players must be negotiated. Hence a Ministerial perambulation around the cluster of officials into the Finance Minister's office takes place on high ground. There have been several occasions where the Finance Minister has set up an earmarked fund for a particular project.16

But here we are less interested in the effectiveness of the system for centralizing, routinizing and rationalizing all resource demands (there will always be some "political" appeals that are handled outside the ideal process if only because there will always be some Ministers too powerful to take a rational, majoritarian "no" for an answer) than in its success in "rationalizing" most normal resource allocation. The criteria of rationalization would be that the system ensures that most or at least many programs are evaluated and their objective worth is determined, that the system is rich in up-to-date information on roughly

250

comparable programs that are in contemporary competition for funds, and that the information is reliable enough and convincing enough to play an important role in the decision-making. That is, while control over use of resources may well have been concentrated in the new system, we are primarily interested here in whether or not control is being exercised in accordance with rationalist principles.

We see problems in several areas. These we have called 1) incomplete implementation, 2) slippage on the "model of proof" that guides the production of evidence about program accomplishment, and hence production of unreliable information, or information whose reliability cannot be assessed, and 3) the general muddying of the political culture and the covert politicization of the administrative level, (particularly the external audit function).17 These are by no means perfect categories , but they suggest in a concrete manner the difficulties that emerge in the field under a drive to establish comprehensive rationality. They are all manifestations of the intrinsic problems described earlier.

b)   Incomplete Implementation

Under this heading are included all the major practical reasons that the new system has been only partly implemented.

First, we must admit that dollar costs of trying to run the new system are not even approximately known. The top central agency apparatus to administer the new system is indeed newly implemented, and the budgets of new organizations can be summed. But this exercise, although tempting, is not quite fair because some parts of the new strucures were taken from existing organizations, hence not all of the cost is due to the new system. In any case, it would be difficult to interpret any figures that emerged.

Perhaps the easiest tactic to get a rough idea of the overhead imposed by the Canadian idea of rational government is to compare the weight of the central agency structure in Canada with that in culturally similar jurisdictions having less-ambitious management sytems. Available comparisons of Canadian effort with that of the American and British govenments indicate that the central agency structure--the articulation of the system just below the political apparatus--is

251

proportionately several times larger. Indeed, some U.S./
Canada comparisons indicate that there are Canadian
central agencies that are larger in absolute terms, let
alone proportionate.18 Much of the growth in the executive levels of the Canadian central agency structure
has come about since the new system was put in place.

Another indicator is the "external" legislative
auditor's budget. It is fair to include this budget as
part of the system costs, because the Office of the
Auditor General is a necessary part of the overall game.
It is the "tough cop", funded by government to report on
adequacy and fairness of government's own information.
Its budget has increased from 14 million dollars a year
just before the 1977 enhancement of the mandate to 38
million in 1983; an increase of 173 percent whereas the
growth of the federal government overall has been at a
rate of 108 percent for the same period. In addition,
the special-purpose central agency that was set up in
1978 to ensure that internal information-gathering is
complete and timely (The Office of the Comptroller
General) has seen its own budget increase more rapidly
than general government growth, although not so quickly
as that of the "external" auditor.

At the top, then, at the level of consumers of
information, one can say that implementation of the new
system was energetic. But the story is different at
working levels. The government-wide initiative to gather
empirical information on the effectiveness of all programs was not itself conceived to be a separate "program"
at departmental level. Resources for conforming to the
government-wide policy have had to come from the "fat
of the land" in each department at a time of severe
restraint on overall levels of spending. It is not
surprising then that pragmatic adjustments have been
made to the ideal of a complete grid of studies.

The "cycles" of five years during which all elements of the departmental program framework were to be
studied has lengthened dramatically in some departments.
In 1978, the Comptroller General of Canada estimated
that there were roughly 2,200 entities that would
require investigation ("evaluation components", "chew-
able chunks") in the federal government's expenditure
base. All were to be assessed for their suitability
for investigation through "evaluation research." As it
now stands, 41 of the 56 departments and agencies
falling under the OCG's responsibility have established
the program evaluation function.19 It is not known

what proportion of the total of program components identified by these departments was eventually (if it is yet completed) scheduled for evaluation, but OCG policy definitely assumes that exclusions should be rare. For illustrative purposes, we can assume that fewer than one-half would be excluded. If the whole expenditure base were to be covered in the five-year cycle, then, it would be necessary to evaluate at most 440 entities each year, and at least 220.

One need only look at the "facts" about the numbers of studies that have been completed. In December of 1983, the federal government released a list of studies completed in 1982 and 1983.20 The titles add to 111 sutdies, of which 52 were completed in the first eleven months of 1983. Some of these are very specialized-- studies of the education programs of five native Indian bands are counted as five evaluations, for example--so there can be little doubt that the list is inflated. Thus even the most optimistic observer could not argue that the government would get much more than half through its "evaluable" base during the five-year cycle.21 Some departments evaluate a lot, others little. There is no wish to castigate the government side for basic good sense in not forcing the issue further, but one can on the evidence insist on the point that program evaluation in the Canadian federal government, despite policy and central apparatus, is not even reasonably broad in coverage. It is really quite selective. The selectivity is focussed largely from administrative levels. The manager who is about to have his or her program evaluated may well ask "why me?"22

It has not always been possible to acquire suitable personnel to staff the function, nor are the most sophisticated analysts distributed homogeneously through the system. Time constraints have forced heavy use of contract researchers, often inadequately guided and set impossible tasks. Research designs have not been standard in any administrative sense, although "affordability" has been a major concern. In important policy areas the object of study is, in a real sense, the fabric of Canadian society (for example, the impact of changes to the penalties for rape and assault)--small wonder that the results cannot be fitted into idealized research designs.

The end result is that no one expects to live to see an up-to-date grid of empirical information assessing some reasonable proportion of sensibly-comparable components of the sectoral effort, so that programs could be compared with one another, the best rewarded, and the worst denuded of resources. Somewhat ironically, the centralization of control and power needed to use the information is in place, while the information itself proves considerably more elusive. But it is not surprising, given the intrinsic impossibilities of the quest as outlined in the first part of the chapter, that resources in even a wealthy, determined jurisdiction should prove grossly inadequate.

c)   Slippage on the Model of Proof

Scientific research in the Western positivist sense is conducted according to formal standards. It is also better conceived as a process of investigation, review, critique and re-investigation on a controlled problem than as a way of providing one-off proofs of whatever we might like to know. Above all, scientific work is conducted in an open way for an expert public. The first tentative standards post-1977/78 for the conduct of the empirical work on programs were exhortations to work at "the state of the art"--to adopt the best methods of academic social science research. Indeed, the characteristic that was intended to distinguish the new effort from other kinds of assessment conducted in the bureaucracy (e.g. management reviews, or common garden analysis) was that findings were to be produced in the form of demonstrable knowledge about program outcomes--objectives and authoritative.

The external auditor's first "demonstrations" of what he expected the public service's studies to tell about program accomplishments continued to strongly aspire to the scientific model of proof.23 The office's paradigm was rationalist, designed to yield conclusive information that would hold the government to account for quality and effectiveness of management. If blame were to be laid, it should be on the basis of incontrovertable evidence. If more of the taxpayer's money were to be spent in an area, s/he should be assured that s/he would receive an utterly precise effect for that sacrifice.

The Office of the Comptroller General (the government side) then spent some time thinking about methods and reviewing the first studies generated by the departments in conformity with the new policy on program evaluation. Official guidelines for the conduct of evaluation research were first promulgated by the government in 1981.24 Pragmatism ruled, and the agency did not attempt to codify the research process in a pocket guide. Its message to departments was, "do the best you can with what you've got." Its view was that there are a great many "approaches" for conducting program review, some better than others depending on the context, and that the main thing was to get the work done in timely fashion. It also admitted in at least two places that research results would be but one contribution to the decision-making process. In other words, the one government agency with a direct responsibility for obtaining certain kinds of research products from all departments assumed not a rationalist perspective, but an administrative perspective.

A thousand flowers, therefore, continued to bloom. The program evaluation function is what each department allows it to be. It is unnecessary to say that none of the work done under the policy is useful. It is only necessary to say that the core of the system-wide rationalist scheme is empty, because the kind of work envisioned--timely, comprehensive across the expenditure base, "objective" and therefore allowing comparability of one program's results with another--has been impossible to produce in a mechanical way. The quality of work is as variable as the people performing the tasks and the problems they face.25 The completed studies are recognizable as the offspring of the parent program, but they bear no family resemblance one to another. They see the amount of daylight that the organizational culture of the sponsoring department can tolerate, but in an informal way. The work is not routinely published, nor is it routinely tabled in Parliament.26

d)   Muddying of the Political Culture

The task of deciding how to evaluate programs for outcomes is so complex that there is no publicly-comprehensible standard to dictate the choice of methods. Instead, there is exercise of "professional discretion" in the task.27 This complete discretion in a task wide open to the play of values is exercised in the administrative culture. Where the myths that guide the individual in daily conduct become so complex, and where their demands begin to conflict, one can expect to see signs of strain.

In the Canadian federal system, the covert conduct of politics in the guise of management issues is most apparent in the annual reports of the Office of the Auditor General. In successive reports since 1978 the

Auditor General has strongly and dramatically criticized
the government's incapacity to demonstrate that its programs are indeed effective. He has pressed for statement of measureable objectives in any number of politically significant areas such as industrial policy while,
calling for statement of measureable objectives for
Crown corporations that the government uses to pursue
national policy aims (and for their accountability
directly to Parliament rather than through the government). He has demanded that the government cease incur-
ring deficits. He has even demanded access to the
complete system of Cabinet papers and confidences
(including minutes of Cabinet meetings) so that his
Office can ascertain whether the policy-making process
leading up to cabinet decision is adequate: he thinks
he should legitimate it. (But the legitimate process
aleady exists--it is the one that Cabinet accepts as
adequate or appropriate to its needs, and can change
from Cabinet to Cabinet--and the right decision is the
one that emerges).

All this from an official whose "audits" can only
be believed if one can also believe utterly in his
policy impartiality. Because Canada has has a government of the one political stripe for some 15 years, and
because the "objective" research method leads to an
almost blanket demonstration of lack of effectiveness,
the effect is of a broad attack of considerable ideological consequence. Not even the political opposition,
while grateful for the ammunition, is in such consistent
opposition to the government or so scornful of its
attempts to direct the bureaucracy. The fact that this
kind of attack is tolerated by the political leadership--
and even very generously funded at the expense of other
initiatives--is a tribute to the sway of the rationalist
ideology in the culture. (The current political leadership is quite unpopular--perhaps a reason that it must
tolerate the rationalist erosion from within, and perhaps
also in part as an effect of the sustained rationalist
critique).

Even firmly grasped, however, this nettle has
plenty of sting left. It can easily be made to sound
like a wish to suppress all dissent and take a "government line." One hastens to say, therefore, that it is
not on the face of it wrong that this government should
be permanently condemned by a self-inflicted critique
of its management capacities. The problem is that such
a critique from supposedly neutral sources, and from
administrative levels, is not simple unvarnished truth.

It is, in important ways, the result of the method--a
system wide demonstration of the rule of the tool.
Nothing works. Energetic demonstrations that "nothing
works" can be selectively focused and selectively publicized, handling the new "scientific" research results in
the same way that the old audit results of fraud and
incompetence were handled. The result is a loss of confidence among the public that the problem, whatever it
is, is a fit one for attention by any government--or
perhaps only that this particular government is fitted
to handle a particular problem. Political goals can be
"tested" and dispensed with more rapidly than they can
be formulated. The rationalist dream has a way of
eating up all other dreams.

Both the political and top bureaucratic levels have
been made all the more vulnerable by the rich resourcing
of the "watchdog" role--the Office of the Auditor
General--while the departments must find resources from
within. The OAG can rightly condemn the departments
for not executing enough evaluation study, and for not
working to sufficiently high standards. But the departments cannot win. Should they begin to work to truly
scientific standards rather than administrator's
standards, "research" could well eat up their budgets.
As a reward, they would find the research difficult to
bring off successfully, difficult to interpret, and the
results would at best damn their programs with faint
praise. The Auditor General would then beat them with
their own stick.

The situation therefore creates strong incentives
for departmental managers to do as little "mandated"
research as possible, and to strategically focus the
work that is done, making the link between the method
of study that will be funded and the results that they
desire to see. They can protect a program that they
think is administratively sound, and offer up programs
that they think do not work well as more-or-less
controlled sacrifices to the "rationality mill." The
officers of the evaluation units are often in untenable
situations. To strive for perfect rationality does not
therefore yield almost-perfect rationality, but instead
creates barriers to informed management. Instead of
being a neutral tool to achieve ends that were chosen on
other grounds (other than their "amenability" to
monitoring by scientific approaches), "research" quite
naturally becomes alternatively a weapon, a danger and
a distraction in the interplay of "small p," bureaucratic politics.28

257

The Auditor General's steadily negative critique will doubtless continue through a change in government, so that in time it will be demonstrated that the Office is not partisan, and indeed that "nothing works" in public policy--not even a complete change in governors. For the moment, however, it appears that one political party has been objectively discredited as to its capacity to devise public policy and to manage the bureaucracy. In fact, its most significant management mistake may have been falling into the rationality swamp. It is unfortunately unlikely to be remedied with a change of political party.

For a variety of political reasons, an explicit rollback of rationality will not be possible for a long time. It would likely appear to the public to be suppression of the "facts"--of scandals of maladministration waiting to be unearthed by the new kinds of "scientific research" on the result of public expenditure.

One wonders how it is that three different kinds of control--scientific control in the sense of control over material forces, administrative control in the sense of ensuring (and monitoring) conformity to guidelines, and political control of the public service in the sense of providing leadership, and monitoring fairness and due process by being attentive to constituents' complaints--could have been allowed to become so intertwined.

What is the real harm is this? Some problems--a loss of faith in the capacity of public policy to affect change, a denigration of the competence of politicians as realists and as managers of the government, and a mounting impression that the bureaucrats are indeed uncontrollable by nature--have been suggested. In Canada, then, we have a mounting public enthusiasm for trimming the size of the central federal bureaucracy. But the "old civil service" of the federal government is by no means the fastest growing part of the public sector in Canada--in fact, if one removes the new central agency framework, the traditional civil service has grown little over the past dozen years. It is merely the most scrutinized part of the total public sector. It is also the most subject to control--much more so than growth of regulation or of crown-owned enterprises or even transfer payments to other levels of government. The effect is not ideologically neutral, because it is the old civil service that traditionally

258

supports what is known as the welfare state. Further, the control-justifying hypothesis that the political level does not have the capability of controlling the bureaucracy can become a self-fulfilling prophesy. Insistence on perfect control over perfectly rational decisions becomes a kind of double-speak in which ideological decisions--those taken on the basis of values and with effects on "who gets what"--are masked as something else and are taken outside the political level. Politicians at all levels stand to lose their capacity to mobilize popular interest and support for their initiatives, and in our federal system that coordinating level of government finds itself at a continual disadvantage in the competition among levels of government for public support. Things come unstuck.

And not at all parenthetically, one must observe that the fact that Canada is a federation increases the difficulty of planning and geting comprehensive, reliable and powerful summary information about program performance. Departmental programs are typically planned in headquarters, with their administration being decentralized to the regional or provincial level to various degrees. The recent government policy to encourage decentralization has meant that for many programs of concern it becomes meaningless to talk about "the program." Information gathered about the effectiveness of the federal government's employment centres in one city should perhaps not be generalized beyond the region and perhaps not past that city. Central resource allocators cannot be expected to master detail about literally dozens of program delivery sites. Still, it is difficult to believe that a summary of common aspects of nation-wide decentralized programs could be more than administrative statistics and truisms in the broadest possible categories. The most decentralized programs will prove least amenable for demonstrating strong effects, because aggregation makes no sense. They are therefore most likely to have to struggle for funds through the system's gate-keeping, despite the political level's emphasis on decentralization as a theme. It is arresting that such a defining characteristic of a political system could seemingly slip out of mind during the planning of the central control system for the federal bureaucracy. In fact, the embrace of rationality ideology has led to a centralization of the capacity to formulate problems and take decisions, but has not and cannot deliver the promised information needed to make the system and the new decisions work. The net effect is pernicious--in effect, one substitutes

259

the intuitions of central, distant resource controllers for the intuitions of those who are closest to the scene and who understand, if not what works, at least what is tolerable. Instead of muddling through, one gains the capacity to make the really big mistake. The regions become steadily more alienated, and the other levels of government become an opposition instead of a co-ordinate authority.

iv)   Toward a Rational Amount of Rationality

Some may say that the lessons to be drawn from the discussion of the intrinsic difficulties of rational systems and from the Canadian case are sufficiently clear: i.e., steer clear.

But the intention is not to justify a complete retreat from research. It is, instead, to suggest that the pre-requisite to a more effective use of research conducted on the positivist model of proof is to save it for the really suitable topic. To substitute for research conducted to scientific standards, one can suggest a more energetic use of kinds of investigation and problem refinement that are pragmatically suited to the administrative environment. In his 1979 article cited earlier, Charles Lindblom makes the point that incremental analysis is not the same thing as incremental politics: it is merely "analysis limited to any calculated or thoughtfully chosen set of stratagems to simplify complex policy problems, that is, to short-cut the conventionally comprehensive "scientific" analysis. 29 Because comprehensive analysis always fails, one is left with a portion of "information" that is not ideologically neutral, but is still "unchosen" in a conscious sense.

In a word, the prescription is that administrators should resist as unsuitable the attempt to generate conclusive, complete sets of information through systematic application of the positivist model of research. (And, by implication, politicians should forcefully resist any attempts by the administrative process to help with systems that will somehow rountinize the choice of goals.) Administrators should apply, instead, the more classical kinds of analysis-- approaches that require much more thinking than energetic creation of new facts. Problems should be selected with a view as to whether movement is or is not possible at the moment. Many useful, craftsmanlike books exist on the kinds of analysis that are fruitful in a variety

of organizatinal settings.30 Still, it may be of use
to list with only minor elaborations a few suggestions
about what this more modest rationality might involve,
if only to convey the flavour of the kind of work we
recommend.

a)   Problem Formulation: The way in which the research
problem is formulated is the single most important
characteristic of any piece of empirical research. In
scientific work, the problem statement is importantly
and closely controlled by the theory of the area of
study. In research conducted in administrative settings,
the problem statement is really very fluid; its quality
and character are open to adjustment. This should be
treated as an opportunity instead of as an embarrassment: a formal stage of problem formulation should be
drawn out and legtimized. The exploratory research
that leads to problem formulation is, it must be noted,
at the opposite end of the induction-deduction continuum
from the strictly deductive mode to which strict
rationality leads. Exploratory research emphasizes
learning, not proving--reaching toward change, and not
toward accountability for the past. The consequences
at the "findings" end of any particular problem statement should be anticipated. If they feel sensitive,
the research should find a political sponsor before it
proceeds.

     Fair questions to ask before one proceeds at the
administrative level are, what kinds of questions and
what kinds of answers will serve whose interests, by
what kinds of rights, with what kinds of outcomes in
mind. The least this stage should do is tease out the
political implications of both problem and proposed
methods--i.e., for each major range of potential
"findings", what will the distributional effects be, and
what kind of political settlement would be required?
The exercise encourages realism (there is often a
Micawberish hope that research will "turn something up"
to solve a problem that will tread on no toes and cost
nothing) and is necessary for coherence. Instead, if
the research is not coherent at this level, one can
anticipate that the results will not be actionable.

b)   Meaningful Precision: It is efficient to be clear
about the degree of precision that is needed. Precision
is worth paying for when the consequences of error are
grave: serious ill effects from administration of a
vaccine, for example. But is probably not worth paying
for precision when a simple tour could establish a rough

idea of the scope of a problem, and when the resources available would in any event dictate the scope of the proposed solution. What does it matter whether the rate of malnutrition in the Canadian north is 15 or 20 percent until a basic decision has been taken about what to do about it? Being reasonable about the kind of precision that is necessary is, of course, related to problem specification. If the question "how much is too much" is imponderable, it may be a sign that energy will be best spent on another substantive approach.

c) Fresh Air: Governments should not attempt to conduct what amounts to basic social research in-house as part of an administrative routine. The result is almost sure to be an expensive failure that no one knows how to evaluate because it was conducted outside the processes and peer networks of normal science. (Normal science and social science should be funded totally apart from the management needs of government. There should be less bullying of researchers as to the immediate "relevance" of their work to "important social problems." Scholars, in any event, are guided by their discipline which is in turn a creature of culture. Direct intervention will more often than not divert them from discipline-based formulations that were about to become productive in the social sense.)

d) Plain Facts: When getting information makes sense--when both society and bureaucratic agency can be aligned to move on a problem--analysts should try for information from as many existing sources as possible, working quickly and inexpensively. The various streams of information will have a "center of gravity" of some probability. Martin Rein stresses the importance of what he calls good "reportage."31

If information being sought for administration and program design does not already exist, and is not quick and inexpensive to obtain, multi-faceted and robust in the fact of tests of ordinary knowledge and customs, it will probably do little to assist choice. The main message of Lindblom and Cohen's Usable Knowledge is that knowledge that is not already rooted in society and culture cannot be created fresh from a standing start through the methods of professional scientific research to inform contemporaneous policy. Confirming a consensus is gratuitous. Suggesting something totally new may be provocative, but unlikely to be accepted because responsible decision-makers would have to be desperate indeed to grasp at a hint against the weight of the

262

accepted knowledge of the past.

e) Plain Methods: Elaborate quantitative methods are founded on the classical rules of logic. Logic is therefore an important test of the coherence of an application of a complex and novel strategy for analysis. If decision-maker and analyst cannot reduce a technique to its basic argument, chances are that they will not be able to draw out its logical implications for implementation. One can retreat to John Stuart Mill's habits of weighing similiarities and differences with very good results. One can formalize basic arguments so that it can been seen that the links are strong and that the evidence adduced is not irrelevant to the main contentions. Grids and charts can be used by the analyst to control information, keep the salient aspects up front, and to ensure that all major participants are talking about the same thing.

f) Reverse Hamlet: Do something. Action can itself be experimental. Even a very small step in a new direction can provoke much information about what a large step would bring about. The trick is to make sure that costs of a retreat would not be too grave. Lindblom and Cohen call this strategy "interactive decision-making."

v) Conclusion

     Facts, one can say, were in the past often most useful when absent. The information-poor official could pore over the problem, identify the major aspects, consult his peers and the people who were affected, weigh, judge, guess and pray--and offer his insights and advice to the political level. People understood that the bureaucrat was not paid to be right, to know exactly "what works". Rather, the official was paid for working up an explanation of what were feasible things to want, given the circumstances, for exercising a judgement built on experience to devise ways to attain the feasible, and for implementing the ultimate strategies. The political task was to assign values to the "feasible", sometimes to deny feasibility and choose bolder directions, and, regardless, to accept responsibility for outcomes. The attractiveness of the ideology of rationality is that it offers an avenue of escape into technique from the burdens of assigning value and of exercising judgement. Indeed, in its emphasis on establishing accountability for "results" judged against supposedly comprehensive objective standards it offers an escape from personal and moral responsibility. But the escape is temporary and its comforts illusory.

Notes

1. An element of the rhetoric says "...even if we can't know where we are going, at least we can know where we have been." And since we must also know where we are, we have the two points necessary for a straight-line projection into the future...The problem is, of course, that when one lacks theory, one does not know where the line is.

2. For this view, see the Auditor General of Canada's 1982 Annual Report, 19, paragraphs 1.80 and 1.81, as well as his remarks about his need to audit the policy-making process at both administrative and political levels, 20-21, paragraph 1.9.

3. Charles Lindblom, "The Science of Muddling Through," Public Administration Review 19 (2) Spring 1959; ..."Still Muddling: Not Yet Through," Public Administration Review 39 (4) November/December 1979, 517-516; and David Cohen, Usable Knowledge: Social Science and Social Problem Solving (New Haven: Yale University Press, 1979). See also Herbert A. Simon, The New Science of Management Decision (Englewood Cliffs: Prentice-Hall, 1977), especially Chapter Two, "The Process of Management Decision," on the problems endemic to synopic rationality.

4. An idea of the general enthusiasm for the movement is communicated by the two volumes of the Annals of the American Academy of Political and Social Science that were devoted to it in 1970 ("Political Intelligence for America's Future") and 1971 ("Social Information for Developing Countries") See also R. A. Bauer (ed.) Social Indicators (Cambridge: MIT Press, 1966), and Andrew Shonfield and Stella Shaw (eds.) Social Indicators and Social Policy (London: Heinemann, 1972).

5. Of great value is Ilene N. Bernstein and Howard F. Freeman Academic and Enterpreneurial Research: The Consequences of Diversity in Federal Evaluation Studies (New York: Russell Sage, 1975). See also Gerald Gordon and Edward V. Morse, "Evaluation Research", Annual Review of Sociology 1, 1975, 339-59; Carolyn Weisse and Michael Bucuvalas, Social Science Research and Decision-Making (New York: Columbia University Press, 1980); and Lee J. Cronbach and Associates, Toward

Reform of Program Evaluation (San Francisco: Jossey Bass, 1980).

6. Christopher Beattie et al _Bureaucratic Careers: Anglophones and Francophones in the Canadian Public Service_ (Ottawa: Information Canada, 1972). Interestingly, the study collected no statistic about the representation of women at any level: the phones had no gender. Exactly because the question was not sufficiently dangerous in a political sense at the time, it was not worth "rationalizing" through empirical research.

7. See, for example, R. Dobell and David Zussman, "An Evaluation System for Government" _Canadian Public Administration_ 24 (3) Fall 1981, 404-428.

8. Richard E. Brown (ed.) _The Effectiveness of Legislative Program Review_ (New Brunswick, N.J.:   Transaction Books, 1979). The book contains several case studies of major evaluations conducted for legislators.

9. See Robert Martinson, "What Works?--Questions and Answers about Prison Reform," _The Public Interest_ 35, 1974, 22-54.

10. PPB was first used to present the government's Estimates to Parliament in 1971. What constitutes a "program" is essentially arbitrary. At the highest level, there are the big "programs" of the Main Estimates--these coincide with the departmental-level organizational framework. Since 1971, Treasury Board Secretariat (TBS) and the Office of the Comptroller General (OCG) have worked to set up guidelines for the definition of sub-department "planning elements" (TBS) or "program components" (OCG). An element/component must be a goal-directed entity in some loose sense, and must be relatable to unique organizational entities and accounting structures. The rate of change that can be allowed is an important concern. Without rules, a department could escape accountability by continually redefining its programs.

11. While an outsider cannot know for sure the extent to which the sectors have been able to find money from within their bases, it is the case that only one major example of a cut in the social sector is frequently cited. This was to a federal granting

program that provided capital to local governments to build sewage treatment plants. The unanticipated down-stream effects, so to speak, of the cancellation for international agreements on water quality resulted in reinstatement a large part of the "saving".

12. His mandate allows him to assess any entity for its economy and efficiency of operation--and to judge the suitability and adequacy of the government's own attempts to measure the effectiveness of any operation's pursuit of its official goals. He can conduct any kind of applied research that he deems suitable, even unsystematic anonymous interviews of a non-probability sample of managers, as he did for the 1983 Report. See Chapter Two, "Constraints to Productive Management in the Public Service."

13. The role of the evaluation units--sketched in the 1977 Policy Directive 1977-47-- is the specification of the total budgets of their departments into empirically evaluable program components/planning elements, and the evaluation of the success of these programs in meeting formal goals. It should be noted then that administrative costs under 1977-47 are conceived to be programs and therefore evaluable. This view of the need for total coverage still holds.

14. The system's tendency is to grow more ambitious rather than less. Tax expenditures have always been in theory part of each sectoral budget (although only one tax expenditure budget was ever made--in 1979--and the OCG is working on ways to incorporate the costs and benefits of regulatory activity in each sectoral budget.

15. See Richard Van Loon, "Ottawa's Expenditure Process: Four Systems in Search of Co-ordination," in G. Bruce Doern (ed.) How Ottawa Spends (Toronto: Lorimer, 1983). (The four systems Van Loon identifies are: a) new policy management, b) ongoing expenditure management, c) budgetary policy and macroeconomic management, and d) major government priorities management--"macro-policy".) See also Sandford F. Borins, "Ottawa's Expenditure 'Envelopes': Workable Rationality at Last?" in G. Bruce Doern (ed.) How Ottawa Spend your Tax Dollars (Ottawa: Carleton University, 1982).

16. A paper delivered to the International Institute of Public Finance's 39th Congress in Hungary in August, 1983, "The Canadian Policy and Expenditure Management System (PEMS): Budget-Making and Social Policy," by Magnus Gunther and Richard Stursberg, gives a history of the important special funds. The danger to the system is, of course, that a proliferation of special funds will make nonsense of the central premise that there are spending limits on a total sectoral budget for the policy area, and that the programs within an area are competitively funded on rational grounds.

17. Although there is a view that the Liberals are, without needing to be subverted into it, naturally mangers at heart. See V. Seymour Wilson, "Mandarins and Kibitzers: Men in and Around the Trenches of Political Power in Ottawa," Canadian Public Administration 26 (3) Fall 1983, 446-462. See also G. Bruce Doern, "Liberal Priorities 1982: The Limits of Scheming Virtuously," 1-37 in the 1982 How Ottawa Spends volume.

18. See, for example, Colin Campbell, Governments Under Stress: Political Executives and Key Bureaucrats in Washington, London and Ottawa (Toronto: University of Toronto Press, 1983) 198. Campbell notes that the Canadian system can more than match the U.S. Office of Management and Budget in rank of officers and absolute numbers. He says that the new PEMS system represents "a tripling of resources for expenditure review in the course of four years."

19. Auditor General's Annual Report, 1983, 110, paragraph 3.6.

20. The full title of the list is "Corporate Evaluation Studies Completed in 1982 and 1983 in Federal Departments and Agencies as of 30 November 1983."

21. In its own five-year trawl of the nearly sixty departments and agencies, the Office of the Auditor General seems to be somewhat further ahead. It has completed 39 unique comprehensive audits, in which it considers the whole department or agency to be a program. Eighteen of the small organizations, for the most part central agencies, have so far been spared a visit.

22. There would seem to be a simple way out: studies could be broader, drawn closer to classical analysis than to applied social research, and, above all, initiated by politicians. The alternative would be to devote at least double the resources so that the original policy to evaluate everything in timely fashion could be accomplished.

23. See the Auditor General's Annual Report, 1978, Introduction and pp. 84 to 96.

24. The Treasury Board of Canada, Guide on the Evaluation Function (Ottawa: Supply and Service, 1981).

25. In his "audit" of the evaluation function published in the 1983 Annual Report, the Auditor General found that more than half the "assessment" stage studies preparatory to evaluation research proper "did not form an adequate basis for sound advice to the deputy for planning evaluation studies." He also found significant weaknesses in the program evaluations themselves, some of them traceable to the inadequate design phase. See p. 38, and the whole of Chapter 3.

26. Only one study has been tabled in Parliament, according to the AG's 1983 Annual Report, p. 29, paragraph 1.119.

27. Interestingly, even the Auditor General works without even the typical general standards set by auditors for most of their other routine tasks. He has repeatedly asked his professional society to join him in the task of publishing "generally accepted audit standards" for the comprehensive audit, and the society has repeatedly evaded the responsibility.

28. This use of research is of course not wholly new, only much more pronounced in more heavily rationalized systems. Douglas Hartle has recently described how the "fatuous nonsense" generated as research for planning by the Privy Council Office, was then used rather effectively in purely strategic ways. See his "Open Letter" in Canadian Public Administration 26 (2) Spring 1983, 95-100.

29. Lindblom, "Still Muddling: Not yet Through", 518.

30.   One of the best texts for analysis in government
      settings is E. S. Quade <u>Analysis for Public Deci-
      sions</u> (New York: Elsevier, 1975).   Another basic
      book that has stood up well over the past nearly-
      twenty years in Charles H. Kepner and B. J.
      Tregoe's <u>The Rational Manager</u> (New York: McGraw
      Hill, 1965).

31.   Martin Rein, <u>Social Science and Public Policy</u>
      (Harmondsworth: Penguin, 1976) 77.   Rein
      continues to advocate the conscious, explicit use
      of metaphors in "stories" to link up the bits that
      are known.   He calls this "construction of
      reality"-- a "what if" approach to building
      patterns out of information.

Appendix

A 1960's Systems Fantasy for the 1980's

In North America, technical progress--the development of modern high-speed computers and mechanisms for
information storage and transmission--has lowered the
costs of gathering and analysing information about the
results of public policy decisions. Now, time series
data collected on fully articulated models follow
developments in each of the major sectors of the economy
and society. Since the rudimentary systems were put in
place and the process of data gathering and analysis was
set in motion during the social indicators movement in
the early 1960's, additional categories have been con-
tinuously defined and refined (always maintaining compa-
tibility with earlier data series) until each sector of
social and economic effort is now represented by a giant
electronic spreadsheet that is updated continously. Any
one of these sectoral spreadsheets might be composed of
literally hundreds of rows and columns filled with values
of variables observed over time, and hundreds of formulae
relating them with one another. Each sectoral spreadsheet is bounded, fully developed internally, and capable
of being linked to similar information systems for all
sectors that share boundaries.

When meta-programs that continually cross-check the
formulae relating series reveal too much variance between predicted value and actual value at any point, the
formulae are flagged for attention of decision-makers
and revised by a method of successive approximation
until accurate predictions can be obtained once more.
The "new" factor that has caused the perturbations is
assesed in context, named, and a new series is begun.
Analysts of the highest calibre assess the event against
the rules of pure theory for the sector. It sometimes
occurs, of course, that a formulation in the past is
found to have been in error, and a phenomenon might be
retroactively deleted in a refreshed version of a sectoral spreadsheet. The same thing is done on a larger
scale to relate variables across sectors. It was the
fourth generation of computers--their miniaturization
and their consequent great power and speed of calcula-
tion--that allowed success of the head-on empirical
approach to problem identification and solution. This
"brute force" method causes every avenue to be investi-
gated--the time and resource costs of the full search
have been made bearable. Applications of fifth genera-

tion computers, those using artificial intelligence, show much promise for reducing the labour of assessing the variety of possible solutions to choose the "best" against soft criteria that embody social and political prejudices.

Full information collected without fear or prejudice almost always reveals co-operative strategies that falsify the zero-sum prediction. If need be, one player can always be found to accept "altruistic" losses in expectation of future benefits. Information, as the writers of the 1960's had hoped, has in 1984 de-politicized most aspects of decision-making. The exceptions are intransigently emotional areas. An example of the public policy area that is hard to rationalize is the parole of criminals. Even though the probability of harm from a paroled offender is much less than the threat from traffic or food carcinogens, the public is unwilling to accept the most negligible losses. Perhaps a little discretion is necessary in communicating such facts. On the other hand, the population has been grateful for the steady if modest prosperity of the 1970s and early 1980s. When, for example, the energy information systems first flagged possible future shortfalls, industry and consumers accepted a new way of life without difficulty. Life, if a little dull, is steadily good: it is assuredly the best of all possible worlds.

Chapter Eleven

The State and Economic Development in Africa

P. A. Muma

That development constitutes about the greatest challenge in our century there can be little doubt. Indeed, no single problem has tasked the able minds of so many experts for so long. It was in order to confront this challenge that the United Nations declared the 1960s and 1970s the development decades of action. Like the 60s before it, the 70s have now come and gone with very few concrete results. Of course there have been some achievements in growth terms (notably in those very few countries where some growth has been attained). But there has been very little success in real development as distinct from growth. Gandhi's reference to 'the dumb-semi-starved millions' highlights a serious development concern of poverty in India as well as in Africa; the truism remains almost as true in our day as during his time. To be sure, the concern now seems even more serious in most parts of Africa in which many children are dying from malnutrition and such related diseases as erasmus.

So massive is the development problem that it is often not clearly understood nor adequately grasped. Conceptually, the experts disagree about what it entails. Methodologically, there are also disagreements with regards to different practical approaches in the search for solutions. Most economists have tended to view the problem in purely economic terms; and although there is currently a shift in emphasis from 'economic growth' to 'economic development', the accent is still on the adjective rather than on the noun. The more radical economists argue for transcending the bounds of economic relations: to consider non-economic as well as economic factors. For the non-economists, the development process is one of 'modernization'. Undoubtedly, such disagreements are a reflection of professional orientations. But they are also a function of ideological schools of thought or strategic approaches to the problem, as well as of divergent views as to what development is all about. I pause, therefore, to question what development actually entails.

According to Rogers and Dickson (1975: 3) "development is about power." This view of development draws attention to the dependency syndrome in which African states and other Less Developed Countries (hereinafter LDCs) find themselves; these countries depend on the Advanced Countries (ACs) not only for development aid but also for their raw materials exports. The view is echoed by the declaration of the South-North Conference on 'The International Monetary System and the New International Order' held in 1980 in Arusha. This Conference maintained that "money is power," and concluded that "This simple truth is valid for national and international relations. Those who wield power control money. Those who manage and control money wield power." This conclusion is based on the activities of the international monetary system which serves as "both a function and instrument of the prevailing power structure." Undoubtedly, the conclusion is a powerful one, coming as it does from part of a document adopted by forty parliamentarians, planners, bankers, international and national officials, and economists from twenty Third World as well as industrialized countries. It is even more powerful in the sense that it is made in the context of a critique of what can be described as the nerve-center of the international monetary system--the IMF.

However, for Nyerere (1968), "development is about people." Although more cryptic and succinctly all-embracing, Nyerere's definition hardly contradicts that of Rogers and Dickson. Far from being diametrically opposed these two views of development are but two sides of the same coin. For, as the latter go on to remark, development "is not simply owning cars, color TV or hi-fi." Nor I may add, has it anything to do with skyscrapers. In point of fact, it is not even a situation at all, but a process. This process deals with, as Rogers and Dickson (1975: 3) conclude:

> The complicated social, political
> and economic process by which
> people acquire greater control over
> their own lives, participating in
> decisions affecting their future,
> and becoming active and creative
> members of their society (authors'
> emphasis).

Nevertheless, these two views of development beg a number of quite serious questions. To weave a web

between them is to address such questions. For
instance: How far does the lack of development bear on
the power of external forces or the internal weaknesses
of African states? What can African states do to
increase their bargaining strength and political and
economic power so as to enable them to realize their
common goal of development? In what sense, and to what
extent, does the prevailing power structure underlining
international relations militate against the efforts of
African states to effectively confront the development
challenge? More importantly, what policy and other
measures are needed by African states in order to cope
adequately with the problem?

Obviously, these, among others, are very significant questions. The aim of this chapter is to examine
the profound issues which they raise and to discuss
their implications in the light of the role and function of the state in Africa in grappling with the
development challenge.

i)   A Three Ps Approach

The above views of development define the theme of
this discussion; in the light of foregoing questions
this relates to the power of the state in Africa, and
emphasizes the welfare needs of the people through a
process of policy formulation (and implementation)
vis a vis socio-institutional changes. There is
deliberate emphasis on the three Ps--Powers, People and
(Policy) Process--to help spell out the approach to
analyzing the main issues, which are in themselves
inextricably linked. Thus, the need for increasing the
state's power has national and international significance; not only in terms of its organizational strength
in domestic economic management, but also in regard to
enhancing its bargaining strength in international
relations. It therefore bears heavily on the effort
enlisted to realize development goals so as to benefit
the masses of people. Similarly, it reflects considerably on the process of transformation through meeting
the policy demands and making the required institutional
and structural changes.

Nor can any discussion of the process of transformation be detached from an examination of existing
obstacles to change. The difficulties entailed in the
implementation of policy measures and introduction of
the needed socio-institutional reforms are part of a
much wider syndrome of political and economic

275

subjugation with both national and international
dimensions. Therefore, to grasp the demands of the
transition process requires some appreciation of the
reasons for the existing socio-structural rigidities,
as a result either of colonial intrusion or the impact
of external forces of the capitalist-imperialist
scenario. The mechanics of the very process of change
involves dismantling colonial and imperialist hurdles on
the path to economic improvement. These obstacles stem
from the inherited, distorted resource and institutional
patterns which are bound up with unequal exchange
relations within the world capitalist system. By the
same token, it calls for the formulation of effective
policies and implementation of relevant decision
measures by the state whose importance therefore comes
into focus.

And yet, in practice this importance of the state
is hardly matched by the development functions and
responsibility of the state. Why? To understand the
variety of reasons for this requires a brief sketch of
the theoretical view of the state and the confusion to
which it gives rise in practice. This, in turn, demands
touching upon the constraints and contradictions
relating to the state in Africa.

ii) The State in Traditional Theory and Analysis

Textbook theory offers no coherent theory of the
state. Accordingly, orthodox analysts simply regard
the state in normative terms, being mainly pre-
occupied with when it 'ought' to intervene in the
economy. They base their prescriptions on scientific,
albeit unrealistic, considerations of welfare maximization. Equally, they consider the need for state
intervention as merely a response to failures in market
mechanisms. The tendency is to treat the institutions
of the state as an exogenous 'black box' whose basic
features are never fully examined (vide: Nore--in Green
and Nore (eds.), 1977).

Thus, the importance and role of the state as a
political machinery which operates to intervene even in
a capitalist society are ignored. This underlines the
weakness of orthodox theory; it also highlights the
empirical irrelevance of textbook concepts in trying to
explain the movement and magnitude of state expenditures
over time. The economic role of the state and its
function in engendering development especially in Africa
is thus dismissed with a sleight of hand. Analytically,

the link betwen normative insights and state policy
needs to be established; so too should the connection
between economists qua scientists and government action.
Where the government has no idea of the welfare maximization of the people it cannot embark upon an effective
program of action to satisfy the welfare goals of the
people it represents. It follows that, in this case,
normative economics has no power for our purpose.

The same logic holds even if the information about
welfare maximization is made available to the government
which does not act upon economic insight. The basis of
this logic is the positive-normative distinction of
theory. This distinction arises from the scientific
claims of traditional analysis and leads to a half-
hearted position. In practice, there is therefore some
modest theoretical modification (on the basis of second
best theory, since application of the first best principle is wide of the mark!). The alternative is to
contradict the very existence of the positive-normative
link: a government which fails to provide the public
or merit goods it ought to provide is thrown out of
office. But since any theory of the state would have
to be based on the establishment of such a link, the
latter would therefore conflict with the validity of
most of the basic assumptions of theory and contradict
its scientific claims.

It was Keynes who sought to draw attention, perhaps
indirectly, to the significance of the state, although
his main purpose was apparently to stabilize capitalism.
He emphasized government spending through which relative
high employment and boom conditions have been maintained,
and the possibilities of a permanent stabilization of
capitalism is being realised. This significance of
government expenditure is aptly portrayed in the words
of Joan Robinson (1972): "when there is unemployment
and low profits the government must spend on something
or other, it does not matter what. As we know, for 25
years serious recessions have been avoided by fostering
this policy." Nevertheless, the neo-classical theory
of the state continues to serve an ideological function,
in being based on a vision of the market economy as the
most efficient allocation of resources. Hence the
state is regarded endogenously as a permanent and
integral part of economic life, which constantly reciti-
fies the shortcomings of the market.

To understand the logic behind state intervention
we have to turn to Marxist analysis of the state under

277

capitalism; after all, it was Marx who discovered the special law of development of the present-day capitalist mode of production, and of the bourgeois system of society. According to Marxist explanations, state action cannot be understood except as a response to historical trends. Nor can such understanding be based on vague and naive references to such concepts as public good. Rather, it must draw on a firm grasp of the genesis and basic motivations for state action over time. There is need to understand the 'present as history'; for the totality of the existing institutions of the state can only be understood as the expression of the day-to-day policies they formulate and which tend to act so as to perpetuate the existing relations of production. The obvious question to ask therefore is: What insights are provided by history into the under-standing of the 'present' development situation of African states, and for the lack of state action in effective policy responses? The answer to the first part of this double-barrelled question lies in the colonial experience; that for the second is to be found in inherited institutions.

iii)   The Colonial Experience: economic consequences

So strong was the colonial intrusion of an alien economic element in the African states that the inextricable link that now exists in the minds of the African people between colonialism and capitalism was firmly established. The process of colonization involved a process of creating outposts of the capitalist system: African states became mere extensions of metropolitan economies. But 'enclave economies' had a minimal impact on the rest of the domestic economy. There was a heavily built-in economic dependence in the important sectors inherited by the new nation states on attaining so-called political independence: the key sectors were predominantly under the ownership and control of aliens including international companies or settler minorities.

The political and economic structures imposed on African states thus disarticulated the economies which now became critically dependent on links with the metro-politan core and Western finance capital. The bound-aries carved out by the colonial powers in their scramble for bits of African territories and their wealth had no regard to either economic, ethnic or geo-graphic realities. Nonetheless, the economic conse-quences of colonialism fell within well-defined, if diverse, patterns of economic penetration. The

Compagnie Francaise de l'Afrique Occidentale, the United
African Company or the British East African Company pre-
ceded the subsequent plantations, banks and mines. In
the same way, these colonial hinterlands and commercial
outposts were to influence the economic structure and
policy of the colonial states and later to become the
outposts of monopoly capitalism. African states thus
depended on metropolitan sources of capital, technology
and managerial manpower. And the transformation of the
mainly subsistence peasants into cash crop farmers was
developed so as to bind the colonial territories to the
metropolitan and world capitalist system. The result
was the transformation of vast land areas of the continent into mini- or pseudo-economies.

    Developmentally, most African states now belong to
the world's least developed group of countries, usually
with a per capita income of less than $200 in 1976.
Even in those countries in which the per capita income
appears higher than this figure, the majority of their
denziens have a living standard not much better off;
due to unequal distribution the bulk of the people live
below the poverty line. Despite huge natural resources,
the pattern of institutions and structures imposed in
the colonial and post-colonial period has condemned the
bulk of African's people to abject poverty. For
example, such was the pattern of colonial taxation, or
credit and marketing structures, in white settler
communities that African efforts to develop modern farms
was greatly hampered. Similarly, the development of
handicraft industries was inhibited by importation of
mass-produced manufactured goods from the British
'workshop of the world'; 'made in Great Britan' was
made to carry psychological overtones of effective, if
subtle, propaganda to create demand by distorting the
tastes of the 'native.' To obtain the wherewithal to
pay taxes people were compelled to drift to the towns
or to leave the country in search of paid jobs.

    In consequence, few African countries can today
claim to account for more than 10% production in manufactured goods. The heavy dependence on trade outside
Africa means less intra-African trade. For the colonial
structure of most Africn economies was highly commodity
and export-oriented, consisting mainly of raw-materials
hinterlands of the metropolitan power. Such an orientation was designed to be unrelated either to the development demands of the mainly subsistence domestic economy
or economic relations with other African economies.
Even after independence structural rigidities have

continued to persist. Improvements and attempts at diversification have been reduced to the creation of essentially mono-product economies, relying on the production of one or two cash crops for export to the metropole and other ACs.

The nature of this pattern of heavy dependence is particularly characterized by the export trade of the Arican states south of the Sahara (Muma, 1982). In this case, the pattern is reflected by the quite marked commodity concentration of most of these states. Three main features highlight this situation. The first concerns the huge dependence of foreign exchange on "mono-products." Thus, in 1965, when most African states had only just become politically independent, only one commodity accounted for more than one quarter of total export earnings in each of the states in the region. This feature of "mono-product" foreign exchange dependence was in fact more than one-third of earnings in twenty-two, and more than one-half in fifteen cases. It seems staggering that two commodities accounted for up to seventy per cent of export receipts in seventeen African countries, and for more than fifty per cent in another twelve.

The second feature relates to the almost total absence of diversified export structures in African states. Only four (Cameron, Kenya, Mozambique, and Somalia) could claim at least six separate exports, each accounting for more than five per cent of total revenue, in 1965; the number of such exports was four or less in up to twenty-six cases. Third, the marked concentration on a few products for exports in each state is a significant feature in the region as a whole. An aggregation of exports in 1965 reveals that there was a marked regional concentration on a very few commodities: only four (copper, coffee, oilseeds and cocoa) accounted for forty-three per cent of total export earnings, while roughly ten (petroleum, cotton, timber, iron and diamonds as well as the above four) accounted for almost seventy per cent of total regional export earnings.

Nor has the above situation changed dramatically-- if at all--since most of the countries became politically independent. Indeed, in those African states that have neither been blessed with oil, nor discovered any high-priced mineral resources, the situation has steadily grown worse. In many of these countries the diversification of the single cash crop export has proved to be a major problem.

280

Conceivably the most significant feature of the
entrenched pattern of trade dependence is also the one
which presents the strongest case for inter-state cooperation. This deals with the high degree of dependence of most, if not all, African states on one market:
the European Common Market (EEC). Most African states
depend on the EEC as a market for more than half their
exports. This concentration has become even more
marked as the number of associated members has increased
from 18 in 1965, consisting mainly of former French
states, to embrace Commonwealth countries under the Lome
conventions covering the ACP (African, Caribbean and
Pacific) countries. Indeed, the imbalance in trade
relations highlights the unequal competition between the
ACP and the EEC; it underlines the argument of those in
favor of non-reciprocity being given to the ACP by the
EEC. Basing their argument on the way international
relations currently operate, they emphasise the fact
that the ACP countries "are mainly producers of raw
materials, for which the prices and markets are outside
their control, fluctuating severely and usually to their
disadvantage." (Pagni, 1976: 17).

The converse is true in the case of EEC countries
which are industrialized; although they may also produce
raw materials, these countries are great exporters of
manufactured and capital goods, the prices of which are
forever going up by comparison to the raw materials from
ACP countries. The fact that the EEC countries also
have a great capacity for international monetary manipulation is also another aspect of unequal relations. Not
only does it further reinforce the relatively weak
position of the ACP countries, it also underlines the
dependency syndrome in which they find themselves. By
such manipulation the ACs can easily dominate and
control international markets. Their use of such competitive weapons to defend their trade and protect their
self-intrest is not merely restricted to good times; in
fact, they are even more effectively used in times of
crisis such as during the mid-1970s. During such times
their desire and ability to gang up so as to maintain
and consolidate their power gather even greater momentum.
By contrast, African states neither have the capacity
of take-off, nor the power to demand a fair share of
the world's resources. To understand the reasons for
this it is necessary to critically examine the concept
and role of the state in Africa.

iv) The State in Africa: mono-product economic
     enclaves and mini-states:

     It is reasonable to argue that without colonial
imposition there would, conceivably, be no African
states as we know them: the artificial creations which
now constitute what are actually mini-states were
designed to suit the imperialist aims of metropolitan
capitalism. Nor, perhaps, would there be the current
development problem of such daunting size and scale.
The basis of this argument stems from the relationship
between capitalism and colonialism or neo-colonialism,
as between capital and the state itself. Its logic lies
in the relation between money and power, best understood
in terms of the economics of international politics and
the politics of international economics (Kindleberger:
1970). Prebisch sees the relationship in terms of the
downward trend of the relative prices of raw materials
from LDCs (the periphery) as against manufactured goods
from the ACs (the center); he concludes that this trend
is the result of persistent differences in monopoly
power--greater in the latter than in the former.

     Indeed, this argument can be varied or extended:
to reveal the relation between the capitalist concept
of the state, and how this impinges both on the pera-
meters of African states, governments and societies; or
bears on the concentration of capital whose logical
essence is profit and private property. For the intensification of this concentration highlights the sinister
relations between the concept of the state and capital
in capitalist countries and their need for economic
expansion in alleged backward societies.

     In so-called primitive societies factors of produc-
tion implied communal ownership. The concept of private
property stems from the capitalist development process;
within this process economic antagonisms grew among the
propertied interests and between property owners and the
property-less. Kinship was destroyed. It was replaced
by political society, the basis of which was territorial, while property was the ground work of social
relations. New social relations gave rise to new
social institutions that, in turn, created new economic
conditions. To avoid possible conflicts due to the
clash of interest there was need for social order and
some discipline. Property then became the basis of
political power while the property class used its
economic power to enforce social order in its class
interest: it captured the control of government by

282

raising its members to the ruling class. Thus, by means of the state the function of government in capitalist societies has been to organize society in the interests of profit and property rather than on behalf of the community.

Historically, the state has been the weapon to hold workers in subjection; and to preserve the interests of capital and property and conquer and colonize foreign lands including Africa. The tendency of capitalism towards intensification of capital has meant the need for capitalist ACs to promote its economic security and profit through colonialism and economic imperialism which, in turn, gave vent to intensified nationalism via the organs of the state. Thus, capitalism in alliance with state organs of government has organized through the political machinery. The basic question that is posed is whether the replication of the original capitalist conception of the state in Africa does not represent a blatant contradiction with its declared aims and goals of development.

There is a sense in which the constraints and con-tradictions of the 'state' in African development bears heavily on colonial intrusion. The political dimension of the stalemate stems from colonialism over the last 300 years, and the artificial creations of pseudo- or mini-states. Sometimes these exist without the self-conscious collective will for life in common; sometimes they are helpless entities, or are too small to be viable. In their various stages of "statehood in miniature" many seem confused as to the direction of their development. Frequently, they fall short of being the major instrument for the construction of the nation; their inherited administrative institutions fail to provide the major essential tool for the economic development of the nation.

The concept of the state must therefore transcend the "agglomerations of tribes" and encompass an ideolo-gical dimension which must reflect on the importance of the state in the process of development. Thus, in one sense, the issues hinge on the question of self-identification through which the modern state becomes realized as a consciously-determined reconstruction. The process, then, is organizational; by it the nation comes of age. This involves the logical development of the process of reshaping society, and the extension of state action into economic as well as political life. It also includes <u>inter alia</u>, the taking of measures to strengthen the bargaining power of the weaker groups and improving their conditions of bargaining and living under the state umbrella. Thus, the development of state policies is the main plank of state organization and the basic means of "humanization."

Economically, however, the conditions created by colonialism underpin the structural rigidities of African states. Most of these are basically due to the crude transformation of the inherent communalism of African society into a pale reflection of pseudo-capitalism with capitalist and pre-capitalist relations. African society now exhibits an overall structure that is complex. Apart from the rural-urban 'dualism' a range of other disparities exists: these are characterized by the distinction between the formal versus the informal sectors, as well as the problem of urban unemployment etc. Moreover, African countries are now integrated into a global economy. Historically, the nature of this world economy changed considerably; the current per capita income of most ACs is roughly three or four times as high as those of Africa, and the level of the agricultural productivity of the latter is a lot lower than that of the former, making the disparity between their agricultural and non-agricultural incomes a lot larger.

To the extent that the economic pattern was firmly rooted in various aspects of foreign control and ownership, efforts to decolonize and localize the economy were a sine qua non for sustained economic growth. Thorough-going nationalization by African states was considered as the only way to increase national control and ownership of the domestic economy. But how this was to be achieved raised questions of ideology. Was the policy to be adopted by the state to be one of socialization of the foreign enterprises or localization of capitalism?

Most African states have tended to fall somewhere between these two extreme cases. Those states that have allegedly chosen the socialist path have contrived to replace foreigners with a bumper crop of petty bourgeoisies. Similarly, those which sought to localize the foreign-owned enterprises through the creation of domestic capitalists have equally been inclined, to varying degrees, to introduce equity participation through parastatal bodies. The means adopted by the different states have therefore been as diverse as to be often imprecise and frequently self-interested.

284

Perhaps for this reason the commitment to the development cause has been both less total and not at all successful.

But while any strict categorization of the different African states in ideological terms can therefore be misleading, it seems obvious that the pressures exerted on them by the whole complex of international capitalism are profound, as dependency is huge. Not least are those due to the strength and power of multinationals in Africa, the self-interest of local capitalists, the actions and policies of metropolitan governments and international agencies, and even of foreign advisers and consultants. Since, by their very nature, these pressures are inevitably fraught with ideological overtones, it is necessary to discover the extent to which ideology plays a role in traditional analysis of the development process, especially in explaining the different conditions of the LDCs from those of the ACs.

v)   Traditional Analysis of the Development Process

In discussing the development process such analysis draws on conflicting approaches: in terms either of a historical periodization of the experience of the ACs or the existence of certain barriers which need to be overcome by African countries. The starting point of the two aproaches explicitly assumes that the LDCs are traditional stagnant societies. In both approaches there is no analysis of the history of underdevelopment. Rather, stress is placed on how to take-off like the ACs which thus become the model of development. The assumption is that there are no alternative approaches to development from the Western capitalist model of growth.

Nevertheless, because development must be regarded as a concept that is flexible enough to leave the options open, the assumption of the traditional theory is therefore misleading on three scores. First is the fact that there is actually no particular Western way of development, but rather different patterns of development along the capitalist path. The second-- related to the first--is historical: not only was the scale of industrial plant and enterprise determined by the relative backwardness of European industrial development, especially during the last century; they also depended on the degree of readiness to enter into monoplistic agreements. As such, the amounts of capital

285

needed for take-off increasingly became greater in order to undertake industrial production. And third, as the corresponding amount of investment-capital gradually grew, the role of the banks (e.g. in France and Germany <u>vis-a-vis</u> Britain) expanded, and with it the role of the state also increased.

Therefore, to expect the LDCs to follow exactly the same strategic development path as these countries seems unreasonable for a number of reasons. First, these are capital-scarce countries; they rely for their investment capital on outside nations and bodies, often on terms which are prohibitive and, it can be argued, somewhat development-inhibiting within the capitalist frame of things. Second, their socio-institutional environments impose conditions that are a far cry from those of Western capitalist nations; for example, most of the existing economic institutions are either largely externally-imposed and/or foreign-dominated. The banking and other financial institutions are largely foreign-owned, existing domestically as outposts of monopoly capitalism; real financial jurisdiction regarding matters of major economic importance and many domestic national investments are usually in external hands.

Moreover, bourgeois explanation of underdevelopment is based on a conception of the differences between the ACs and LDCs viewed merely in quantitative terms; it aims at preserving one of the cherished beliefs of neo-classical economics regarding its claim of universal applicability. But such are the assumptions of text-book economic theory that they do not accommodate the social and institutional setting of these countries. Not only are the conceptual categories inadequate, being largly concerned with the problems of capitalist deve-lopment of the ACs, the theory lacks any real relevance to the problems of Africa. The twin assumptions of high degree of factor mobility and flexibility of res-ponses (e.g. to price changes, technical progress etc) offer examples of textbook fallacies which do not reflect existing conditions in Africa.

But perhaps the most dangerous assumption relates to the government. Not only is the existence of an effective government assumed; its efficiency is taken for granted. Thus, the apparatus of the government is considered to be so effective as to be able to impose and collect taxes efficiently and to restore the economy to a state of bliss (and Pareto optimality!) in times of crisis. One example which underlines the fallacy of this assumption is the consumption-investment distinction. To draw the neat distinction between consumption and investment in such countries is misleading: some consumption items in these countries are needed to increase productivity and output for future development. Certain government expenditures (e.g. on health, education, literacy, nutrition etc.) therefore constitute investment. And, unlike other needed investment expenditures, these are induced and cannot be regarded as autonomous. Government expenditures are thus needed to create jobs as well as to increase wage labor so as to raise future output, particularly in African situations where paid employment is not at all widespread.

The traditional view of the development process, therefore, has strong ideological overtones in seeking to explain underdevelopment as a state of society from which the ACs 'took-off' into the advanced phase of high capitalist development. The obvious (implicit?) emphasis on harmony rather than on conflict in economic relations does not take account of the unequal relations in trade, nor of the international (development) dualism in the global economic order. The imbalance in economic power, of which such unequal relations are as much cause as effect, has therfore prompted cries from the poor countries for a New International Economic Order.

Further, in assuming the absence of conflict between the development of Africa and the interests of the advanced capitalist countries, the traditional view also provides a basis for the perpetuation of neo-classical relationships through aid and preferential trading. Thus, it exonerates the ACs from any responsibility for having underdeveloped the African countries (Rodney, 1972). It comes as no surprise, then, that with the decolonization of much of Africa and the gradual proliferation of newly independent states, most of them become committed more-or-less to a radical break with the old colonial patterns of capitalist development. Equally, it is not surprising that the alternative view which regards development as two sides of the same coin is unpalatable to the ACs; this view is particularly regarded with hostility by adherents of the neo-classical explanation of development.

The obvious ideological suggestion of the traditional view is that development is only possible for African countries by following the same capitalist path.

And while the barriers to development include population growth and lack of capital, these could be overcome through birth control (introduced with Western technical assistance--however dangerously!) and capital flows (through foreign aid and foreign ivestment--despite the terms and conditions regarding cost of repayments, effects of debt-servicing, etc.). The logical conclusion is that for African countries to develop they must maintain close links with the West and tow the ideological line!

vi) The Distribution of Income and Power in LDCs

The above conclusion also seems evident in the strategy of development under foreign domination. This strategy reveals a package deal which highlights the distribution of income and power in Africa, seemingly intended to serve the long-term interests of the foreign capitalists and those of the African ruling elites. The package inherently stresses the redistribution of power and income that is inconsistent with the development demands of Africa. For instance, the skewed demand resulting from the prevailing distribution of income can only be met by imports, or through import-substitution. To satisfy the demands of the elites requires producing the elite consumer items by capital-intensive production techniques using imported equipment. However, a strategy based even on import substitution would lead to generating capital and intermediate goods imports, profit outflows, expatriate employee remittances, etc. The result is the perpetuation of an ever-growing strain on the balance of payments as well as a perpetually over-valued exchange rate which, in turn, has negative feed-back in terms of worsening the crisis by further cheapening capital.

Moreover, elite products are unprofitable at the scarcity price because they are capital-intensive; for their production they require the ruling elite to grant a range of favors which now come under the banner of tax incentives, allegedly to encourage foreign investments in the domestic economy. Instead of widening the tax base of the state, the growth of industry--where there is any at all--creates conditions which require state subsidies. Thus, the demand on state expenditure and foreign exchange increases. Indeed, it turns out that most of the so-called 'attracted' industries catering for elite goods production are parasitic; they require outlays on capital as well as import-intensive infrastructure (such as electricity and water--frequently state-owned and supplied below or at cost--transport and other amenities that are usually urban-biased). This urban-bias of the required infrastructure characterises planning: the tendency of planners and decision-makers to gear policies towards a "centers-of-growth" strategy which generally reflects a "technocratic" approach to development. One of its consequences is the congregation of skilled and literate people in cities. Not only does this widen the already wide village-city gap, it further distorts the balance of power and frequently leads to a hardening of attitudes.

The development strategy of most African nations therefore draws on a package which imposes heavy demands on foreign exchange and state expenditures that increase over time, so that the increased burden on the state is itself actually maintained by means of foreign aid and debt-servicing. Thus to the extent that the package-deal explains the reasons behind the existing domestic inequality, to that extent does the overall strategy also reflect upon the scenario of foreign capitalist domination, the structural imbalance and the dependency syndrome, all of which underscore the basic contradiction of economic development through capitalism. Particularly in a labor-abundant economy, the growth of parasitic industries using capital-intensive techniques has consequences in terms of unemployment while such industries only cater for a narrow elitist market. The production of one or two products in the agricultural sector thus seems important only in so far as it helps to generate the needed foreign exchange to import the necessary capitals equipment and plant and so raise the needed taxes to finance the development expenditure of the parasitic sector's infrastructure. Frequently, however, the main source of finance for such investments is foreign aid which increases the burden of debt-servicing on the state and with it heavy dependence on the ACs.

vii) Dependence Through 'Aid' and No Trade

In practise, foreign aid and foreign capital merely fill up the holes that they themselves created (Dos Santos in Livingstone (ed.), 1981: 145). The history of aid to Africa now spans a generation. Instead of helping the recipient countries the so-called 'aid' has in most cases proved to be more of a trojan horse: most African states are not any better-off than they were two or so decades ago. The strings attached through conditions imposed by the donor countries have made the

289

development task an even greater challenge. These conditions include overcharging due to restrictive terms, payment of high proportions of aid in local currency, as well as the 'tying' of credits which greatly reduces the real component of foreign aid. Thus the meaning of aid to help foster development now seems to have been almost entirely replaced by that of helping to bail them out of crises; perhaps in view of the harsh conditions and terms of most aid-donors this may well have been their original long-term aim.

For African states south of the Sahara aid now totals roughly 20 billion dollars annually. The accumulated debts faced by these countries runs to the tune of $500 billion. Most of these states are low-income oil-importing countries. As such, they now face certain and almost total collapse without aid. The whole situation is even more depressing against the spiralling increases in the prices of oil and manufactured goods; at the same time as the trade terms for developing countries as a whole has been severely battered by world-wide industrial growth and protectionist policies of the ACs. Not only are raw materials at an all-time low, the prices the raw materials exports fetch abroad has been declining rapidly for the past decades. Cries for 'trade not aid' have met with little response from the ACs, so as to reduce the magnitude of the crisis. Nor has constant bickering over measures of price protection done anything to help African states which have sunk deeper into the abyss of debt burden, paradoxically in their bid to merely stay afloat.

All that the World Bank could do is to make too neat a suggestion about the need for more aid. The Bank's recommendation about doubling aid by 1990 is perhaps understandable considering the fact that it is an international institution mainly dominated by already developed donors. Especially those African states that have honestly sought to experiment with a socialist path to development as the only way out of the dilemma, having been convinced of the total failure of anything else, their problem situation is further deepened by the special brand of ready-made pre-conditions before any lending by the Bank, by far the largest donor.

Regretably, the Bank now demands a greater say as to the development direction which the tiers monde should take. The Bank even ignores the priority that ought to be placed on agricultural production. Instead, it stresses the production of cash crop exports, the prices of which are neither guaranteed nor stable. This is a senseless procedure which seems aimed at benefitting the multinationals which control the imports of vast quanties of cereals that now have to be imported to feed the hungry. Although most African states were self-reliant in food production prior to political independence many now have to rely on food imports and food aid.

Now, like most LDCs Africa is economically trade dependent. Such dependency inhibits the extent of self-reliance that can be achieved in the drive towards development. Such is the dependency syndrome that the amount of loss to the LDCs as a whole as a result of gradually declining terms of trade, remission of profits and dividends and loan repayments far exceed the much-touted gains from the inflow of so-called aid and foreign investment. Thus, the argument that it is the LDCs that are aiding the ACs and not vice versa is not far-fetched.

Aid should primarily be aimed at supporting sub-sistence agriculture, particularly in African states whose economies are predominantly agricultural. This support should be based on achieving self-sufficiency in food production through which the aid should also be directed towards achieving regional cooperation. Without broad-based self-sufficiency and collaborative efforts at joint development action aid cannot serve any useful function. It can only serve a negative, not to say wicked, purpose under conditions in which it is quite pointless to launch spectacular projects which will benefit outside investors while peasants continue to starve. Any aid program or transaction that expects a poor African nation to, in the words of the European Commissioner for Third World Relations, Egard Pisani, "import cereals and buy oil to run export ventures and new industries" (in Pagni, 1976) cannot be considered as seeking to help the recipient countries. In such circumstances especially the development res-ponsibility of individual states is reinforced.

viii)   State Responsibility and Government Action

The significance of the responsibility of the state is two-fold. First, it focuses our attention on the role of the state in devising effective policies and executing a development program which enables realiza-tion of economic and social improvement for its citizens. The second flows from this, and stresses the functions

291

of the state in terms of social organization, a means
of bringing human nature into social harness. Both
aspects are realized through the machinery of government. Thus government action is as necessary to beat
inflation as to eradicate poverty and reduce inequality,
so that, as Dalton (1979: 204) points out, "regardless
of ideology governmental economic activities are important to development."

In pure economic terms, the problem therefore fades
into that of the making of economic society (Heilbroner,
1968). In which case, it involves two fundamental
inter-related tasks of the state: a) organization of
a system to assure the production of enough goods and
services for the survival of its people, and b)
arranging the distribution of produced goods and
services so as to foster and facilitate production of
the required items and basic needs.

Execution of these two fundamental tasks is
obviously pregnant with difficulties relating to matters
of mobilization, allocation and distribution. But the
degree of difficulty involved, or with what ease the
tasks are confronted, in each of these major economic
areas is very much a function of the extent of state
participation and the efficiency of government in supply
management. This is especially so in Africa where, by
their very nature, economic organizations and activities
are dominated by socio-cultural norms and subject to the
vagaries of international relations and the pressures
of external economic forces.

Take the task of mobilization. This represents an
important problem relating to the acquisition of skills
and capacity utilization. Both the development of skills
and utilization of capacity are optimally achieved
through harnessing the social effort and avoidance of
waste in mobilizing available resources. They entail
marshalling total energies by the state in carrying out
the productive process called development. At the same
time, they also require grappling with the scarcity of
nature through devising an efficient social mechanism.
Such a mechanism should ensure participation by all in
the productive process so as to yield maximum results
in terms of individual and collective contributions.
Thus, the design and development of an effective socio-
political mechanism aimed at the efficient mobilization
of resources is a challenge to issues of organization
of social effort. On the effectiveness of such organization depends the success or failure of the role of the

state and the tasks its leadership sets for itself.

There is also the problem of allocation of effort. This problem also impinges on issues of skills improvement, as much as it relates to questions of production of goods and services to satisfy societal needs and welfare requirements. A prime prerequisite to the effective utilization of capacities and viable allocation of social effort is the establishment of socio-economic institutions which are directed at assuring maximum welfare for all the people. For Africa--as indeed any LDC--the task presented here is challenging; it is more complicated than in ACs. The reason for this is two-fold. First, the basic needs of society for food, fodder and fuel are paradoxically less demanding: they constitute items of basic needs that the local (village) people produce naturally. They do not make as many demands in terms of skills and techniques as in the so-called advanced industrial societies.

By contrast, the task of allocation is more complicated than in the ACs where the demands of food, fodder and fuel extend beyond the notion of meallie bread and firewood; in these countries the people's needs also include such luxuries as automobiles requiring an extraordinary spectrum of special (technological) tasks well beyond the simple process of 'natural' production. It is this paradox which further complicates the complex development demands of the tasks to be performed by the state in Africa. Not only does development require a transformation process from traditional natural production to a mechanical production system; the process of transformation itself requires grappling with difficulties entailed in the spectrum of special tasks at each stage and direction of progress in productive terms. The task of allocation must seek to match productive supply with effective demand at all levels. It is pointless to devote social effort to the production of luxuries for the rich few while the poor majority starve. Similarly, to be unable to channel the society's productive effort into areas of critical importance is to court disaster.

This then brings me to issues of distribution: the most crucial issue upon which the whole idea of mobilization and allocation impinge. The fundamental question which the process of production seeks to address is that of survival. As such, the issues of mobilization and allocation bear on questions of distribution to meet the requirements of survival. And yet distribution questions pose even greater problems. The collective contribution of the state is made up of the sum total of the contribution of individual members of society. Individually, each member's contribution of effort depends on his/her share of the national cake--i.e. received from the state to fulfil his/her needs and human requirements. The daily horsepower-hour of effort supply of each individual requires a minimum of society's output to run its human engine to full capacity. And yet how often have the 'haves' and well-to-do complained of the laziness of the 'have-nots' even while the latter languish in their daily toil: eking out a bare subsistence in the teeth of poor conditions, at the same as the grainries burst with excess grain. Economic viability and welfare improvement thus demand confronting squarely the stringencies and hardships posed by nature and, equally, contenting with the inherent constraints and contradictions of society.

Together, the mobilization, allocation and distribution dimensions of the task place a much greater accent on the state's role in engendering development and fostering the well-being of its people. Although they stress the economic aspects of the problem they actually bear heavily on the human factor in, and non-economic aspects of, development. It is this emphasis on the human aspect that delineates--as nothing else does--the precise meaning and function of the state, as well as the need for government action or intervention.

Having outlined the broad tasks, albeit in more or less economic vein, it is necessary to broaden the analysis so as to embrace the socio-political as well as economic dimensions without which development is difficult, if not impossible. For any clear appreciation of the means for realizing the tasks is only possible within the framework of the socio-political and economic matrix of the development situation. To undertake the tasks requires effective utilization of institutions of government, parliament and public services through all of which the state not only becomes incarnate; it also achieves nationhood by taking important policy decisions both within and without parliament. Particulary in Africa, such policy measures and decisions are primariy aimed at generating and promoting development. They are put into effective action by the formal and non-formal structures of the state: i.e. either statal, parastatal or non-statal organs of administration.

294

Further, since the inherited policies and institutions had sought to play, with invariable success, on ethnic conflicts in order to break up national cohesion and political unity, the need to overcome such obstacles places even greater accent on political mobilization of the people. The same need also suggests increasing the control of the 'bureaucratic bourgeoisie' of the state machinery so as to assume effective state control over the commanding heights of the national political economy--in banking and financial institutions, in industry and in foreign and domestic wholesale trade etc. The state therefore requires institutional and policy changes which ensure such control; which is only possible from a position of democratic political strength based on popular support and democratic participation.

There is also need to ensure and maintain a reasonable degree of co-ordination; in order to carry out the public will, national planning is necessary. Only the state, as the central organ for co-ordination of public policies in a national community, is equiped to meet this need. The necessity for planning is thus pressed upon it by the need for state intervention and the growth of mass participation. Individual entities within a state represent special interests, rather than the general and common interest of the nation. Such representation leads to a lack of co-ordination. For example, primary and higher education, and structures of public health and care need to be planned. So too do the redistributional reforms such as the welfare and security schemes or measures to care for the sick, disabled, aged, unemployed and children. All these require complexes of socio-economic intervention by the state in the bid to secure redistributional and social welfare for all.

A similar logic underlines the case for public intervention in other fields: housing and construction of habitable homes or provision of clean pipe-borne water. It is the responsibility of the state to influence decisively--indeed provide--such conditions; it seeks to meet these through a complex of interventions concerning rents, availability and prices of houses, mortgage facilities, labor market conditions, etc. Thus, the various organs for public policy should seek to create the opportunities for mass participation; and to rectify the conditions for the smooth operation of organized markets regarding wages, prices and incomes or other conditions of the ordinary business of life; such that all prices and wages, incomes and other welfare conditions constitute demand and supply curves that are in a sense "political." It is not by accident that Adam Smith, concerned with the "Wealth of Nations," wrote of political economy, redefined by Kindleberger (1970) as "the study of how the economy and polity work in settling questions of public policy."

The preoccupation of Smith and other classical economists was basically with problems of change and development issues which cannot be restricted to the confines of economics as a metaphysical science (Muma, 1983). Actually, from the time of Smith up to that of the neo-classicists, economics and politics were part of moral philosophy. Then, gradually, first economics followed by political science moved away to be concerned with description, analysis and measurement. Nevertheless, the two branches remained joined to each other, at least in analytical techniques and conceivably in subject matter, if not to philosophy. This is particularly true in the case of development, the analysis of which calls for a multi-dimensional approach. The "un-success" of a unistic, essentially economic, approach in the 70s and preceding decades, bears testimony to this fact. Being "economic" as well as "political," the development problem requires state policy responses which transcend the scope of mere scientific proof (Muma, 1982).

ix) The Way Forward: emergent issues

This chapter has focused basically on the political economy of the state regarding its role and function in the process of development. The set of interrelated issues which emerge is mainly three-fold. The first highlights the urgency of development as a pressing problem which must be regarded as a serious challenge by African states. The second bears heavily on the responsibility of the state, and thus stresses its function in terms of the formulation of policies and implementation of relevant programs of action in order to cope effectively with the challenge. And the third transcends the concept and role of the state as an isolated entity; it embraces not only the question of economic viability of the indivitual state but also its relations with other African states, as well as their power and strength in joint co-operative action in dealing with ACs, external agencies or other forces.

As a summing up, a brief outline of the first two seems necessary in order to reinforce the main thrust of the basic argument. This will also provide the main plank for stressing the more important question regarding the need for inter-state people's participation in the affairs of the national community.

The importance of the state's role in fostering development also lies in maintaining and strengthening, through its central organs of government, a number of positive and fundamental policy structures in a number of fields: in international trade and exchange, labor and employmnt, taxation and social security matters, education and health, transport and communication. It is the state's responsibility to seek the people's mandate not least by the organization of the national community in accordance with the public will as well as collective (state) interest and community welfare.

The formulation and implementation of the relevant policies should basically be to address the fundamental problem of the weakness of the state's assymetrical economy: non-viable either in terms of creditable capital that can be nationally raised, or the markets for a range of domestically produced goods now imported from the capitalist industrial countries of the world. The lack of capital has meant the exploitation of domestic resources by transnational corporations which, as an important element of the world capitalist system dominated by the industrial core of Western nations, have retained full control of the commanding heights of peripheral economies. Any solution to the problem must therefore entail wresting control of these commanding heights. Further, it will also require joint action and co-ordination of efforts along with other states through the synchronization of policies, inter-state or cross-boundary sectoral co-operative programs of action; which brings me to the important issue of cooperation and the question of integration.

Co-operation: vertical or horizontal integration?

For many years many African states have not been able to mobilize the capital or markets required to prop up the viability of their assymetrical economies. This is due to the truncated nature of their economies with an in-built feature of dependence on importing basic plant and machinery to undertake any basic industrialization programs. Moreover, most African states are so small that they are generally unable to develop fully their extensive known resources as a basis for cooperation and joint action in confronting a common problem.

Confronting the Challenge: radical policies

African states need to awake to the realization that
half-hearted solutions have so far not produced any concrete results in terms of improvements in the general
welfare of their peoples. The fact that the problem
remains pressing and inherently endemic calls for a more
radical approach. Such an approach needs to be based
on a historical view of underdevelopment; it thus calls
for vigorous socio-institutional reforms to which the
needed policies should be geared. Accordingly, such
policies should be directed towards countering the
effects of three main types of dependence: a) colonial
dependence (the domination of economic relations through
commercial and financial capital and the colonial monopoly of land and manpower of the state by metropolitan
powers); b) dependence due to the emergence and domination of financial and industrial monopoly capital; and
c) multinational corporation-based dependence.

The above three features of dependence also
characterize the nature and type of obstacles that need
to be tackled. For the forces behind the dependency
syndrome explain the vulnerability of African countries
to the vagaries of international relations and the weakness of most of their domestic economies. Apart from
measures to cope with needed social and structural
reforms, the failure of the hitherto foreign-oriented
strategy underlines the need for radical policy responses by the state in order to increase its control
and management of the local ecomony.

Effective Policies and Management and Control

In order to manage effectively the economy, the
state must assume greater responsibility than is at
present the case in most African countries. Thus
policies aimed at effective state control could facilitate the marketing of processed exports, and help raise
foreign exchange earnings by seeking alternative markets
in other (socialist or developing) countries beyond
those provided by traditional metropolitan capitalist
sources. By means of a variety of measures such
policies should be aimed at spurring the development of
local production by the use of local human and natural
resources to meet the needs of the people. Through the
provision of regular political processes and organizations within the institutional infrastructure the state

298

could embark upon important public policies, and such schemes could advance building modern industrial networks of relevant factories; as such they are not able to offer the needed increasing employment opportunities to their growing populations. At present the population of most states are relatively small in market terms; in many cases they do not even match those of the capital cities of the core industrial nations such as New York, London, Paris or Tokyo. The smallness of the states in population size does not provide optimally viable markets for doemstically produced manufactures. With low per capita incomes (usually less than a tenth of those of the ACs) it is also difficult, if not impossible, to generate the required savings to finance basic industries on any economically viable scale.

For example, the combined GDP of the ten SADCC states is little more than is little more than that of South Africa, the southern flank of the industrial core of capitalist ACs. Individually, the respective invest-able surplus of each state is hardly adequate to finance more than one or two industrial projects. Investment projects on a scale necessary to permit full utilization of the natural and human resources of most African states is therefore such as to make the develop-ment demands (in terms of capital and markets) greater than can be easily met by individual mini-nation states.

Through balkanization of the continent Africa was reduced to clusters of small artificial states, each with an insufficient population, with limited natural products and with inadequate markets. Often the optimum size of infrastructural projects are, for most states, larger than can be effectively utilized. Accordingly, the fact that behind the notion of economic size is the idea of a market large enough to offer the necessary base for the optimum zone of devlopment rein- forces the argument for stronger economic cooperation and united action. It is particularly in this context that the responsibility of the individual African states is greatest: i.e. in taking steps to ensure that it belongs to a common market, economic federation or some form of commission to promote economic cooperation and ; in ensuring that the advantages of doing so are realized by every member state rather than impeded by the self-interest of particular national entities.

Such advantages can be explained in terms of the anomalies that have been created by arbitrarily located national boundaries; in some cases the artificial

creation of 'mini-states' have limited the utilization
of natural resources or prevented development altogether.
Foreign firms have thus succeeded in playing one state
against another to obtain more favorable tax and royalty
rates, and so are able to reduce the share of revenue
from mineral exports obtained by African states.
Further, these states are deprived of the value added in
the more advanced production stages where they fail to
develop their own industrial complexes based on their
own mineral and agricultural raw materials. They are
also prevented from producing low cost intermediate
goods and finished products essential not only to
further national industrial growth but also to the
development of relevant technological knowledge and
technical skills.

Thus most of the anomalies in these areas can be
circumvented by means of cooperation and joint economic
action. In themselves, the anomalies bear testimony to
"the fact that the challenges facing African states are
so numerous and varied as to require multinational
approaches to their solutions" in the words of Green
and Krishna (1967: 7): a fact, "that constitutes the
best hope of African economic integration."

Presumably, the political essence of the logic for
cooperation can be found in the Senghorian argument for
some form of federation for the states of former French
Africa (Markovitz, 1969: chapter 4): to promote unity
and prevent the emergence of isolated helpless entities
or balkanization and to provide domestic markets. At a
higher, more dynamic, level a similar logic underpins
Nkrumah's original conception fo the OAU: a more
comprehensive integration in terms of unity of action
along the lines of political as well as economic, if not
military, matters. African states need to increase their
power through cooperation initially on a regional basis.
Not only should such cooperation be more greatly
emphsized by each state then hitherto; the emphasis
should also be aimed at greater unity of political action
on most questions affecting Africa. Further, this aim
should be geared towards increasing strength by collective action and agreement, always conscious of the
obvious short-term interest of the ACs in "discouraging
ganging up of the poor countries in a region or the
world for concerted action " (Myrdal, 1960, 177).

At the same time, any effective cooperation and
unity of action must be based on clear thinking and
determined effort of concentrated action as a matter of

300

principle. It is no use belonging to a customs union
the main thrust of whose progams violates the basic
overall aims of presenting an overall collective front
on economic and political matters. One underlying
objective of this aim should be that of altering the
heavy metropolitan colonial orientation--i.e. "vertical
integration" due to colonial imposition--and to replace
it with increased cooperation among African states
themselves--"horizontal integration." For example,
certain SADCC countries are very much integrated within
the so-called Southern African Customs Union; they offer
tax concessions to South African investors on such
generous terms and conditions as to make advantages far
in excess of any real economic benefits to the domestic
economy, to say nothing of the huge tax revenue forgone.
The investors leave after the expiration of the period
of tax holiday, gathering their profits with compara-
tively little received in return by the countries
either in terms of trained personnel and skills, employment creation or the establishment of a useful infre-
structure for future industrial projects (Seidman and
Makgetla, 1980).

But the need for cooperation is further reinforced
by the fact that schemes of regional and inter-regional
cooperation, as the Lome Convention (Protocol number 2,
chapter 4, article 7) points out, "is desirable to
smoothen the commercial relations and reduce the
imbalance which stems from unequal competition between
African States and the Industrial (Advanced) Countries"
(Pagni, 1976). The present level of trade between
African states is ridiculously low; this is all the
more so in view of geographical proximity. Conceivably,
then, the most fundamental reason for some form of
horizontal integration or economic cooperation in the
search for solutions is the fact that the requirements
for tackling a common, if urgent, problem of all African
states is the same; these stress the progressive adapta-
of production so as to accommodate both the tastes and
consumer habits of the African people. I must therefore
give the last word to Green and Krishna (1967), experts
of long standing research experience on integration and
development issues: "The situation in many African
countries is such that in the absence of cooperative
action of some kind, they would permanently be disabled
from overcoming the barriers that seriously inhibit
their development today"; they thus conclude as do I
that "under such circumstances cooperation becomes not
a matter of choice but of necessity."

Bibliography

Dalton, H. (1979). *Economic Systems of Society*. (Harmondsworth: Penguin).

Dos Santos. (1981). "The Structure of Dependence" in I. Livingstone (ed.) *Development and Economic Policy: Readings*. (London: George Allen and Unwin).

Green, R. H. and Krishna, K. G. V. (eds.) (1967) *Economic Cooperation in Africa: retrospect and prospect.* (London: OUP).

Heilbroner, R. (1968). *The Making of Economic Society*, (Englewood Cliffs: Prentice-Hall).

Kindleberger, C. P. (1970). *Power and Money: the economics of international politics and the politics of international economics*. (New York: Basic Books).

Markovitz, I. L. (1969). *Senghor and the Politics of Negritude*. (London: Heinemann).

Muma, P. A. (1981). "The Therapy of Distance: economics with a human face", *Development Studies Association*, University of Oxford, September.

Muma, P. A. (1982). *Economics Teaching for Economic Development: the case of Africa*. Unpublished Ph.D. Thesis, University of London.

Muma, P. A. (1983).. "Economic Theory and Development Analysis". *Swaziana Occasional Paper 11*, University of Swaziland.

Myrdal, G. (1960). *Beyond the Welfare State: economic planning in the welfare states and its international implications*, (London: Duckworth).

Nyerere, J. K. (1968). *Ujaama--Essays on Socialism*. (London and Dar es Salaam: OUP).

Pagni, L. (1976). "Unequal Competition" *The Courier*, 36, March-April.

Robinson, Joan, (1972), "The Second Crisis of Economic Theory" *American Economic Review, Papers and Proceedings*, May.

Rodney, W. (1972). How Europe Underdeveloped
Africa. (Dar es Salaam: Tanzania Publishing House).

Rogers, P and B. Dickson. (1975). Producer Power--
the third world hits back. (London: World Development
Movement).

Seidman, Ann and Neva Makgetla. (1980). Outposts
of Monopoly Capitalism--Southern African in the
changing global economy. (London: Zed Press).

Chapter Twelve

Regional Development in Zambia:

Political and Administrative Issues

B. C. Chikulo

i)   Introduction

Regional development was made the top priority of
the First, Second and Third National Development Plans
in Zambia. While regional development is a top priority
of the national development effort, it is also a
strategy which aims at not only stimulating rapid socio-
economic development in rural areas but also reducing
inherited regional imbalances through a process of
decentralization of political and administrative
authority to lower levels of government. Thus, since
the attainment of independence in 1964, the energies of
the Zambian government have been concentrated on the
creation of appropriate politico-administrative structures which could not only stimulate but also sustain
the pattern of socio-economic development desired by
the center in the regions. Emphasis on regional development reflects the center's desire to increase its
ability to co-ordinate, plan and implement development
programs at the local level.

However, inspite of such emphasis, a wide gap has
emerged between rhetoric and reality in regional development in Zambia. The major issue in this development
strategy has been the degree of political and administrative authority that should be devolved to the
provinces in order to enable them to perform the stated
objectives of regional development. The centrality of
political and administrative issues is reflected by an
increasing concern with political an administrative
organization at the provincial level.1 Accordingly, the
objective of this chapter is to highlight how political
and administrative issues have affected the smooth
implementation of regional development in Zambia. My
focus is on provincial administration, a genetic term
used in Zambia to describe regional administration;
i.e., administration at all levels except the center.

305

ii) Background

At independence on 24 October 1964, Zambia inherited an under-developed economy characterized by sharp socio-economic inequalities between the rural areas and the rapidly growing urban centers. Socio-economic inequalities were particularly marked by the backwardness of the rural areas and the affluence of the urban centers.2 For purposes of administration, the country was divided into eight provinces and forty-four districts and sub-districts.3 The provinces could be grouped into three main macro-regions:

a) central macro-region, which includes Central, Copperbelt, Lusaka and Southern Provinces-- the line-of-rail provinces;

b) rural eastern macro-region, which covers Eastern, Luapula and Northern Provinces; and

c) rural western macro-region, which incorporates North-Western and Western Provinces.

Of the three macro-regions, the central one was the most prosperous.

Although Zambia has great agricultural potential, development efforts were largely concentrated upon high income urban enclaves (the central macro-region) thereby neglecting the majority of African subsistence farmers in the rural areas. This duality was further complicated by the parallel interracial inequality, with the best socio-economic facilities being monopolized by European settlers and poor, limited facilities reserved for Africans.4 Thus at independence the new Zambian government faced the problem of how to correct inherited regional socio-economic imbalances. There was, however, an added major impetus for correcting the regional imbalance. During the terminal years of colonial rule, nationalist political parties were compelled to address themselves to the rural electorate. There they capitalized on widespread discontent over the distribution of power and wealth in society. Attainment of independence accelerated demands for socio-economic improvement in rural areas where the bulk of the population--about 70 per cent--lived. The rural inhabitants duly expected rapid delivery of their share of the "fruits of independence." Thus, in an effort to reduce not only inherited regional socio-economic imbalances but also to meet the high expectations among the rural population following

306

independence the government pledged itself to stimulate rapid rural development. This strategy of development from "above", however, was to depend on mass participatory inputs from "below." Active popular participation was seen to be crucial to the accelaration of socioeconomic development in rural areas; it was also seen to be in accord with the principles of the national ideology of Humanism. As President Kaunda has argued:

> In our Humanist Revolution, <u>decentralization</u> of power in <u>all spheres</u> of <u>human</u> endeavour is central to all we think, say and do. It follows, therefore, that the program of <u>decentralization of this power</u> must be pursued with all the vigour at our command. What then should be done in order to make an effective start towards establishing a decentralized administration which should take <u>power</u>, all power, where it belongs--to the people. 5

In pursuance of this policy, attempts have been undertaken to develop effective politico-administrative institutions, especially at provincial and district levels.

iii) <u>Provincial Administration (PDG): organization and structure 1964-1980</u>

Regional development is not attained merely by according it top priority in national development plans. Political and adminstrative structures must be created to bring about a dynamic interaction between public policy and popular aspirations of the people in the rural areas. What is at issue here is how political and administrative structures may be patterned in order to realize the socio-economic developmental goals espoused by the center. Accordingly, the regional development strategy adopted by the Zambian political leadership postulates an ensemble of participatory, democratic politico-administrative structures as vehicles for regional development.6 Under such circumstances, the manner in which the center links up with the periphery and activates the population becomes a matter of critical importance.

At independence, Zambia inherited eight provinces and 35 rural districts with a PDG administrative structure which was neither oriented towards nor adequate to bring about the rapid socio-economic development envisaged by the new government. The magnitude of this problem was exacerbated by high expectations following independence among the rural population, which expected the promised "fruits of independence" and an immediate change in socio-economic situation.7 Thus the priority given to rural development by the new African government was a political necessity. The problem which confronted it was that of transforming the inherited PDG--which had come to be associated with colonial oppression in the eyes of the African population--into a dynamic organ of development administration.

In order to re-orient provincial administration, the PDG--the "kingpin" around which the colonial system of government was built--ceased to exist in its old form on 31 August 1964.8 For reasons of a political and 'legitimation' nature, the PDG retained only a skeletal presence, losing its political power and administrative backbone. This was a necessary move since it was at the provincial and district levels that the extraordinary autocratic powers of the colonial government were visible. It was therefore decided that PDG should lose its power and its distinct autocratic identity, which had alienated the African population. The government deliberately instituted a process of drastic and consistent reduction in the scope of the PDG. The latter yielded most of its powers to newly created central government departments and ministries.

The primary issue which concerned the political leadership at this stage was that of establishing political control over the civil service and the country as a whole. Politicization of the PDG was seen to be essential to both political control and rapid socio-economic development in the rural areas. The main problem of control arose from the fact that in the terminal years of colonialism and in readiness for independence a bureaucratic apparatus, not easily subject to political control, was created.9 As a condition for the granting of independence nationalist leaders had to accept a multi-party system and a politically neutral civil service modelled upon metropolitan lines.10 In consequence, civil servants were instructed to adhere to 'universalistic criteria' and to insist on the separation of powers; i.e. on the distinction between politics and administration. This meant that the new political masters were inhibited in exerting effective control over the civil service. This problem was complicated by the deeply-felt suspicion of the civil service among the African politicians, borne out of their experience of the white-dominated colonial service. The politicians resented the attempt to foster political neutrality, maintaining that the colonial civil service had never been politically neutral.11 They pointed, for instance, to the leading role of the colonial PDG in suppressing the nationalist movement and in selling the idea of a federation for Rhodesia and Nyasaland.

The concern with the loyalty of the civil service was exacerbated, first and foremost, by heavy dependence on former colonial civil servants most of whom despite being foreign personnel, occupied senior positions and whose loyalty, therefore, could not be taken for granted and, second, by the shortage of Zambians in responsible positions. For example, in February 1964, only 28 of the 848 administrative and professional posts were filled by Zambians and only 26 per cent of division I and II posts,12 while PDG only had 18 Zambians out of a staff complement of 227 Administrative Officers.13. This critical shortage of qualified Zambian personpower was the result of the adverse economic legacy of the Federation and European settler rule. The inherited personpower situation was weaker than in most of Zambia's neighbors to the North.14 The result was that President Kaunda's new and inexperienced Cabinet had to rely heavily on expatriate senior civil servants, even though they doubted the latter's loyalty. This was especially critical in the racially-charged atmosphere of central Africa in 1964. The negative attitudes of colonial civil servants has been note by many scholars,15 the most explicit being Ian Henderson, who wrote: "The 'South African' ideas of the lower reaches of the civil service had their advocates at a higher level."16 Similarly, James Scarritt noted how colonial civil servants "bemoaned the need to take political factors into account in post-independence Zambia."17 There was thus an urgent need to Zambianize the field of personnel not only to reduce dependence on expatriates but also to create a new image for PDG.

The political leadership's strategy was twofold. First, rapid Zambianization of PDG. For instance, by early 1967, all of the eight Resident Secretaries were Zambians and thirty-three out of forty-two District Secretaries were Zambians. In all, eighty-five per cent of all administrative and executive grade posts were Zambianized by that time. Zambianization has subse-

quently become total.18 As Subramaniam has argued,
Zambianization in itself constituted a stage of "indirect" politicization of the civil service because "there
comes a 'flush' of patriotism among the newly-elevated
members of the civil service slowly building up personal
loyalty to the leader of the freedom struggle."19 And
second, the politicians adopted a policy of strategically
placing UNIP politicians in the PDG hierarchy.

In consequence, politicization of PDG became the
prime goal and was seen to be an essential pre-
requisite for a politically-committed PDG. Accordingly, a UNIP politician called 'Minister' (later
changed to Resident Minister and much later to Minister
of State) was posted to each of the eight provinces as
the politico-administrative leader and alter ego of the
President. He was directly responsible for his conduct
to the President. The Resident Minister took over the
chairmanship of the Provincial Development Committee as
well as the Provincial Information Committee, whose main
role was to provided the Government with up-to-date
reports on welfare and the general security situation in
each province. The appointment of a UNIP politician to
the post of Resident Minister gave a Zambian politician
the right, for the first time, to control actions of
the PDG. As Ian Scott has noted, one of the main
reasons for the introduction of Resident Minister was to
ensure tougher control over a still European--dominated
civil service and to attempt closer supervision of the
local UNIP organization. At the same time, other senior
UNIP politicians were appointed to specially created
posts of Political Assistant; by the end of 1968 there
were twenty-six of them. Their role was to assist the
Provincial Ministers on political matters. A vital
part of their function was to explain government
policies to the people, maintain contact with them and
report reactions to government policies to the Minister

Following the 1968 administrative reforms, a
Cabinet Minister was posted to each of the eight provin-
ces as the politico-administrative head. The Provincial
Cabinet Minister was assisted by a Minister of State.
In 1976, the President argued that political problems
in the provinces required the fullest attention of the
Central Committee of UNIP. He therefore appointed a
senior politician--Member of the Central Committee
(MCC)--to take over from the Provincial Cabinet Minister
as the politico-administrative head of the province.
The MCC is assisted on the political side by a Provincial
Political Secretary (PPS), who deputizes for the MCC in

in the latter's absence.

On the administrative side, the MCC is assisted by a senior civil servant--the Provincial Permanent Secretary--who is the supervising officer for all government personnel in the province and as such is the supreme disciplinary authority. As a sub-warrant holder from permanent secretaries of central ministries in Lusaka, the Provincial Permanent Secretary accounts to them for expenditure in the development projects of their ministries. The Permanent Secretary is assisted by an Under-Secretary and an Assistant Secretary and through one of his subordinates--the Provincial Local Government Officer--he controls the activities of local authorities in the province.

The MCC and PPS are expected to perform their developmental role in the province through the Provincial Development Committee (PDC). This Committee meets quarterly under the chairmanship of the MCC, its main function being to coordinate the work of all the development agencies in the province. The PDC scrutinise the progress reports and estimates of expenditure from the districts before forwarding them to Lusaka. Besides providing an important forum where people concerned with implementing development programs can exchange information, consider complaints, clear up misunderstandings and reconcile divergent views, the PDC channels provincial needs and grievances to the center. In addition, the PDC, through a sub-committee--the Finance, Economic and Planning Committee--distributes resources among the districts within the provinces from the provincial budget.

At district level, however, no corresponding politico-administrative heads were appointed until the end of 1966. Each district was in charge of a district Secretary (DS) who was still a civil servant and chaired the District Development Committee (DDC). In 1967 the DS was replaced as chairman of the DDC by the UNIP Regional Secretary. The prominent role given to the DS had created friction due to the resentment of his position by district-level UNIP activists, particularly the UNIP Regional Secretary. By replacing the DS as chairman of the DDC, the Regional Secretary assumed responsibility within the provincial administration framework. Following the 1968 administrative reforms, a political appointee called District Governor (DG) became the politico-administrative head of each of the 53 district and sub-districts. The DG also assumed the chairmanship of the DDC. In consequence, civil servants in provincial administration came to be increasingly watched by UNIP politicians.

At the sub-district level, a network of development committees such as Village Productivity (VPCs), Ward Councils (WCs) and Ward Development Committees (WDCs)-- was established. As President Kaunda pointed out:

> The role of Village and Ward Development Committees will be...to consider, discuss and approve their own development plans and submit them to the District Development Committee for approval and inclusion in the district plans.20

The Registration and Development of Villages Act, 1971, laid down the organization and functions of these committees and legalized them as structures for grass-roots participation. The development committee network was intended to provide the much needed political and administrative linkage between the government and the governed. It was to provide horizontal linkages between government agencies in any given area and thus provide a forum both for the expression of local needs and enforcement of central goals.

iv) Political and Administrative Issues in Regional Development

Political and administrative issues have been the most crucial component of the regional development strategy. Despite a policy commitment to regionalization as a development strategy, many problems have emerged which have seriously impeded the attainment of objectives of regional development. Political and administrative issues are probably the most crucial in the development strategy. The main issue has been how much political and administrative power to devolve to the provinces for them to perform developmental tasks effectively. In other words, what should be the proper allocation of power and functions between central government and provincial administration? Another related issue is the role of popular participation in this development process.

Inspite of a policy commitment to decentralize power to the provincial level, there has been a wide gap between political rhetoric and reality. There has been little devolution of power to the provinces on either substantive matters (policy and development

312

programmes) or administrative (budget and personnel) matters to enable provinces to undertake their functions effectively. Let me illustrate briefly.

Personnel

One of the indicators to determine the commitment of the center to regional development is the movement of qualified staff to the provinces. Indeed, a corollary of decentralization is the realization of skills from the Capital to the provinces, since the decentralized system will not work without staff of real calibre. Yet, apart from the transfer to senior Party officials from Lusaka to the provinces as politico-administrative leaders, there has been no significant parallel movement of senior civil servants; many of the key administrative, technical and professional staff are still congregated in the capital. On the contrary, there has been a flight of capable civil servants to the center since independence. The result was that there was a fall in the average education and experience of Provincial Administration staff, whose prestige among other public servants declined. In short, although the administrative load of the Provincial Administration increased after independence, there was a run-down of staff. Inevitably, the Provincial Administration was less able to perform its functions, especially those of coordinating and implementing the regional development programmes, than previously.21

Departmentalism

The effectiveness of Provincial Administration has been further hampered by the reluctance of central government ministries both to share policy determination with the provinces and to vest a high degree of discretion in their field officers. As a result, provincial officers cannot respond speedily to PDG resolutions as they have to spend much of their time corresponding with their superiors at headquarters and seeking approval for provincial action. Such a state of affairs reflects the limited degree of deconcentration of authority to the province and is a major factor hindering the rapid implementation of development projects. Thus, although central ministries recognize the provinces as an administrative unit, the latter is not regarded as an autonomous unit.

The emphasis has been on functional decentralization; ie. the creation of field offices by the various

313

sectoral agencies--and not areal decentralization. The
emphasis on functional decentralization has created
both horizontal and vertical linkage problems. The
dilemma has been how to reconcile the 'functional principle' underlying the organization of specialist departments of central government with the 'areal principle'
which provincial administration involves. The conflict
between these two principles of organization has limited
the scope and authority of provincial administration.

Regional Development Planning

        The limited scope and authority at provincial
level has a major impact on planning since it prevents
the proper economic evaluation of proposals emanating
from the districts. The result has been a lack of
integrated planning at provincial level: planning has
tended to be done on a project-by-project basis by
individual ministries and departments represented in
the province without any real effort to relate them to
an overall regional development strategy. In spite of
numerous recommendations to improve the administrative
machinery and planning at provincial level, little has
been done and the machinery still remains weak.22 This
has remained the situation, even though the Second
National Development Plan had promised to set up the
"nuclei of competent regional planning units in each
province."23 The Third National Development Plan
promised to rectify the above problem, by establishing
autonomous planning units in each of the nine provinces
under the direct supervision of the National Commission
for Development Planning.

        An essential complement to provincial (regional)
planning is the decentralization of the means for
implementing development projects. However, only meagre
means of development are committed directly to the
Provincial Administration. In fact, the Provincial
Administration's share of the central government total
expenditure is rather small. The small provincial
share of both capital and recurrent funds underlines
the provincial administration's limited role in
regional development planning: provincial funds under
direct provincial adminstration control account for
less than ten per cent of central government expenditure though there are central government projects
located in the provinces.

Resource Distribution

One of the major objectives of the regional investments programme was to redress the disparities and
imbalances existing between and within regions. In
other words, while the development strategy aimed to
accelerate regional development, it was also concerned
with equity goals--i.e., effecting a more balanced and
equitable distribution of resources between regions.
This is an issue of primary importance, in view of the
inherited disparities in resource endowments and capabilities. Although the government has increased
expenditure in the poor rural macro-regions, the central
region, which prospered during the colonial period,
still maintained its privileged position after independence.

Reversing the imbalance, however, proved difficult
to achieve and the expenditure pattern continued to
favor the line-of-rail provinces. During the SNDP,
public expenditure turned out to be higher than planned
in the urban provinces and lower in the rural provinces
According to the SNDP, this state of affairs did not
signify partiality on the part of planners but
reflected the "need to apply scarce resources to areas
and lines of investment which offer the best economic
returns to the country as a whole."24 Elsewhere, the
SNDP argued that the reinforcement of the inherited
regional imbalances should be viewed as a "manifestation of the superior capacity of the more developed
provinces on the line of rail to absorb planned
investment as against their rural neighbours."25

However, an analysis of the TNDP's provincial
investment program shows a higher per head investment
for outlying provinces, and this pattern was reflected
in the annual plans for 1980 and 1981.26 Nonetheless,
we have to bear in mind that the provincial investment
plan accounts for only 8 per cent of the total capital
budget for 1980 and 10 per cent of the total public
expenditure for 1981.

Thus, the provincial capital budget is so meagre
that it cannot significantly bring about the socio-
economic development of the under-privileged provinces;
only central ministerial capital budgets can be
expected to have a noticeable impact in the provinces
and only if there is a positive move to discriminate
against the better-off regions. One of the factors
responsible for the ineffectiveness of the provincial

budget to redress the existing imbalances is the limited
aborptive capacity of the rural provinces in spite of
their strong enthusiasm for project implementation.
For instance, during the FNDP capital expenditure in
these provinces amounted to K211.9 million, or 79 per
cent of the plan's K269.6 million target. At the same
time, the two urbanized provinces (Central and
Copperbelt) over-spent by 52 per cent on the plan's
K269.6 million target.

Popular Participation

        Inspite of the stated official commitment of
popular participation, the tense political atmosphere
in the early 1970s resulted in the development committee
network being turned primarily into an instrument of
control and management.27 The desire for political
control resulted in membership of the development
committees being co-opted or selected by the UNIP
machinery. In most cases, the public had little say in
the matter, as Kapteyn and Emery observed:

                the feeling of real participation is
                not strong among the common villager;
                he rather tends to look up to these
                committees as created for him, over
                him, and without him.28

Measures directed at "taking power to the people" were
primarily aimed at incorporating provincial, district
and village politico-administrative institutions into a
nationally-articulated and centrally-directed hierarchy.

        As a result, the provision of a full complement of
political appointees to the provinces was not
accompanied by devolution of power. On the contrary,
there has been a steady political drive to achieve
greater centralization of authority and to tighten
control over the periphery. This trend meant that the
full compliment of central political appointees at the
provincial and district levels with no local power bases
assumed responsibility for provincial administration--
the effect has been to bring the influence of the
center closer to the people. This state of affairs has
obstructed popular participation and made provincial
administration unresponsive to local demands.

        To sum up thus far: an analysis of government
attempts between 1964 and 1980 to institutionalize a
regional development strategy raises profound questions

about its commitment to devolving power to the provinces. There is an apparent contradiction between the centralization trend and policy statements calling for 'participatory democracy.'

v) Concluding Remarks: problems and prospects

From the above discussion it is obvious that provincial administration has had limited impact on regional development, the main reason being the centrally-controlled and compartmentalized nature of central administration. To overcome the problems entailed by such an administrative structure, a Local Administration Act 1980 came into force in January 1981. The objective of this Act was to restructure the pattern of local administration in Zambia into an integrated system of local government, with a single politico-administrative structure called District Council created in each district to which significant powers were to be devolved. The 1980 Act was not only to decentralize significant functions to the local level but also to ensure an effective integration of primary organs of the Party and other local administration units in the district. In short, the objective of the 1980 Act was to establish a decentralized, integrated local government system. The major structural change entailed by the Act was the abolition of the distinction between the Party on the one hand and central and local government on the other. This involved the creation of an administrative structure composed of party functionaries, central and local officials. As a result, a single politico-administrative structure has been created in each of the 55 districts, to which has been assigned the totality of government and party activity. By replacing the former triparite local government system and also incorporating the partry organization into the new system of local administration, the latter goes beyond what Leemans calls a "fused" or single hierarchy model of government in the district.29

The 1980 Act has transferred a substantial measure of operational autonomy to the provinces. Responsibility for regional development administration has been devolved to the provincial administration. It was hoped that the new system of administration entailed by the Act would facilitate the expeditious implementation of regional development projects. Nonetheless, a number of issues still remain to be resolved: (a) the relationship and degree of power sharing between Lusaka, the province and even the district; and (b) the

317

appropriate institutional structure to be created at the central level as a result of the changes being made at district and provincial levels. It has been stated that central ministries in Lusaka will have an important role in coordinating and overseeing the work of the provinces and in providing them with resources. But this needs to be spelt out clearly; at the moment, the main concern is with the implementation of the new system at district level.

Notes

1. The appointment of several commissions in recent years to review the system of administration has been the inevitable consequence of this realization, and underscores the concern with political and administrative penetrative structures. See, for instance, the following: Report of the Working Party Appointed to Review the System of Decentralized Administration (Lusaka, 1972); Decentralized Government: proposals for integrated local government administration (Lusaka, 1979); Towards Another Development in Rural Zambia (Lusaka, 1979); and The Local Administration Act, 1980.

2. See J. A. Hellen, Rural Economic Development in Zambia 1890-1964 (Munchen, 1968), 250-268, and C. Elliot, "Growth, Development ... or Independence?", in H. and U. E. Simonis (eds.) Socioeconomic Development in Dual Economies: the example of Zambia (Munchen, 1970).

3. J. C. Stone, A Guide to Administrative Boundaries of Northern Rhodesia (O'Dell Memorial Monograph No. 7, Department of Geography, University of Aberdeen).

4. D. Rothchild, "Inter-sectional Conflicts and Resource Allocation in Zambia", African Studies Association, (Denver, November 1971), and C. Harvey, "The Structure of the Zambian Development", in U. G. Dimachi (ed.), Development Paths in Africa and China (London, 1976), 136-137.

5. Humanism in Zambia and a guide to its implementation, Part II, (Lusaka: Government Printer, 1976), 33; emphasis in the original.

6. For a brief outline of the political and administrative network envisaged see: UNIP, National Policies for the Next Decade 1974-1984 (Lusaka), and Communocracy: a strategy for constructing a peoples economy under Humanism (Lusaka, 1976).

7. See, T. Rusmussen, "The Popular Basis of Anti-Colonial Protest", in W. Tordoff (ed.) Politics in Zambia (Manchester, 1974), 47

8. Provincial and District Government, Annual Report for 1964 (Lusaka, 1965), 2.

319

9. See for example, F. Burke, "Public Administration
    in Africa: the legacy of inherited colonial insti-
    tutions", International Political Science Associa-
    tion, Brussels, September 1967, 10-11, and F. W.
    Riggs, "Bureaucrats and Political Development: a
    paradoxical view", in J. La Palombara (ed.)
    Bureaucracy and Political Development, (Princeton:
    Princeton University Press, 1963), 125.

10. For a critique of British colonial policy as a
    "preparation" for self-rule, see B. B. Schaffer,
    "The Concept of Preparation" in his The Administra-
    tive Factor (London, 1973), 219.

11. See K. D. Kaunda, Zambia's Guidelines for the Next
    Decade (Lusaka, 1968), 13.

12. Hon. K. H. Nkwabilo, Chairman of the Zambianization
    and Training Committee of the Public Service,
    "Remarks on Manpower and Zambianization", Univer-
    sity of Zambia, 26 June 1969, mimeo.

13. PDG, Annual Report for 1966 (Lusaka, 1967), 1.

14. Manpower Report: a report and statistical handbook
    on manpower, education, training and Zambianization
    1965-66 (Lusaka, 1966).

15. R. Molteno, "Zambia's Political History-Colonial
    and Since Independence", University of Zambia
    PA 210/73/7a 1973 mimeo, and J. Scarritt, "Elite
    Values, Ideology and Power in Post-Independence
    Zambia", African Studies Bulletin, 14 (1) 1971.

16. Henderson, "Zambia's Colonial Administrators
    1900-1964", University of Zambia PA 210/72/27
    (mimeo) 1972.

17. Scarritt, "Elite Values, Ideology and Power in
    Post-Independence Zambia".

18. PDG, Annual Report 1966, 1 and Cabinet Office,
    Government Directory, (Lusaka, 1967).

19. V. Subramanian, "The Zambian Administrative
    Experiment and Experience", Quarterly Journal
    of Administration, 6 (3), 1972, 293.

20. President Kaunda's Address to Parliment,
    22 January 1969 (Lusaka, 1969).

21. Decentralized Government, 20.

22. M. Chikzuk, "Provincial/Regional Planning in Zambia: an outline", (Lusaka, 1976, mimeo).

23. Second National Development Plan (Lusaka, 1971), 176.

24. Ibid., 167.

25. Ibid., 168.

26. Third National Development Plan (TNDP), Annual Plan 1980 (Lusaka, 1980), 109-110; and TNDP, Annual Plan 1981 (Lusaka, 1981), 189-245.

27. See for example, C. Gertzel, "Administrative Reform in Kenya and Zambia", in G. Hyden (ed.), A Decade of Public Administration in Africa (Nairobi: EALB, 1975), 205.

28. R. C. E. Kapteyn and C. Emery, District Administration in Zambia (Lusaka, 1972), 18.

29. A. F. Leemans, Changing Patterns of Local Government (The Hague, 1970).

List of Contributors

Timothy M. Shaw is Professor of Political Science at
Dalhousie University. In 1984/5 he has been President
of the Canadian Association of African Studies. His
latest book is Towards a Political Economy of Africa:
the dialectics of dependence.

H. M. Stevenson is a member of the Political Science
Department at York University in Toronto. He is author
of Black Africa: a comparative handbook and of several
comparative, quantitative analyses of African politics.
He has taught at the University of Ibadan, Nigeria and
continues to teach African politics despite a recent
concentration on Canadian politics.

Jean Laponce is Professor of Political Science at the
University of British Columbia in Vancouver. A past-
president of the Canadian and International Political
Science Associations, he has published widely on
language and politics. His most recent books are
Left and Right and People vs. Politics.

Okwudiba Nnoli is Professor of Political Science and
Dean of Social Science at the University of Nigeria,
Nsukka. He is author of, inter alia, Self-Reliance
and Foreign Policy in Tanzania and Ethnic Politics
in Nigeria, editor of Path of Nigerian Development
and President of AAPS.

Marcel Leroy is Associate Professor of Social Science
at the University College of Cape Breton in Sydney,
Nova Scotia. His work on environment, population and
international development has appeared in International
Journal and Peace and the Sciences. He is author of
Population and World Politics.

Edmond Orban is Professor of Political Science at the
University of Montreal. He has published widely on
Quebec, Canadian and American politics, most recently
on La dynamique de la centralisation dans l'Etat
federal, Quebec, State and Society in Crisis, Mecanismes
de transformation constitutionelle and Quebec: un pays
incertain.

Geoffrey R. Weller is Dean of the Faculty of Arts and Professor of Political Studies at Lakehead University, Thunder Bay, Ontario. He has published widely in the areas of Canadian and comparative health policies and politics in the Canadian north.

Peter Aucoin is Professor of Public Administration and Political Science and Director of the School of Public Administration at Dalhousie University. Among his works on the public policy of health and of technology are The Structures of Policy-making in Canada, Public Policy in Canada (both with G. Bruce Doern) and The Politics and Management of Restraint in Government.

Maureen Covell is Assistant Professor in the Department of Political Science at Simon Fraser University in Burnaby, British Columbia. She has worked on regional and local politics in Africa and Europe, particularly in Malagasy and Belgium, with articles in Canadian Journal of African Studies and West European Politics.

Ian McAllister is Professor of Economics and Director of the Pearson Institute for International Development at Dalhousie University. He has written widely on regional development in Africa, Canada and Europe.

Sharon Sutherland is Associate Professor in the School of Public Administration at Carleton University in Ottawa and Secretary-Treasurer of the CPSA. Previously with Dalhousie University and the Canadian Department of Health and Welfare, Dr. Sutherland has published on political behavior and public policy in Canadian Public Administration, Canadian Review of Sociology and Anthropology and Signs. She is author of Patterns of Belief and Action.

Patrick Muma is Lecturer in Economics at the National University of Lesotho in Roma.

B. C. Chikulo is Lecturer in Political and Administrative Studies at the University of Zambia, Lusaka.

Yash Tandon is Research and Publications Director of AAPS and has published widely on African political economy and international relations, including Readings in African International Relations and Horizons of African Diplomacy. Dr. Tandon was for many years of Makerere University, Uganda and the University of Dar es Salaam, Tanzania.

.